T-1 Nonimmigrant Visa

Being a Victim of Sex Trafficking or Work Exploitation can result in Getting a T Visa

Attorney Brian D. Lerner

LAW OFFICES OF
BRIAN D. LERNER
A PROFESSIONAL CORPORATION

ATTORNEY DRAFTED IMMIGRATION PETITIONS

By

Brian D. Lerner

Attorney at Law

Disclaimer and Terms of Use:

Effort has been made to ensure that the information in this book is accurate and complete. However, the author and the publisher do not warrant that this particular petition will mirror or be exactly as your situation. There has not been any attorney-client agreement created by the purchase of this petition or application. No legal advice has occurred. The cases, regulations and/or statutes cited may change at any time without notice.

INTRODUCTION

There are a multitude of different immigration petitions and applications. They are complex and full of requirements. Obviously, it would be best to hire an immigration attorney to best prepare the petitions and applications. However, this can certainly cost thousands of dollars.

The next best option is to get a sample of the petition written by an experienced immigration attorney. The samples cost a fraction what would be charged by an immigration attorney. However, while the reader has to alter, amend and change the parts of the sample petition to reflect their actual situation, it is a fantastic roadmap for them to use. If the reader has purchased the entire petition or application, they will have real live samples of cover letters, forms, declarations, affidavits and the necessary exhibits to use. The samples come from real cases and the names of those clients have been redacted to protect the privacy of that person or corporation.

These are petitions and applications that have been drafted by an experienced immigration attorney with over 25 years of experience. Get the benefits of that experience without the costs.

CONTENTS

About the Law Offices of Brian D. Lerner

Brian D. Lerner has been a licensed attorney since 1992 and started the Law Offices of Brian D. Lerner, APC. The law practice consists of Immigration and Nationality Law and everything involved with and regarding immigration which includes citizenship, investment visas, family and employment visas, removal and deportation hearings, appeals, waivers, adjustment, consulate processing and all types of immigration and citizenship matters. Thousands of families have been reunited and/or permitted to stay in the U.S. and/or return to the U.S. because of the successful work of Immigration Attorney Brian D. Lerner.

This law offices handles all types of immigration cases including family based and employment based. Immigration issues range from immigration court proceedings to trying to fix what paralegals may have done that was neither correct nor proper. Foreign nationals must have experience lawyers admitted to practice law.

The Law Offices of Brian D. Lerner, APC, handles cases arising from business visas, work permits, Green Cards, non-immigrant visas, deportation, citizenship, appeals and all areas of immigration. The Law Offices of Brian D. Lerner, APC does EB-5 Investor Visas, H-1B Specialty Occupation, L-1 Intracompany Transferee, E-2 Treaty Investor, E-1 Treaty Trader, O-1 Extraordinary Ability among others. Regarding immigrant visas for the Green Card, the firm does PERM and advanced degree PERM, Family Petitions, and Extraordinary Alien Petitions. In addition to affirmative petitions, the Law Firm represents people in people in deportation and removal hearings, including political asylum, withholding of removal, and convention against torture cases.

Brian D. Lerner has been certified as an expert in Immigration & Nationality Law by the California State Bar, Board of Legal Specialization since 2000 and has been re-certified three times. He now passes on his decades of experience by allowing the Reader, Law Schools, Professors and other Immigration Attorneys to purchase sample petitions on every facet of Immigration Law.

About the T-1 Nonimmigrant Visa

T nonimmigrant status is a temporary immigration benefit that enables certain victims of a severe form of trafficking in persons) to remain in the United States for an initial period of up to 4 years if they have complied with any reasonable request for assistance from law enforcement in the detection, investigation, or prosecution of human trafficking or qualify for an exemption or exception. T nonimmigrant status is also available to certain qualifying family members of trafficking victims. T nonimmigrants are eligible for employment authorization and certain federal and state benefits and services. T nonimmigrants who qualify may also be able to adjust their status and become lawful permanent residents (obtain a Green Card).

- Sex trafficking: When someone recruits, harbors, transports, provides, solicits, patronizes, or obtains a person for the purpose of a commercial sex act, where the commercial sex act is induced by force, fraud, or coercion, or the person being induced to perform such act is under 18 years of age; or
- Labor trafficking: When someone recruits, harbors, transports, provides, or obtains a person for labor or services through the use of force, fraud, or coercion for the purpose of involuntary servitude, peonage, debt bondage, or slavery.

These are the victims that can apply for the T Visa. Therefore, if you qualify, you should apply for this.

This particular sample is an actual T Visa Petition for somebody who was a victim of sex trafficking or trafficking illegally in work. Of course, it would be sure that the ultimate beneficiary had the requisite requirements needed to fulfill the T visa and that in fact they were such a victim. Note that our library also has all the other types of preference petitions for your perusal. Note that our library includes not only this family petition and other family preference petitions, but nonimmigrant visa petitions such as the L-1A Intracompany Transferee Petition and other types of applications and petitions such as the Humanitarian Reinstatement application, multiple types of work-permits such as the H-1B Specialty Occupation Visa Petition, the O-1 Extraordinary Alien Petition, B-2 examples, I-140 Applications and many more. If you enjoy this family 2nd preference petition and it makes your life easier, then come back and try the other immigration applications and petitions.

Remember this T Visa Petition does need the cooperation of a government official to ultimately succeed and could eventually get the Green Card. If granted, you will be given an T Visa which will allow you to work and then some time afterwards, you can apply for the Green Card.

We certainly hope you find this petition useful and helpful and hope for the best immigration experience you can have. We do have petitions on every subject area of immigration, and you might look at those if needed as well. If you do need to actually have a consultation, you can call our U.S. Immigration Law office at 562-495-0554 for an initial free consultation to determine what must be done to help you and your family.

ATTORNEY COVER LETTER

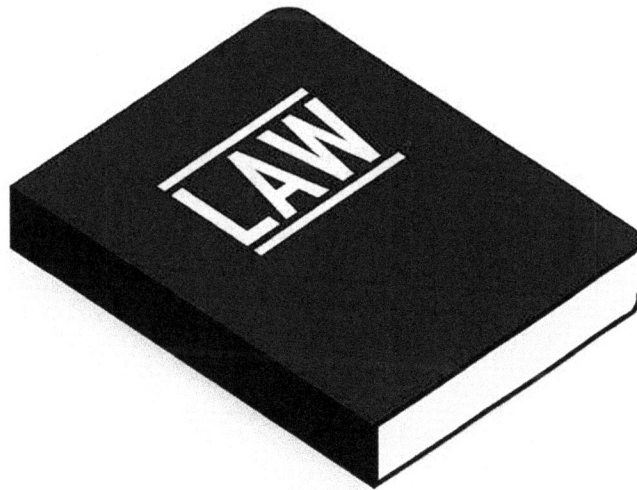

Law Offices of Brian D. Lerner

A PROFESSIONAL CORPORATION

CERTIFIED SPECIALIST IN IMMIGRATION AND NATIONALITY LAW
ADMITTED TO THE U.S. SUPREME COURT

LONG BEACH, CALIFORNIA
(562) 495-0554

CARSON, CALIFORNIA
(310) 684-5420

October 15, 2018

USCIS – Vermont Service Center
Attn: T VISA UNIT
75 Lower Welden Street
St. Albans, VT 05479-0001

> **Re: I-914, Application for T Nonimmigrant Status**
> **Applicant:** ▮▮▮▮▮▮▮▮
> **Alien Number:** ▮▮▮▮▮▮▮

Dear Officer:

Enclosed please find an application for T nonimmigrant status (form I-914), filed on behalf of ▮▮. ▮▮▮▮▮▮▮▮ (hereinafter "Applicant") pursuant to the Trafficking Victims Protection Act of 2000.

We enclose the following in support of Applicant's I-914:

Forms:	Description:
G-28	Notice of Entry of Appearance as Attorney or Accredited Representative; and
I-914	Application for T Nonimmigrant Status.

EXHIBITS

Tab:	Description:
1.	Applicant's Declaration;
2.	Applicant's Current Passport (Bio Page Only);
3.	Applicant's Expired Passport, Visa and Entry Stamp;
4.	Applicant's H-1B Approval Notice and Current I-94;
5.	Applicant's Marriage Certificate and Evidence of Pending Dissolution/Divorce;
6.	Applicant's Daughter's Birth Certificate;
7.	Applicant's Master of Science in Finance Degree;
8.	Hillsborough County Sheriff's Arrest/Incident Report;
9.	Final Judgment of Injunction for Protection Against Domestic Violence Against Applicant's Husband and In-Laws;
10.	Applicant's Husband's and In-Law's Conviction Documents;
11.	Applicant's Initial Assessment and Diagnostic Impression (PTSD);
12.	Applicant's Medical Records;
13.	Photographs of Applicant's Injuries;
14.	New Articles Regarding Applicant's Abuse and Suffering;
15.	Indian Country Summary – Human Rights Watch (January 2018);

16.   India 2017/2018 Annual Report – Amnesty International;
17.   India Travel Advisory – U.S. Department of State (January 10, 2018);
18.   2018 Trafficking in Person Report: India – U.S. Department of State; and
19.   2017 Human Rights Report: India – U.S. Department of State.

I.
T NONIMMIGRANT

Section 101(a)(15)(T) of the Immigration and Nationality Act (hereinafter "INA" or "Act") defines a T nonimmigrant as an alien who the Secretary of Homeland Security determines--

> (I) is or has been a victim of a severe form of trafficking in persons, as defined in section 103 of the Trafficking Victims Protection Act of 2000;

> (II) is physically present in the United States, American Samoa, or the Commonwealth of the Northern Mariana Islands, or at a port of entry thereto, on account of such trafficking, including physical presence on account of the alien having been allowed entry into the United States for participation in investigative or judicial processes associated with an act or a perpetrator of trafficking;

> (III) has complied with any reasonable request for assistance in the Federal, State, or local investigation or prosecution of acts of trafficking or the investigation of crime where acts of trafficking are at least one central reason for the commission of that crime; and

> (IV) the alien would suffer extreme hardship involving unusual and severe harm upon removal;

See also 8 C.F.R. 214.11(b).

II.
APPLICANT IS THE VICTIM OF A SEVERE FORM OF TRAFFICKING IN PERSONS.

Pursuant to 8 C.F.R. 214.11(a), "severe form of trafficking in persons" means:

> sex trafficking in which a commercial sex act is induced by force, fraud, or coercion, or in which the person induced to perform such act is under the age of 18 years; or the recruitment, harboring, transportation, provision, or obtaining of a person for labor or services through the use of force, fraud, or coercion for the purpose of subjection to involuntary servitude, peonage, debt bondage, or slavery.

Pursuant to 8 C.F.R. 214.11(a), "coercion" means:

> threats of serious harm to or physical restraint against any person;

any scheme, plan, or pattern intended to cause a person to believe
that failure to perform an act would result in serious harm to or
physical restraint against any person; or the abuse or threatened
abuse of the legal process.

Pursuant to 8 C.F.R. 214.11(a), "involuntary servitude" means:

a condition of servitude induced by means of any scheme, plan, or
pattern intended to cause a person to believe that, if the person did
not enter into or continue in such condition, that person or another
person would suffer serious harm or physical restraint; or a
condition of servitude induced by the abuse or threatened abuse of
legal process. Involuntary servitude includes a condition of
servitude in which the victim is forced to work for the defendant
by the use or threat of physical restraint or physical injury, or by
the use or threat of coercion through the law or the legal process.
This definition encompasses those cases in which the defendant
holds the victim in servitude by placing the victim in fear of such
physical restraint or injury or legal coercion.

In this case, Applicant's husband physical, sexually, verbally and emotionally abused her throughout
their 10-year relationship and in 2014, through fraud and coercion, convinced Applicant to return to the
United States after a trip abroad to continue said abuse including involuntary domestic servitude as
described below.

A. Involuntary Servitude.

Involuntary servitude "includes a condition of servitude induced by means of (A) any scheme, plan, or
pattern intended to cause a person to believe that, if the person did not enter into or continue in such
condition, that person or another person would suffer serious harm or physical restraint; or (B) the abuse
or threatened abuse of the legal process." 22 U.S.C. § 7102(5).

In the present case, Applicant was a victim of physical, sexually, verbally and emotionally abuse,
including involuntary servitude, when her husband forced her to cook and clean and do any other chores
that he thought were necessary, threatened to have her deported or take away their daughter if she left,
and isolated her from the outside world.

1. Applicant's Husband Physically, Sexually, Verbally and Emotionally Abused Applicant and Kept Her Isolated from the Outside World.

In the present case, Applicant's husband kept Applicant in a state of involuntary servitude through
physical, sexual, verbal and emotional abuse and isolation. Applicant's husband was both manipulative
and controlling, and would regulate when and where Applicant could go, what she could wear, who she
could be friends with and who could visit their home. Applicant's husband would also force her to cook
and clean and do any other chores as necessary.

When he got upset, he would curse at Applicant, call her degrading names and even threaten to have her
deported or take away their daughter. When things escalated, which was often, he would physically
abuse Applicant; spit in her face, punch and kick her, and slap and pull her hair. Applicant's husband
would also sexually abuse her and force her to have rough and violent sex and even tying her up at

times.

See Exhibits 1 and 8.

2. Applicant's Husband Coerced Her into Staying with Him with Threats of Harm.

Applicant's husband also kept Applicant in a condition of involuntary servitude through threats of what would happen to her if she left him. Applicant's husband threatened that if Applicant ever left, that he could call the police, have her deported and even take away their daughter. These threats particularly scared Applicant because of the years of abuse she suffered, her immigration status, her young daughter's age and her lack of family ties in this country.

Fortunately though, on September 2, 2017, after years of abuse, Applicant was able to escape her husband's control with the help of her parents in India, her brother in Florida and the local police.

See Exhibits 1 and 8.

II.
APPLICANT IS PHYSICALLY PRESENT IN THE UNITED STATES ON ACCOUNT OF A SUCH TRAFFICKING.

In this case, Applicant's husband physical, sexually, verbally and emotionally abused her throughout their 10-year relationship. In 2014, Applicant and her husband returned to India for Applicant's husband's brother's wedding and which point, Applicant contemplated leaving her husband and staying in India. However, through fraud and coercion, Applicant's husband convinced her to return to the United States with him so that he could continue said abuse.

Applicant is still present in the United States as a result of the initial trafficking that brought her here. She has been dealing with effects of being traumatized by her husband, before and since that time, and is afraid to return to India as a result.

See Exhibits 1, 3 and 8-19.

Accordingly, she is present in the United States as a result of the initial act of trafficking that brought her here.

III.
APPLICANT HAS FULLY COOPERATED WITH LAW ENFORCEMENT.

Pursuant to 8 C.F.R. 214.11(a), "reasonable request for assistance"means:

> a request made by an EA to a victim to assist in the investigation or
> prosecution of the act of trafficking in persons or the investigation
> of crime where act of trafficking are at least one central reason for
> the commission of that crime.

In the present case, Applicant assisted the police and the prosecutors every step of the way, doing everything that was asked of her, including giving a full statement to the police, identifying possible witnesses and testifying/speaking at her husband and in-laws' trial. She also sat through a deposition in regards to the orders of protection that she filed against her husband and his parents, and she provided a statement to Immigration authorities requesting that any bond be denied in her husband's case. *See*

Exhibits 1 and 8-10.

As such, Applicant has fully cooperated with law enforcement in this case.

IV.
APPLICANT WOULD SUFFER EXTREME HARDSHIP, INCLUDING UNUSUAL AND SEVERE HARM, IF FORCED TO RETURN TO INDIA.

There is little doubt that Applicant would suffer extreme hardship if forced to return to India. On information and belief, both Applicant's husband and his parents have been ordered removed to Indian and Applicant fears that if forced to return to India, she would suffer the same abuse as she suffered in the United States, if not worse, and that the government in India would not be able to protect her.

In addition, Applicant has been severely traumatized by the acts of trafficking that were committed against her, resulting in Post Traumatic Stress Disorder (PTSD). However, since escaping from her husband, she has benefited substantially from various social services and the support of her community. If Applicant were forced to return to India, these services and support would no longer be available to her. In fact, the 2018 U.S. Department of State Trafficking in Persons Report notes that India does not fully meet the minimum standards for the elimination of trafficking and that victim protection remains inadequate and inconsistent and that the government sometimes penalized victims through arrest for crimes committed as a result of being subjected to human trafficking. The report also notes that the government's conviction rate and the number of investigations, prosecutions, and convictions was disproportionately low relative to the scale of trafficking in India, particularly with respect to bonded and forced labor. In addition, the 2017 Department of State Human Rights Report notes that significant human rights abuse exist in India, including police and security force abuses, widespread corruption, lack of criminal investigation or accountability for cases related to rape, domestic violence, dowry-related deaths, honor killings, sexual harassment and violence and discrimination against women. Thus, there is little to no likelihood that Applicant could continue to receive the services and support that has been so critical to her recovery.

Furthermore, Ms. CLIENT still aspires to pursue her career in this country and at the same time, raise her U.S. born daughter here, which would not be possible if she were forced to return to India.

See Exhibits 1, 6, 11-12 and 15-19.

Accordingly, Applicant would suffer extreme hardship, including unusual and severe harm, if forced to return to India.

//
//
//

V.
CONCLUSION.

For the foregoing reasons, Applicant respectfully requests that her application for T Nonimmigrant status be approved. If you should have any questions, please feel free to contact our office at (562) 495-0554.

Sincerely,

Brian D. Lerner
Attorney at law

FORMS

Notice of Entry of Appearance
as Attorney or Accredited Representative

Department of Homeland Security

DHS
Form G-28
OMB No. 1615-0105
Expires 05/31/2021

Part 1. Information About Attorney or Accredited Representative

1. USCIS Online Account Number (if any)

   ▶ [ ][ ][ ][ ][ ][ ][ ][ ][ ][ ][ ][ ]

Name of Attorney or Accredited Representative

2.a. Family Name (Last Name) **Lerner**

2.b. Given Name (First Name) **Brian**

2.c. Middle Name **David**

Address of Attorney or Accredited Representative

3.a. Street Number and Name **3233 E. Broadway**

3.b. ☐ Apt. ☐ Ste. ☐ Flr. [ ]

3.c. City or Town **Long Beach**

3.d. State **CA**   3.e. ZIP Code **90803**

3.f. Province [ ]

3.g. Postal Code [ ]

3.h. Country **USA**

Contact Information of Attorney or Accredited Representative

4. Daytime Telephone Number
   (562) 495-0554

5. Mobile Telephone Number (if any)
   [ ]

6. Email Address (if any)
   blerner@californiaimmigration.us

7. Fax Number (if any)
   5626088672

Part 2. Eligibility Information for Attorney or Accredited Representative

Select all applicable items.

1.a. ☒ I am an attorney eligible to practice law in, and a member in good standing of, the bar of the highest courts of the following states, possessions, territories, commonwealths, or the District of Columbia. If you need extra space to complete this section, use the space provided in Part 6. Additional Information.

Licensing Authority

Supreme Court of California

1.b. Bar Number (if applicable)

158536

1.c. I (select only one box) ☒ am not ☐ am subject to any order suspending, enjoining, restraining, disbarring, or otherwise restricting me in the practice of law. If you are subject to any orders, use the space provided in Part 6. Additional Information to provide an explanation.

1.d. Name of Law Firm or Organization (if applicable)

Law Offices of Brian D. Lerner, APC

2.a. ☐ I am an accredited representative of the following qualified nonprofit religious, charitable, social service, or similar organization established in the United States and recognized by the Department of Justice in accordance with 8 CFR part 1292.

2.b. Name of Recognized Organization

[ ]

2.c. Date of Accreditation (mm/dd/yyyy)

[ ]

3. ☐ I am associated with

[ ]

the attorney or accredited representative of record who previously filed Form G-28 in this case, and my appearance as an attorney or accredited representative for a limited purpose is at his or her request.

4.a. ☐ I am a law student or law graduate working under the direct supervision of the attorney or accredited representative of record on this form in accordance with the requirements in 8 CFR 292.1(a)(2).

4.b. Name of Law Student or Law Graduate

[ ]

Part 3. Notice of Appearance as Attorney or Accredited Representative

If you need extra space to complete this section, use the space provided in Part 6. Additional Information.

This appearance relates to immigration matters before (select **only one** box):

1.a. ☒ U.S. Citizenship and Immigration Services (USCIS)

1.b. List the form numbers or specific matter in which appearance is entered.

I-914

2.a. ☐ U.S. Immigration and Customs Enforcement (ICE)

2.b. List the specific matter in which appearance is entered.

3.a. ☐ U.S. Customs and Border Protection (CBP)

3.b. List the specific matter in which appearance is entered.

4. Receipt Number (if any)

   ▶

5. I enter my appearance as an attorney or accredited representative at the request of the (select **only one** box):

   ☒ Applicant ☐ Petitioner ☐ Requestor
   ☐ Beneficiary/Derivative ☐ Respondent (ICE, CBP)

Information About Client (Applicant, Petitioner, Requestor, Beneficiary or Derivative, Respondent, or Authorized Signatory for an Entity)

6.a. Family Name (Last Name) ▮▮▮▮▮

6.b. Given Name (First Name) ▮▮▮▮▮

6.c. Middle Name

7.a. Name of Entity (if applicable)

7.b. Title of Authorized Signatory for Entity (if applicable)

8. Client's USCIS Online Account Number (if any)

   ▶

9. Client's Alien Registration Number (A-Number) (if any)

   ▶ A- ▮▮▮▮▮

Client's Contact Information

10. Daytime Telephone Number

    ▮▮▮▮▮

11. Mobile Telephone Number (if any)

    ▮▮▮▮▮

12. Email Address (if any)

    ▮▮▮▮▮

Mailing Address of Client

NOTE: Provide the client's mailing address. Do not provide the business mailing address of the attorney or accredited representative **unless** it serves as the safe mailing address on the application or petition being filed with this Form G-28.

13.a. Street Number and Name ▮▮▮▮▮

13.b. ☐ Apt. ☐ Ste. ☐ Flr.

13.c. City or Town ▮▮▮▮▮

13.d. State FL   13.e. ZIP Code 33569

13.f. Province

13.g. Postal Code

13.h. Country

USA

Part 4. Client's Consent to Representation and Signature

Consent to Representation and Release of Information

I have requested the representation of and consented to being represented by the attorney or accredited representative named in Part 1. of this form. According to the Privacy Act of 1974 and U.S. Department of Homeland Security (DHS) policy, I also consent to the disclosure to the named attorney or accredited representative of any records pertaining to me that appear in any system of records of USCIS, ICE, or CBP.

Part 4. Client's Consent to Representation and Signature (continued)

Options Regarding Receipt of USCIS Notices and Documents

USCIS will send notices to both a represented party (the client) and his, her, or its attorney or accredited representative either through mail or electronic delivery. USCIS will send all secure identity documents and Travel Documents to the client's U.S. mailing address.

If you want to have notices and/or secure identity documents sent to your attorney or accredited representative of record rather than to you, please select all applicable items below. You may change these elections through written notice to USCIS.

1.a. ☒ I request that USCIS send original notices on an application or petition to the U.S. business address of my attorney or accredited representative as listed in this form.

1.b. ☐ I request that USCIS send any secure identity document (Permanent Resident Card, Employment Authorization Document, or Travel Document) that I receive to the U.S. business address of my attorney or accredited representative (or to a designated military or diplomatic address in a foreign country (if permitted)).

NOTE: If your notice contains Form I-94, Arrival-Departure Record, USCIS will send the notice to the U.S. business address of your attorney or accredited representative. If you would rather have your Form I-94 sent directly to you, select Item Number 1.c.

1.c. ☐ I request that USCIS send my notice containing Form I-94 to me at my U.S. mailing address.

Signature of Client or Authorized Signatory for an Entity

2.a. Signature of Client or Authorized Signatory for an Entity

➡ [redacted]

2.b. Date of Signature (mm/dd/yyyy) **09/14/2018**

Part 5. Signature of Attorney or Accredited Representative

I have read and understand the regulations and conditions contained in 8 CFR 103.2 and 292 governing appearances and representation before DHS. I declare under penalty of perjury under the laws of the United States that the information I have provided on this form is true and correct.

1.a. Signature of Attorney or Accredited Representative

1.b. Date of Signature (mm/dd/yyyy) **10 15 18**

2.a. Signature of Law Student or Law Graduate

2.b. Date of Signature (mm/dd/yyyy) **09/14/2018**

Part 6. Additional Information

If you need extra space to provide any additional information within this form, use the space below. If you need more space than what is provided, you may make copies of this page to complete and file with this form or attach a separate sheet of paper. Type or print your name at the top of each sheet; indicate the Page Number, Part Number, and Item Number to which your answer refers; and sign and date each sheet.

1.a Family Name
(Last Name) ▮▮▮▮▮▮

1.b. Given Name
(First Name) ▮▮▮▮

1.c. Middle Name

2.a. Page Number   **2.b.** Part Number   **2.c.** Item Number

2.d.

3.a. Page Number   **3.b.** Part Number   **3.c.** Item Number

3.d.

4.a. Page Number   **4.b.** Part Number   **4.c.** Item Number

4.d.

5.a. Page Number   **5.b.** Part Number   **5.c.** Item Number

5.d.

6.a. Page Number   **6.b.** Part Number   **6.c.** Item Number

6.d.

Application for T Nonimmigrant Status

Department of Homeland Security
U.S. Citizenship and Immigration Services

USCIS
Form I-914
OMB No. 1615-0099
Expires 01/31/2019

START HERE - Type or print. *Use black ink. See Instructions for information about eligibility and how to complete and file this application.*

PART A. Purpose for Filing the Application

Check all that apply:

[X] I am filing for T-1 nonimmigrant status and have not previously filed for such status.

[ ] I am filing for T-1 nonimmigrant status and have previously filed for such status.
Receipt Number (begins with EAC) [   ]

[ ] I have received T-1 status and am applying to bring family members to the United States.

PART B. General Information About You *(Person filing this form as a victim)*

Family Name *(Last Name)*	Given Name *(First Name)*	Middle Name *(if any)*
▮▮▮▮	▮▮▮▮	

Other Names Used *(Include maiden name/nickname)*
[   ]

Home Address - Street Number and Name		Apt. Number
▮▮▮▮		

City	State/Province	Zip/Postal Code
Riverview	FL	33569

Safe Mailing Address (if other than above) - Street Number and Name   Apt. Number
[   ]

C/O (*in care of*):
[   ]

City	State/Province	Zip/Postal Code

Home Telephone Number *(with area code)*   Safe Daytime Phone Number *(with area code)*
▮▮▮▮   ▮▮▮▮

E-Mail Address *(optional)*   A-Number *(if any)*
▮▮▮▮   ▮▮▮▮

U.S. Social Security Number *(if any)*   Gender
▮▮▮▮   [ ] Male   [X] Female

Marital Status:
[ ] Single/Never Married   [X] Married   [ ] Divorced   [ ] Widowed

Date of Birth *(mm/dd/yyyy)*	Country of Birth	Country of Citizenship
11/28/1983	India	India

Passport Number	Place of Issuance	Date of Issue *(mm/dd/yyyy)*
▮▮▮▮	▮▮▮▮	03/21/2016

Place of Last Entry	Date of Last Entry *(mm/dd/yyyy)*
Chicago, IL (ORD)	03/10/2014

Form I-94 Number *(Arrival-Departure Record)*	Current Immigration Status
▮▮▮▮	H-1B

For USCIS Use Only

Returned	Receipt
Date	
Date	
Resubmitted	
Date	
Date	
Reloc Sent	
Date	
Date	
Reloc Rec'd	
Date	
Date	

Validity Dates
From:
To:

Remarks

Conditional Approval
Stamp #   Date

Action Block

To Be Completed by *Attorney or Representative, if any*

[X] Fill in box if G-28 is attached to represent the applicant.

ATTY State License # 158536

Form I-914 02/27/17 Y

Page 1

11 | P a g e

PART C. Additional Information

Answers to the following questions about your claim require explanation and supporting documentation. You should attach documents in support of your claim that you are a victim of a severe form of trafficking in persons and the specific facts on which you are relying to support your claim. **You must** attach a personal narrative statement describing the trafficking. If you are only applying for T derivative status for a family member subsequent to your (the principal applicant) initial filing, evidence supporting the original application is not require to be resubmitted with the new Form I-914.

Attach additional sheets of paper as needed. Write your name and Alien Registration Number (A-Number), if any, at the top of each sheet and indicate the number of the item that you are answering. Include the Part and letter or number relating to the additional information you provided (example: Part C, 3).

1. I am or have been a victim of a severe form of trafficking in persons. *(Attach evidence to support your claim.)* ☒ Yes ☐ No

2. I am submitting a law enforcement agency (LEA) declaration on Form I-914, Supplement B, Declaration of Law Enforcement Officer for Victim of Trafficking in Persons. *(If "No," explain why you are not submitting the LEA Certification.)* ☐ Yes ☒ No

3. I am physically present in the United States, American Samoa, or the Commonwealth of the Northern Mariana Islands, or at a port of entry, **on account of trafficking,** or have been allowed entry into the United States to participate in investigative or judicial processes associated with an act or perpetrator of trafficking. *(If "Yes," explain in detail and attach evidence and documents supporting this claim.)* ☒ Yes ☐ No

4. I fear that I will suffer extreme hardship involving unusual and severe harm upon removal. *(If "Yes," explain in detail and attach evidence and documents supporting this claim.)* ☒ Yes ☐ No

5. I have reported the crime of which I am claiming to be a victim. *(If "Yes," indicate to which law enforcement agency and office you have made the report, the address and phone number of that office, and the case number assigned, if any. If "No," explain the circumstances.)* ☒ Yes ☐ No

Law Enforcement Agency and Office	Address	Phone Number	Case Number
Florida State Attorney's Office	800 East Kennedy Boulevard Tampa, Florida 33602-4199	(813) 272-5400	17-CF-013214A-C

Circumstances:
Battery/Domestic Violence; Kidnapping/False Imprisonment; Tampering/Harassing a Witness; Child Abuse; Aggravated Assault w/ Deadly Weapon. See attached.

6. I am under *the age of 18 years. (If "Yes," proceed to Question 8.)* ☐ Yes ☒ No

7. I have complied with requests from Federal, State, or local law enforcement authorities for assistance in the investigation or prosecution of acts of trafficking, or am unable to cooperate with such requests due to physical or psychological trauma. *(If "No," explain the circumstances.)* ☒ Yes ☐ No

8. This is the first time I have entered the United States. *(If "No," list each date, place of entry, and under which status you entered the United States for the past five years, and explain the circumstances of your most recent arrival.)* ☐ Yes ☒ No

Date of Entry	Place of Entry	Status
03/10/2014	Chicago, IL (ORD)	H-1B

PART C. Additional Information (continued)

9. My most recent entry was on account of the trafficking that forms the basis for my claim. *(Explain the circumstances of your most recent arrival.)* ☒ Yes ☐ No

10. I want an Employment Authorization Document. ☒ Yes ☐ No

11. I am now applying for one or more eligible family members. *(If "Yes," complete and include a Form I-914, Supplement A, Application for Immediate Family Member of T-1 Recipient, for each family member for whom you are now applying. You may also apply to bring eligible family members to the United States at a later date.)* ☐ Yes ☒ No

PART D. Processing Information

Answer the following questions about yourself. For purposes of this application, if applicable, you must answer "Yes" to the following questions, even if your records were sealed or otherwise cleared or if anyone, including a judge, law enforcement officer, or attorney, told you that you no longer have a record. *(If your answer is "Yes" to any one of these questions, explain on a separate sheet of paper. Additionally, explain if any of the acts or circumstances below are related to you having been a victim of a severe form of trafficking. Answering "Yes" does not necessarily mean that you will be denied T nonimmigrant status or are not entitled to adjust your status or register for permanent residence.)*

1. Have you EVER:

   a. Committed a crime or offense for which you have not been arrested? ☐ Yes ☒ No

   b. Been arrested, cited, or detained by any law enforcement officer (including DHS, former INS, and military officers) for any reason? ☐ Yes ☒ No

   c. Been charged with committing any crime or offense? ☐ Yes ☒ No

   d. Been convicted of a crime or offense (even if violation was subsequently expunged or pardoned)? ☐ Yes ☒ No

   e. Been placed in an alternative sentencing or a rehabilitative program (for example: diversion, deferred prosecution, withheld adjudication, deferred adjudication)? ☐ Yes ☒ No

   f. Received a suspended sentence, been placed on probation, or been paroled? ☐ Yes ☒ No

   g. Been in jail or prison? ☐ Yes ☒ No

   h. Been the beneficiary of a pardon, amnesty, rehabilitation, or other act of clemency or similar action? ☐ Yes ☒ No

   i. Exercised diplomatic immunity to avoid prosecution for a criminal offense in the United States? ☐ Yes ☒ No

If you answered "Yes" to any of the above questions, complete the following table. If you need more space, use a separate sheet of paper to give the same information.

Why were you arrested, cited, detained, or charged?	Date of arrest, citation, detention, charge (mm/dd/yyyy)	Where were you arrested, cited, detained, or charged? (City, State, Country)	Outcome or disposition (e.g., no charges filed, charges dismissed, jail, probation, etc.)

2. Have you:

    a. Engaged in prostitution or procurement of prostitution or do you intend to engage in prostitution or procurement of prostitution?   ☐ Yes ☒ No

    b. EVER engaged in any unlawful commercialized vice, including, but not limited to illegal gambling?   ☐ Yes ☒ No

    c. EVER knowingly encouraged, induced, assisted, abetted, or aided any alien to try to enter the United States illegally?   ☐ Yes ☒ No

    d. EVER illicitly trafficked in any controlled substance, or knowingly assisted, abetted, or colluded in the illicit trafficking of any controlled substance?   ☐ Yes ☒ No

3. Have you EVER committed, planned or prepared, participated in, threatened to, attempted to, or conspired to commit, gathered information for, or solicited funds for any of the following:

    a. Hijacking or sabotage of any conveyance (including an aircraft, vessel, or vehicle)?   ☐ Yes ☒ No

    b. Seizing or detaining, and threatening to kill, injure, or continue to detain, another individual in order to compel a third person (including a governmental organization) to do or abstain from doing any act as an explicit or implicit condition for the release of the individual seized or detained?   ☐ Yes ☒ No

    c. Assassination?   ☐ Yes ☒ No

    d. The use of any firearm with intent to endanger, directly or indirectly, the safety of one or more individual or to cause substantial damage to property?   ☐ Yes ☒ No

    e. The use of any biological agent; chemical agent; or nuclear weapon or device; explosive; or other weapon or dangerous device, with intent to endanger, directly or indirectly, the safety of one or more individuals or to cause substantial damage to property?   ☐ Yes ☒ No

4. Have you EVER been a member of, solicited money or members for, provided support for, attended military training (as defined in section 2339D(c)(1) of title 18, United States Code) by or on behalf of, or been associated with an organization that is:

    a. Designated as a terrorist organization under section 219 of the Immigration and Nationality Act?   ☐ Yes ☒ No

    b. Any other group of two or more individuals, whether organized or not, which has engaged in or has a subgroup which has engaged in:

        1. Hijacking or sabotage of any conveyance (including an aircraft, vessel, or vehicle)?   ☐ Yes ☒ No

        2. Seizing or detaining, and threatening to kill, injure, or continue to detain another individual in order to compel a third person (including a governmental organization) to do or abstain from doing any act as an explicit or implicit condition for the release of the individual seized or detained?   ☐ Yes ☒ No

        3. Assassination?   ☐ Yes ☒ No

        4. The use of any firearm with intent to endanger, directly or indirectly, the safety of one or more individual or to cause substantial damage to property?   ☐ Yes ☒ No

        5. Soliciting money or members or otherwise providing material support to a terrorist organization?   ☐ Yes ☒ No

        6. The use of any biological agent; chemical agent; or nuclear weapon or device; explosive, or other weapon or dangerous device, with intent to endanger, directly or indirectly, the safety of one or more individuals or to cause substantial damage to property?   ☐ Yes ☒ No

5. Do you intend to engage in the United States in:

   a. Espionage? ☐ Yes ☒ No

   b. Any unlawful activity, or any activity the purpose of which is in opposition, to control, or overthrow of the government of the United States? ☐ Yes ☒ No

   c. Solely, principally, or incidentally in any activity related to espionage or sabotage or to violate any law involving the export of goods, technology, or sensitive information? ☐ Yes ☒ No

6. Have you ever been or do you continue to be a member of the Communist or other totalitarian party, except when membership was involuntary? ☐ Yes ☒ No

7. Have you, during the period of March 23, 1933, to May 8, 1945, in association with either the Nazi Government of Germany or any organization or government associated or allied with the Nazi Government of Germany, ever ordered, incited, assisted, or otherwise participated in the persecution of any person because of race, religion, nationality, membership in a particular social group, or political opinion? ☐ Yes ☒ No

8. Have you EVER been present or nearby when any person was:

   a. Intentionally killed, tortured, beaten, or injured? ☐ Yes ☒ No

   b. Displaced or moved from his or her residence by force, compulsion, or duress? ☐ Yes ☒ No

   c. In any way compelled or forced to engage in any kind of sexual contact or relations? ☐ Yes ☒ No

9. a. Are removal, exclusion, rescission, or deportation proceedings pending against you? ☐ Yes ☒ No

   b. Have removal, exclusion, rescission, or deportation proceedings EVER been initiated against you? ☐ Yes ☒ No

   c. Have you EVER been removed, excluded, or deported from the United States? ☐ Yes ☒ No

   d. Have you EVER been ordered to be removed, excluded, or deported from the United States? ☐ Yes ☒ No

   e. Have you EVER been denied a visa or denied admission to the United States? *(If a visa was denied, explain why on a separate sheet of paper.)* ☐ Yes ☒ No

   f. Have you EVER been granted voluntary departure by an immigration officer or an immigration judge and failed to depart within the allotted time? ☐ Yes ☒ No

10. Have you EVER ordered, incited, called for, committed, assisted, helped with, or otherwise participated in any of the following:

   a. Acts involving torture or genocide? ☐ Yes ☒ No

   b. Killing any person? ☐ Yes ☒ No

   c. Intentionally and severely injuring any person? ☐ Yes ☒ No

   d. Engaging in any kind of sexual contact or relations with any person who was being forced or threatened? ☐ Yes ☒ No

   e. Limiting or denying any person's ability to exercise religious beliefs? ☐ Yes ☒ No

11. Have you EVER:

   a. Served in, been a member of, assisted in, or participated in any military unit, paramilitary unit, police unit, self-defense unit, vigilante unit, rebel group, guerrilla group, militia, or insurgent organization? ☐ Yes ☒ No

   b. Served in any prison, jail, prison camp, detention facility, labor camp, or any other situation that involved detaining persons? ☐ Yes ☒ No

PART D. Processing Information (continued)

12. Have you EVER been a member of, assisted in, or participated in any group, unit, or organization of any kind in which you or other persons used any type of weapon against any person or threatened to do so? ☐ Yes ☒ No

13. Have you EVER assisted or participated in selling or providing weapons to any person who to your knowledge used them against another person, or in transporting weapons to any person who to your knowledge used them against another person? ☐ Yes ☒ No

14. Have you EVER received any type of military, paramilitary, or weapons training? ☐ Yes ☒ No

15. Are you under a final order or civil penalty for violating section 274C (producing and/or using false documentation to unlawfully satisfy a requirement of the Immigration and Nationality Act)? ☐ Yes ☒ No

16. Have you EVER, by fraud or willful misrepresentation of a material fact, sought to procure, or procured, a visa or other documentation, for entry into the United States or any immigration benefit? ☐ Yes ☒ No

17. Have you EVER left the United States to avoid being drafted into the U.S. Armed Forces? ☐ Yes ☒ No

18. Have you EVER been a J nonimmigrant exchange visitor who was subject to the two-year foreign residence requirement and not yet complied with that requirement or obtained a waiver of such? ☐ Yes ☒ No

19. Have you EVER detained, retained, or withheld the custody of a child, having a lawful claim to U.S. citizenship, outside the United States from a U.S. citizen granted custody? ☐ Yes ☒ No

20. Do you plan to practice polygamy in the United States? ☐ Yes ☒ No

21. Have you entered the United States as a stowaway? ☐ Yes ☒ No

22. a. Do you have a communicable disease of public health significance? ☐ Yes ☒ No

   b. Do you have or have you had a physical or mental disorder and behavior (or a history of behavior that is likely to recur) associated with the disorder which has posed or may pose a threat to the property, safety, or welfare of yourself or others? ☐ Yes ☒ No

   c. Are you now or have you been a drug abuser or drug addict? ☐ Yes ☒ No

PART E. Information About Your Family Members

Provide the following information about your spouse and all of your sons and daughters. If you need more space, attach an additional sheet of paper.

1. ☒ Spouse

Family Name (Last Name)	Given Name (First Name)	Middle Name (if any)	Date of Birth (mm/dd/yyyy)
███████	████████	██████	04/29/1984
Country of Birth		Current Location	
India		USA/India	

2. ☒ Children

a.

Family Name (Last Name)	Given Name (First Name)	Middle Name (if any)	Date of Birth (mm/dd/yyyy)
■■■■■	■■■■■		12/13/2016

Country of Birth		Relationship	Current Location
USA		Child	Riverview, FL USA

b.

Family Name (Last Name)	Given Name (First Name)	Middle Name (if any)	Date of Birth (mm/dd/yyyy)

Country of Birth	Relationship	Current Location
	-	

c.

Family Name (Last Name)	Given Name (First Name)	Middle Name (if any)	Date of Birth (mm/dd/yyyy)

Country of Birth	Relationship	Current Location
	-	

Complete Form I-914, Supplement A, Application for Family Member of T-1 Recipient, for each family member listed above for whom you are now applying to have join you in the United States, and attach it to this application.

PART F. Applicant's Statement, Contact Information, Declaration, Certification, and Signature

NOTE: Read the Penalties section of the Form I-914 Instructions before completing this part.

Applicant's Statement

NOTE: Select the box for either Item A. or B. in Item Number 1. If applicable, select the box for Item Number 2.

1. Applicant's Statement Regarding the Interpreter

   A. ☒ I can read and understand English, and I have read and understand every question and instruction on this application and my answer to every question.

   B. ☐ The interpreter named in **Part G.** read to me every question and instruction on this application and my answer to every question in [   ],

   a language in which I am fluent, and I understood everything.

2. Applicant's Statement Regarding the Preparer

   ☒ At my request, the preparer named in **Part H.,** | Brian D. Lerner | ,
   prepared this application for me based only upon information I provided or authorized.

PART F. Applicant's Statement, Contact Information, Declaration, Certification, and Signature (continued)

Applicant's Contact Information

3. Applicant's Daytime Telephone Number

▮▮▮▮▮▮▮▮▮▮▮

4. Applicant's Mobile Telephone Number (if any)

▮▮▮▮▮▮▮▮▮▮

5. Applicant's Email Address (if any)

▮▮▮▮▮▮▮▮▮▮

Applicant's Declaration and Certification

Copies of any documents I have submitted are exact photocopies of unaltered, original documents, and I understand that USCIS may require that I submit original documents to USCIS at a later date. Furthermore, I authorize the release of any information from any and all of my records that USCIS may need to determine my eligibility for the immigration benefit that I seek.

I authorize the release of any information from my record that USCIS needs to determine eligibility for the benefit I am seeking to investigate my claim, and to investigate fraudulent claims. I further authorize USCIS to release information to law enforcement agencies and prosecutors investigating crimes of trafficking or related crimes. I further authorize USCIS to release information to Federal, State, and local public and private agencies providing benefits, to be used solely in making determinations of eligibility for benefits pursuant to 8 USC 1641(c).

I furthermore authorize release of information contained in this application, in supporting documents, and in my USCIS records, to other entities and persons where necessary for the administration and enforcement of U.S. immigration law.

I understand that USCIS may require me to appear for an appointment to take my biometrics (fingerprints, photograph, and/or signature) and, at that time, if I am required to provide biometrics, I will be required to sign an oath reaffirming that:

1) I reviewed and understood all of the information contained in, and submitted with, my application; and

2) All of this information was complete, true, and correct at the time of filing.

I certify, under penalty of perjury, that all of the information in my application and any document submitted with it were provided or authorized by me, that I reviewed and understand all of the information contained in, and submitted with, my application and that all of this information is complete, true, and correct.

Applicant's Signature

6. Applicant's Signature (sign in ink)

➡ ▮▮▮▮▮▮▮▮▮▮▮▮▮

Date of Signature (mm/dd/yyyy)

09/14/2018

NOTE TO ALL APPLICANTS: If you do not completely fill out this application or fail to submit required documents listed in the Instructions, USCIS may deny your application.

PART G. Interpreter's Contact Information, Certification, and Signature

Provide the following information about the interpreter.

Interpreter's Full Name

1. Interpreter's Family Name (Last Name)

   Interpreter's Given Name (First Name)

2. Interpreter's Business or Organization Name (if any)

Interpreter's Mailing Address

3. Street Number and Name

   Apt. Ste. Flr. Number
   ☐ ☐ ☐

   City or Town

   State

   ZIP Code

   Province

   Postal Code

   Country

Interpreter's Contact Information

4. Interpreter's Daytime Telephone Number

5. Interpreter's Mobile Telephone Number (if any)

6. Interpreter's Email Address (if any)

Interpreter's Certification

I certify, under penalty of perjury, that:

I am fluent in English and _____, which is the same language specified in Part F., Item B. in Item Number 1., and I have read to this applicant in the identified language every question and instruction on this application and his or her answer to every question. The applicant informed me that he or she understands every instruction, question, and answer on the application, including the **Applicant's Declaration and Certification**, and has verified the accuracy of every answer.

Interpreter's Signature

7. Interpreter's Signature (sign in ink)

   Date of Signature (mm/dd/yyyy)

PART H. Contact Information, Declaration, and Signature of the Person Preparing this Application, if Other Than the Applicant

Provide the following information about the preparer.

Preparer's Full Name

1. Preparer's Family Name (Last Name)

   Lerner

   Preparer's Given Name (First Name)

   Brian

2. Preparer's Business or Organization Name (if any)

   Law Offices of Brian D. Lerner, APC

Preparer's Mailing Address

3. Street Number and Name

   3233 E. Broadway

   Apt. Ste. Flr. ☐ ☐ ☐ Number

   City or Town

   Long Beach

   State CA   ZIP Code 90803

   Province

   Postal Code

   Country USA

Preparer's Contact Information

4. Preparer's Daytime Telephone Number

   (562) 495-0554

5. Preparer's Mobile Telephone Number (if any)

6. Preparer's Email Address (if any)

   blerner@californiaimmigration.us

Preparer's Statement

7. A. ☐ I am not an attorney or accredited representative but have prepared this application on behalf of the applicant and with the applicant's consent.

   B. ☒ I am an attorney or accredited representative and my representation of the applicant in this case

   ☒ extends ☐ does not extend beyond the preparation of this application.

   NOTE: If you are an attorney or accredited representative, you may be obliged to submit a completed Form G-28, Notice of Entry of Appearance as Attorney or Accredited Representative, with this application.

Preparer's Certification

By my signature, I certify, under penalty of perjury, that I prepared this application at the request of the applicant. The applicant then reviewed this completed application and informed me that he or she understands all of the information contained in, and submitted with, his or her application, including the **Applicant's Declaration and Certification**, and that all of this information is complete, true, and correct. I completed this application based only on information that the applicant provided to me or authorized me to obtain or use.

Preparer's Signature

8. Preparer's Signature (sign in ink)

   Date of Signature (mm/dd/yyyy)

   09/14/2018

EXHIBITS

EXHIBIT #1

APPLICANT'S DECLARATION

<u>**DECLARATION OF**</u> ██████████

I, ████████ , declare as follows:

1. I am 34-years-old and I was born in Batala, India.

2. I last entered the United States on March 10, 2014 as an H-1B nonimmigrant worker. My current H-1B status expires on June 15, 2019. I was previously in the United States in F-1 student status and completed my Masters in Finance at the University of Illinois Institute of Technology (Illinois Tech) in Chicago, Illinois.

3. I met my husband, ████████████ , through a common friend in November 2008 while studying at Illinois Tech. At the time, my husband was pursuing his Masters in Electrical Engineering. We became friends, started dating and started living together in 2009.

4. We were married in India on May 18, 2013. We were also married in the United States on May 18, 2016, in St. Petersburg, Florida. We have one U.S. citizen daughter together, 22-month-old, Saria.

5. During our relationship, I was a victim of severe psychological, emotional and physical abuse. The abuse started prior to first marriage but got significantly worse after our marriage and continued until we separated in September 2017. The abuse was constant, but the type and severity depended greatly on my husband's mood.

6. My husband was a very manipulative and controlling man, who would say when and where I could go, what I could wear, who I could be friends with and who could visit our home. He would force me to cook and clean and do any other chores that he thought were necessary. When he got upset, he would curse at me, call me degrading names and even threaten to have me deported or take away our daughter. He would do this in front of our daughter and other family and friends, he just did not care. When things got real bad, which was often, he would physically abuse me; spit in my face, punch me, kick me, slap me and pull my hair. He also sexually abused me; forcefully had rough and violent sex with me, tying me up at times, and forced me to try different things which were very painful. He also threatened to hurt me if I refused to have sex with him.

7. When his mother and father would visit, they too would call me names and criticize the way I cared for our daughter and the way I took care of their son.

8. I never told anyone about the abuse, I kept everything to myself. I felt very ashamed. The only people that knew what I was going through and how I was suffering were my parents in India and my brother who lived nearby in Florida. If people ever asked about by injuries, my bruises, I would just lie and make something up. My family would urge

me to leave him, to file for divorce or even call the police but I never did. I wanted to leave, I really did, but I felt stuck and I was scared. I also loved my husband dearly and always believed him when he told me that he was sorry, that he loved me and that it would never happen again.

9. I did have the strength to leave once though, around June 2017, and I stayed with my brother. I returned home in August 2017 because I was afraid of what my husband might do, afraid for my safety and the safety of our daughter.

10. I also thought about leaving my husband and staying in India when we returned there in 2014 for my husband's brother's wedding. I didn't want to go to that wedding in the first place, I didn't feel comfortable, but once in India, I didn't want to return to the United States either. I had a lot going for me in the United States, including my career, but I couldn't imagine going back to our life in Florida, going back to the constant physical, verbal and emotional abuse. I think my husband could sense how I was feeling during that trip and he promised over and over that he would change and that things would be different when we returned to the United States. Of course I believed him and of course, things did not change. My husband never allowed me to return to India after that and I have not been back since.

11. On September 1, 2017, during another argument, my husband called me various names and slapped me while I had our daughter in my arms. I tried to leave our home, but my husband took my cell phone, house keys and car keys and warned me not to call the police. When I insisted on leaving, his parents got involved and grab me by the arms and dragged me back into the house. They all proceeded to hit and slap me and curse at me, and my husband's father got a knife from the kitchen and threatened to kill me. Again, my husband warned me not to call the police and said that he could kill me before they ever came and that he would harm our baby. I called my parents in India later that night and they called my brother in USA and my brother called the police to conduct welfare check and police arrested my husband and his parents the very next day.

12. Shortly after this incident, I filed for divorce.

13. On September 22, 2017, my husband and his parents were charged with various crimes including false imprisonment, armed false imprisonment, aggravated assault with a deadly weapon and domestic violence/battery.

14. On July 16, 2018, my husband was convicted on felony false imprisonment and misdemeanor domestic violence/battery. The same day my father-in-law was convicted of felony armed false imprisonment, felony aggravated assault with a deadly weapon and misdemeanor domestic violence/battery, and my mother-in-law was convicted of felony false imprisonment and domestic violence/battery.

15. My husband and his parents are currently detained by Immigration and I have been told that they should be deported by end of the month.

16. During these proceedings I assisted the police and the prosecutors every step of the way, doing everything that was asked of me, including given a full statement to the police, identifying possible witnesses and testifying/speaking at their trial. I also sat through a very long deposition in regard to the order of protection that I filed again my husband and his parents, and I provided a statement to Immigration authorities requesting that any bond be denied in my husband's case.

17. I have suffered tremendously as a result to the abuse that I have suffered in this country and I would suffer even more if I was forced to return to India. Not only would I lose everything that I have worked for so hard in this country, but my daughter would be forced to return with me. My daughter's life would be truly altered in India where her father will be able to take her away from me, while in the United States his rights have been terminated. She would also be denied being raised in her birth country and lose all the benefits she would have in this country as a U.S. citizen.

18. Returning to India would also put me in a greater risk as I would be returning to a country where my abusers presumably live. I believe my daughter's life would be in danger as well. I would also be returning to a country with significant human rights issues including police and security force abuses, widespread corruption, religious restrictions, and lack of criminal investigations or accountability for cases related to rape, domestic violence, dowry-related deaths, honor killings, and sexual harassment.

19. I have tried to do everything right in this country and I have never violated any criminal or immigration laws in this country and I only pray that I can remain here legally with my daughter.

20. For these reasons, I beg immigration to grant my application for T status.

I declare under penalty of perjury under the laws of the United States that the foregoing is true and correct. Executed in Riverview, Florida.

Date: 10/11/2018

EXHIBIT #2

APPLICANT'S CURRENT PASSPORT (BIO PAGE ONLY)

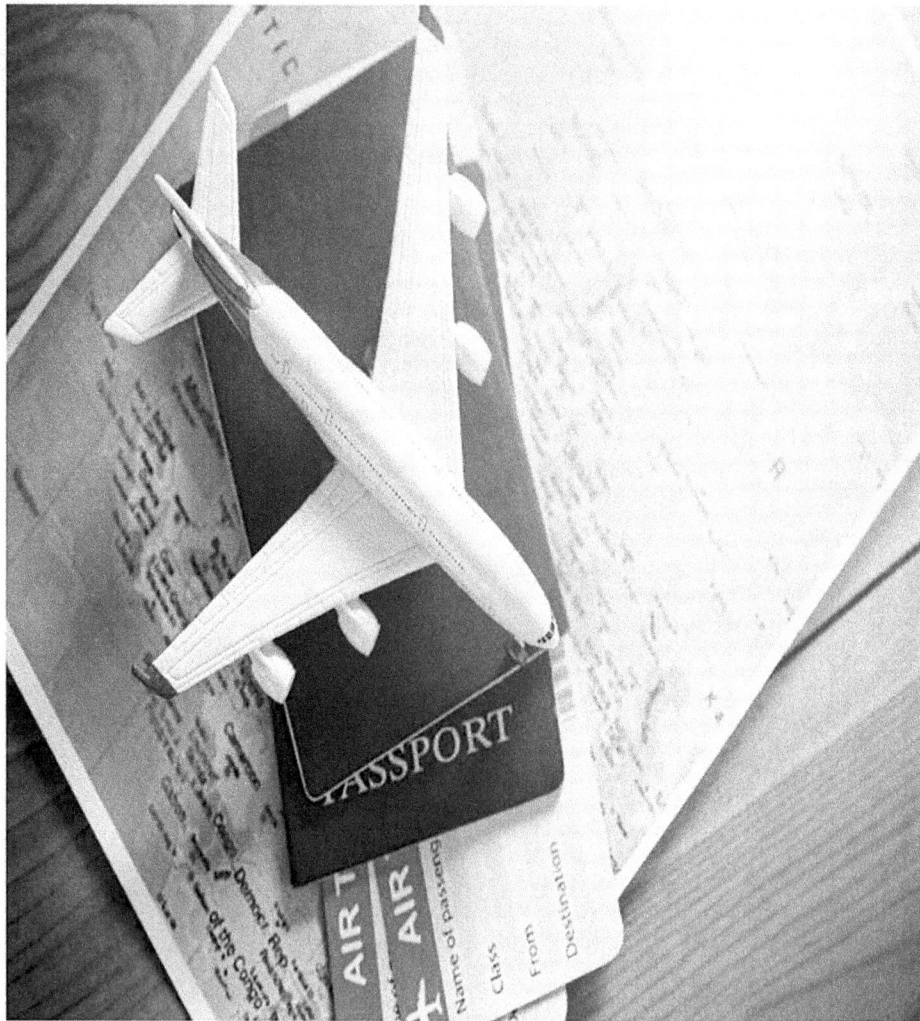

भारत गणराज्य REPUBLIC OF INDIA

ATLANTA

F

28/11/1983

21/03/2016

20/03/2026

भारतीय / INDIAN

P<IND8311287F2603209<<<<<<<<<<<<<<<<<
P1529970<2<<SILKY<<<<<<<<<<<<<<<<<<<<<<

EXHIBIT #3
APPLICANT'S EXPIRED PASSPORT, VISA, AND ENTRY
STAMP

भारत गणराज्य REPUBLIC OF INDIA

शाके द्वारा, भारत गणराज्य के राष्ट्रपति के नाम पर, उन सभ से जिनका एव यह सो सरोकार हो, यह सनिंधा एवं अपेक्षा की जाती है कि वे धारक को दिया रोक-टोक, आजादी से चलने-फिरने दें, और उसे हर तरह की ऐसी सहायता और सुरक्षा प्रदान करें जिसकी उसे आवश्यकता हो ।

THESE ARE TO REQUEST AND REQUIRE IN THE NAME OF THE PRESIDENT OF THE REPUBLIC OF INDIA ALL THOSE WHOM IT MAY CONCERN TO ALLOW THE BEARER TO PASS FREELY WITHOUT LET OR HINDRANCE, AND TO AFFORD HIM OR HER EVERY ASSISTANCE AND PROTECTION OF WHICH HE OR SHE MAY STAND IN NEED.

भारत गणराज्य के राष्ट्रपति के आदेश से दिया गया
BY ORDER OF THE PRESIDENT OF THE REPUBLIC OF INDIA

राज कुमार
RAJ KUMAR
सहायक/Assistant
पारपत्र कार्यालय, जालंधर
Passport Office, Jalandhar

P INDIAN

F 28/11/1983

30/10/2006 29/10/2016

G0497445<7IND8311287F1610291<<<<<<<<<<<<<<<0

VISA UNITED STATES OF AMERICA

Issuing Post Name
NEW DELHI

Control Number
20131289550001

Surname
GAIND

Given Name

Visa Type /Class
R   H1B

Passport Number

Sex
F

Birth Date
28NOV1983

Nationality
IND

M

Issue Date
01MAY2013

Expiration Date
29OCT2015

0101

Annotation

H2192255

PN-COGNIZANT TECHNOLOGY SOLUTIONS US CORP
P#-EAC1303951617   PED-29OCT2015

<<<<<<<<<<<<<<<<<<<<<<<<<<<<<<
G0497445<7IND8311287F1510298H8NWD007X6532234

EXHIBIT #4

APPLICANT'S H-1B APPROVAL NOTICE AND CURRENT
I-94

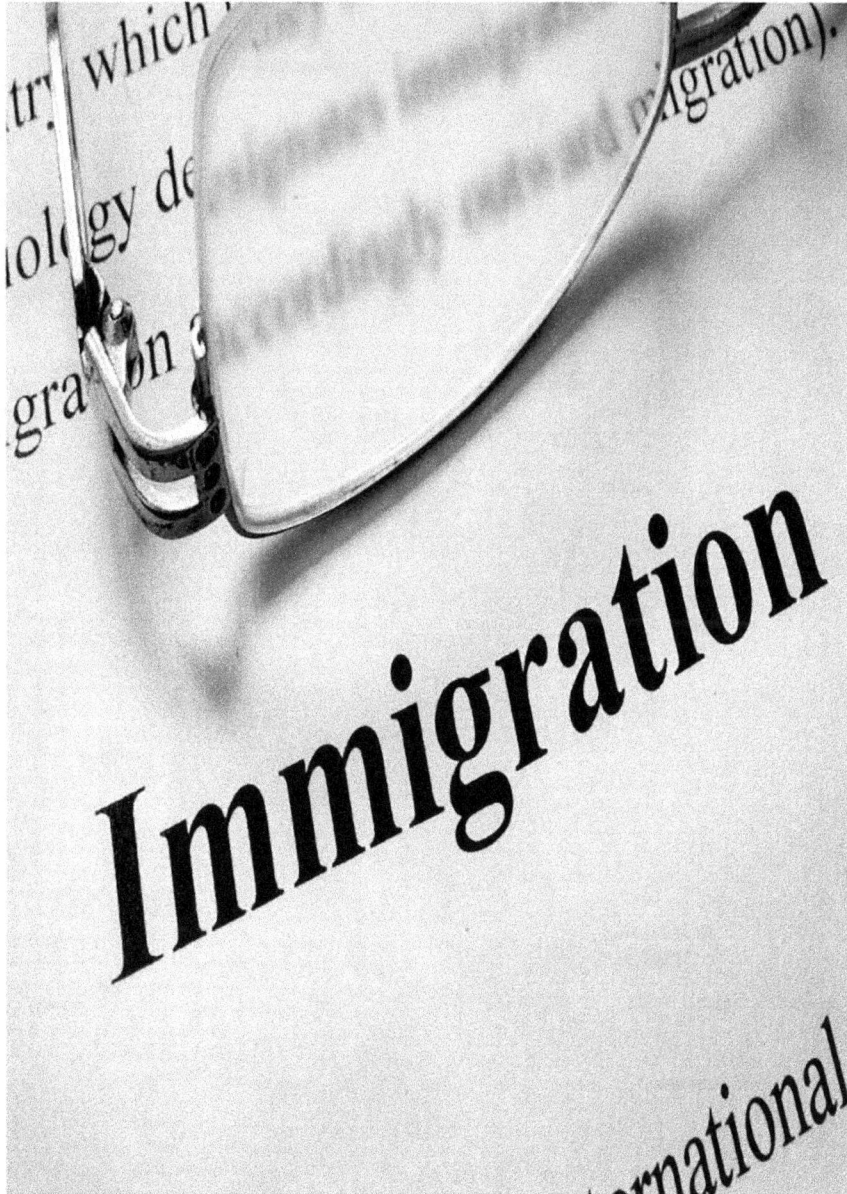

THE UNITED STATES OF AMERICA

I-797A | NOTICE OF ACTION | DEPARTMENT OF HOMELAND SECURITY
U.S. CITIZENSHIP AND IMMIGRATION SERVICES

Receipt Number EAC1704351739		Case Type I129 - PETITION FOR A NONIMMIGRANT WORKER
Receipt Date 12/05/2016	Priority Date	Petitioner COGNIZANT SOLNS US CORP.
Notice Date 03/14/2017	Page 1 of 2	Beneficiary ▉▉▉▉▉▉▉

COGNIZANT SOLNS US CORP
c/o 252262 - CHANDRIKA RACHAKONDA IMG
▉▉▉▉▉▉▉▉
COLLEGE STATION TX 77845

Notice Type: Approval Notice
Class: H1B
Valid from 03/14/2017 to 06/15/2019

The above petition and extension of stay have been approved. The status of the named foreign worker(s) in this classification is valid as indicated above. The foreign worker(s) can work for the petitioner, but only as detailed in the petition and for the period authorized. Changes in employment or training may require you to file a new Form I-129 petition. Since this employment or training authorization stems from the filing of this petition, separate employment or training authorization documentation is not required. The I-94 attached below may contain a grace period of up to 10 days before, and up to 10 days after the petition validity period for the following classifications: CW-1, E-1, E-2, E-3, H-1B, H-2B, H-3, L-1A, L-1B, O-1, O-2, P-1, P-2, P-3, TN-1, and TN-2. H-2A nonimmigrants may contain a grace period of up to one week before and 30 days after the petition validity period. The grace period is a period of authorized stay but does not provide the beneficiary authorization to work beyond the petition validity period. The decision to grant a grace period and the length of the granted grace period is discretionary and final and cannot be contested on motion or appeal. Please contact the IRS with any questions about tax withholding.

The petitioner should keep the upper portion of this notice. The lower portion should be given to the worker. He or she should keep the right part with his or her Form I-94, Arrival-Departure Record. The I-94 portion should be given to the U.S. Customs and Border Protection when he or she leaves the United States. The left part is for his or her records. A person granted an extension of stay who leaves the U.S. must normally obtain a new visa before returning. The left part can be used in applying for the new visa. If a visa is not required, he or she should present it, along with any other required documentation, when applying for reentry in this new classification at a port of entry or pre-flight inspection station. The petitioner may also file Form I-824, Application for Action on an Approved Application or Petition, to request that we notify a consulate, port of entry, or pre-flight inspection office of this approval.

The approval of this visa petition does not in itself grant any immigration status and does not guarantee that the alien beneficiary will subsequently be found to be eligible for a visa, for admission to the United States, or for an extension, change, or adjustment of status.

THIS FORM IS NOT A VISA AND MAY NOT BE USED IN PLACE OF A VISA.

The Small Business Regulatory Enforcement and Fairness Act established the Office of the National Ombudsman (ONO) at the Small Business Administration. The ONO assists small businesses with issues related to federal regulations. If you are a small business with a comment or complaint about regulatory enforcement, you may contact the ONO at www.sba.gov/ombudsman or phone 202-205-2417 or fax 202-481-5719.

Please see the additional information on the back. You will be notified separately about any other cases you filed.

USCIS/Vermont Service Center
U. S. CITIZENSHIP & IMMIGRATION SVC
75 Lower Welden Street
Saint Albans VT 05479-0001

Customer Service Telephone: 800-375-5283

PLEASE TEAR OFF FORM I-94 PRINTED BELOW AND STAPLE TO ORIGINAL I-94 IF AVAILABLE

Detach This Half for Personal Records

Receipt# EAC1704351739

I-94# ▉▉▉▉▉▉▉

NAME ▉▉▉▉▉▉

CLASS H1B

VALID FROM 03/14/2017 UNTIL 06/15/2019

PETITIONER
COGNIZANT SOLNS US CORP.

COLLEGE STATION TX 77845

217647468 30

Receipt Number EAC1704351739
US Citizenship and Immigration Services

I94 Departure Record
Petitioner: COGNIZANT SOLNS US CORP

14. Family Name ▉▉▉▉▉▉	
15. First (Given) Name ▉▉▉▉	16. Date of Birth 11/28/1983
17. Country of Citizenship INDIA	

FORM I-797A (REV. 08/01/16)

THE UNITED STATES OF AMERICA

I-797A | NOTICE OF ACTION | DEPARTMENT OF HOMELAND SECURITY
U.S. CITIZENSHIP AND IMMIGRATION SERVICES

Receipt Number	Case Type
EAC1704351739	I129 - PETITION FOR A NONIMMIGRANT WORKER

Receipt Date	Priority Date	Petitioner
12/05/2016		COGNIZANT SOLNS US CORP.

Notice Date	Page	Beneficiary
03/14/2017	2 of 2	

NOTICE: Although this application or petition has been approved, USCIS and the U.S. Department of Homeland Security reserve the right to verify this information before and/or after making a decision on your case so we can ensure that you have complied with applicable laws, rules, regulations, and other legal authorities. We may review public information and records, contact others by mail, the internet or phone, conduct site inspections of businesses and residences, or use other methods of verification. We will use the information obtained to determine whether you are eligible for the benefit you seek. If we find any derogatory information, we will follow the law in determining whether to provide you (and the legal representative listed on your Form G-28, if you submitted one) an opportunity to address that information before we make a formal decision on your case or start proceedings.

Please see the additional information on the back. You will be notified separately about any other cases you filed.

USCIS/Vermont Service Center
U. S. CITIZENSHIP & IMMIGRATION SVC
75 Lower Welden Street
Saint Albans VT 05479-0001

Customer Service Telephone: 800-375-5283

PLEASE TEAR OFF FORM I-797 BELOW AND STAPLE INFORMATION PART AVAILABLE

Detach This Half for Personal Records

Receipt Number	VOID	VOID	VOID
I-94#			
NAME	VOID	VOID	VOID
CLASS			
VALID FROM	UNTIL VOID	VOID	VOID
PETITIONER	VOID	VOID	VOID
	VOID	VOID	VOID
	VOID	VOID	VOID

Receipt Number	VOID	VOID
US Citizenship and Immigration Services		
VOID	VOID	VOID
I94 Departure Record		
Petitioner VOID	VOID	VOID
14. Family Name		
VOID	VOID	VOID
15. First (Given) Name		16. Date of Birth
VOID	VOID	VOID
17. Country of Citizenship		
VOID	VOID	VOID

FORM I-797A (REV. 09/01/16)

EXHIBIT #5

APPLICANT'S MARRIAGE CERTIFICATE AND EVIDENCE OF PENDING
DISSOLUTION/DIVORCE

CERTIFICATE

This certificate is presented to

SAMPLE TEXT HERE YOUR SAMPLE TEXT YOUR SAMPLE TEXT

NAME SURNAME

YOUR SAMPLE TEXT HERE YOUR SAMPLE TEXT

SAMPLE TEXT HERE YOUR SAMPLE TEXT YOUR SAMPLE TEXT
YOUR SAMPLE TEXT YOUR SAMPLE TEXT
TEXT HERE YOUR SAMPLE

DATE 24.05.18   SIGNATURE *Signature*

Department of Health • Office of Vital Statistics

STATE OF FLORIDA
MARRIAGE RECORD
TYPE IN UPPER CASE
USE BLACK INK
This license not valid unless seal of Clerk,
Circuit or County Court, appears thereon

(STATE FILE NUMBER)

2016 ML 3372976
(APPLICATION NUMBER)

APPLICATION TO MARRY

1. NAME OF SPOUSE (First, Middle, Last)	1a. MAIDEN SURNAME (If applicable)	2. DATE OF BIRTH (Month, Day, Year)
▮▮▮	▮▮▮	04/29/1984

3a. RESIDENCE - CITY, TOWN, OR LOCATION	3b. COUNTY	3c. STATE	4. BIRTHPLACE (State or Foreign Country)
▮▮▮	PINELLAS	FLORIDA	INDIA

5a. NAME OF SPOUSE (First, Middle, Last)	5b. MAIDEN SURNAME (If applicable)	6. DATE OF BIRTH (Month, Day, Year)
▮▮▮	GAIND	11/28/1983

7a. RESIDENCE - CITY, TOWN, OR LOCATION	7b. COUNTY	7c. STATE	8. Birthplace (State or Foreign Country)
ST PETERSBURG	PINELLAS	FLORIDA	INDIA

WE THE APPLICANTS NAMED IN THIS CERTIFICATE, EACH FOR HIMSELF OR HERSELF, STATE THAT THE INFORMATION PROVIDED ON THIS RECORD IS CORRECT TO THE BEST OF OUR KNOWLEDGE AND BELIEF, THAT NO LEGAL OBJECTION TO THIS MARRIAGE NOR THE ISSUANCE OF A LICENSE IS KNOWN TO US AND HEREBY APPLY FOR LICENSE TO MARRY.

9. SIGNATURE OF SPOUSE (Sign full name using black ink)	10. SUBSCRIBED AND SWORN TO BEFORE ME ON (DATE)
> *Dilli*	05/05/2016
11. TITLE OF OFFICIAL	12. SIGNATURE OF OFFICIAL (Use black ink)
DEPUTY CLERK	*Maria Stony*
13. SIGNATURE OF SPOUSE (Sign full name using black ink)	14. SUBSCRIBED AND SWORN TO BEFORE ME ON (DATE)
> *Silky end*	05/05/2016
15. TITLE OF OFFICIAL	16. SIGNATURE OF OFFICIAL (Use black ink)
DEPUTY CLERK	*Maria Stony*

LICENSE TO MARRY

AUTHORIZATION AND LICENSE IS HEREBY GIVEN TO ANY PERSON DULY AUTHORIZED BY THE LAWS OF THE STATE OF FLORIDA TO PERFORM A MARRIAGE CEREMONY WITHIN THE STATE OF FLORIDA AND TO SOLEMNIZE THE MARRIAGE OF THE ABOVE NAMED PERSON. THIS LICENSE MUST BE USED ON OR AFTER THE EFFECTIVE DATE AND ON OR BEFORE THE EXPIRATION DATE IN THE STATE OF FLORIDA IN ORDER TO BE RECORDED AND VALID.

17. COUNTY ISSUING LICENSE	18. DATE LICENSE ISSUED	18a. DATE LICENSE EFFECTIVE	19. EXPIRATION DATE
PINELLAS	05/05/2016	05/08/2016	07/04/2016

20a. SIGNATURE OF COURT CLERK OR JUDGE	20b TITLE	20c. BY D C
> *Ken Burke*	CLERK OF THE CIRCUIT COURT AND COMPTROLLER	ASG

CERTIFICATE OF MARRIAGE

I HEREBY CERTIFY THAT THE ABOVE NAMED SPOUSES WERE JOINED BY ME IN MARRIAGE IN ACCORDANCE WITH THE LAWS OF THE STATE OF FLORIDA.

21. DATE OF MARRIAGE (Month, Day, Year)	22. CITY, TOWN, OR LOCATION OF MARRIAGE
5/18/2016	St Petersburg, Pinellas County, Florida

23a. SIGNATURE OF PERSON PERFORMING CEREMONY (Use black ink)	23c. ADDRESS (Of person performing ceremony)
>	545 1st Avenue N, St Petersburg, FL 33701

23b. NAME AND TITLE OF PERSON PERFORMING CEREMONY (Or show state)	24. SIGNATURE OF WITNESS TO CEREMONY (Use black ink)
HOLLI A SATTEL Deputy Clerk	>
	25. SIGNATURE OF WITNESS TO CEREMONY (Use black ink)
	>

MAY 18 2016

IN THE CIRCUIT COURT OF THE THIRTEENTH JUDICIAL CIRCUIT
IN AND FOR HILLSBOROUGH COUNTY, FLORIDA
FAMILY LAW DIVISION

IN RE: The Marriage of

██████████

    Petitioner/Plaintiff/Wife,

and

██████████

    Respondent/Defendant/Husband.

_____/

CASE NO: 17DR14005
DIVISION: R

SUMMONS

THE STATE OF FLORIDA

TO: ██████████
    Inmate- Hillsborough County Jail
    Booking number 17032339

TO EACH SHERIFF OF THE STATE: You are commanded to serve this SUMMONS and a copy of the Petition for Dissolution of Marriage on the above-named Respondent.

IMPORTANT

A lawsuit has been filed against you. You have **20 calendar days** after this summons is served on you to file a written response to the attached complaint/petition with the clerk of this circuit court, located at Hillsborough County Courthouse , 800 E. Twiggs St., Tampa, Florida 33602 .A phone call will not *RM 101 protect you. Your written response, including the case number given above and the names of the parties, must be **filed** if you want the Court to hear your side of the case.

If you do not file your written response on time, you may lose the case, and your wages, money, and property may be taken thereafter without further warning from the Court. There are other legal requirements. You may want to call an attorney right away. If you do not know an attorney, you may call an attorney referral service or a legal aid office (listed in the phone book).

If you choose to file a written response yourself, at the same time you file your written response to the Court, you must also mail or take a copy of your written response to the party serving this summons at:

Terryn H. Bennett, Esquire
2309 South MacDill Ave. Suite 105
Tampa, FL 33629

Copies of all court documents in this case, including orders, are available at the Clerk of the Circuit Court's office. You may review these documents, upon request. You must keep the Clerk of the Circuit Court's office notified of your current address. (You may file Notice of Current Address, Florida Supreme Court Approved Family Law Form 12.915.) Future papers in this lawsuit will be mailed to the address on record at the clerk's office.

WARNING: Rule 12.285, Florida Family Law Rules of Procedure, requires certain automatic disclosure of documents and information. Failure to comply can result in sanctions, including dismissal or striking of pleadings.

IMPORTANTE

Usted ha sido demandado legalmente. Tiene veinte (20) dias, contados a partir del recibo de esta notificacion, para contestar la demanda adjunta, por escrito, y presentarla ante este tribunal. Localizado en: Hillsborough County Courthouse , 800 E. Twiggs St., Tampa, Florida. Una llamada telefonica no lo protegera. Si usted desea que el tribunal considere su defensa, debe presentar su respuesta por escrito, incluyendo el numero del caso y los nombres de las partes interesadas. Si usted no contesta la demanda a tiempo, pudiese perder el caso y podria ser despojado de sus ingresos y propiedades, o privado de sus derechos, sin previo aviso del tribunal. Existen otros requisitos legales. Si lo desea, usted puede consultar a un abogado inmediatamente.
Si no conoce a un abogado, puede llamar a una de las oficinas de asistencia legal que aparecen en la guia telefonica.

Si desea responder a la demanda por su cuenta, al mismo tiempo en que presente su respuesta ante el tribunal, usted debe enviar por correo o entregar una copia de su respuesta a la persona denominada abajo.

Si usted elige presentar personalmente una respuesta por escrito, en el mismo momento que usted presente su respuesta por escrito al Tribunal, usted debe enviar por correo o llevar una copia de su respuesta por escrito a la parte entregando esta orden de comparencencia a:

Nombre y direccion de la parte que entrega la orden de comparencencia:

Terryn H. Bennett, Esquire
2309 South MacDill Ave. Suite 105
Tampa, FL 33629

Copias de todos los documentos judiciales de este caso, incluyendo las ordenes, estan disponibles en la oficina del Secretario de Juzgado del Circuito [Clerk of the Circuit Court's office]. Estos documentos pueden ser revisados a su solicitud.

Usted debe de manener informada a la oficina del Secretario de Juzgado del Circuito de su direccion actual. (Usted puede presentar el Formulario: Ley de Familia de la Florida 12.915, [Florida Supreme Court Approved Family Law Form 12.915], Notificacion de la Direccion Actual [Notice of Current Address].) Los papelos que se presenten en el futuro en esta demanda judicial seran env ados por correo a la direccion que este registrada en la oficina del Secretario.

ADVERTENCIA: Regla 12.285 (Rule 12.285), de las Reglas de Procedimiento de Ley de Familia de la Florida [Florida Family Law Rules of Procedure], requiere cierta revelacion automatica de documentos e informacion. El incumplimient, puede resultar en sanciones, incluyendo la desestimacion o anulacion de los alegatos.

IMPORTANT

Des poursuites judiciaries ont ete entreprises contre vous. Vous avez 20 jours consecutifs a partir de la date de l'assignation de cette citation pour deposer une reponse ecrite a la plainte ci-jointe aupres de ce tribunal. Qui se trouve a: [L'Adresse] Hillsborough County Courthouse , 800 E. Twiggs St., Tampa,

Florida, 33602. Un simple coup de telephone est insuffisant pour vous proteger; vous etes obliges de deposer votre reponse ecrite, avec mention du numero
de dossier ci-dessus et du nom des parties nommees ici, si vous souhaitez que le tribunal entende votre cause. Si vous ne deposez pas votre reponse ecrite dans le delai requis, vous risquez de perdre la cause ainsi que votre salaire, votre argent, et vos biens peuvent etre saisis par la suite, sans aucun preavis ulterieur du tribunal. Il y a d'autres obligations juridiques et vous pouvez requerir les services immediats d'un avocat. Si vous ne connaissez pas d'avocat, vous pourriez telephoner a un service de reference d'avocats ou a un bureau Florida Family Law Rules of Procedure Form 12.910(a), Summons: Personal Service on an Individual (9/00) C-195 d'assistance juridique (figurant a l'annuaire de telephones).

Si vous choisissez de deposer vous-meme une reponse ecrite, il vous faudra egalement, en meme temps que cette formalite, faire parvenir ou expedier une copie au carbone ou une photocopie de votre reponse ecrite a la partie qui vous depose cette citation.

Nom et adresse de la partie qui depose cette citation:

Terryn H. Bennett, Esquire
2309 South MacDill Ave. Suite 105
Tampa, FL 33629

Les photocopies de tous les documents tribunals de cette cause, y compris des arrets, sont disponible au bureau du greffier. Vous pouvez revue ces documents, sur demande.

Il faut aviser le greffier de votre adresse actuelle. (Vous pouvez deposer O. Florida Supreme Court Approved Family Law Form 12.915, Notice of Current Address.) Les documents de l'avenir de ce proces seront envoyer a l' adresse que vous donnez au bureau du greffier.

ATTENTION: La regle 12.285 des regles de procedure du droit de la famille de la Floride exige que l'on remette certains renseignements et certains documents 4a la partie adverse. Tout refus de les fournir pourra donner lieu a des sanctions, y compris le rejet ou la suppression d'un ou de plusieurs actes de procedure.

WITNESS MY HAND and seal of this Court on _____, 2017.

DATED ___SEPTEMBER 12TH, 2017___

(SEAL)

PAT FRANK
CLERK OF THE CIRCUIT COURT

By: _Sharon D. Dale_
Deputy Clerk

IN THE CIRCUIT COURT OF THE THIRTEENTH JUDICIAL CIRCUIT
IN AND FOR HILLSBOROUGH COUNTY, FLORIDA
FAMILY LAW DIVISION

IN RE: The Marriage of

███████

Petitioner/Plaintiff/Wife,

and

███████

Respondent/Defendant/Husband.

CASE NO:
DIVISION:

_____/

WIFE'S PETITION FOR DISSOLUTION OF MARRIAGE and OTHER RELIEF

COUNT ONE

DISSOLUTION OF MARRIAGE

COMES NOW, the Wife, █████████ by and through the undersigned Attorney,

files this Petition for Dissolution of Marriage, and Other Relief and verifies the following

statements are true:

1. **ACTION FOR DISSOLUTION:** This is an action for Dissolution of Marriage

and other relief.

2. **RESIDENCY:** Wife has been a resident of the State of Florida for more than six

(6) months prior to the filing of this petition.

3. **MARRIAGE:** The parties were married to each other on May 18, 2013 in

Ludhiana, India and separate on or about September 1, 2017.

4. **VENUE:** The venue is Hillsborough County, Florida because the parties last

resided in this county as husband and wife.

5. **GROUNDS:** The marriage of the parties is irretrievably broken.

6. **MILITARY SERVICE DECLARATION:** Neither party is a member of the Armed Forces of the United States nor has either been within a period of thirty (30) days immediately preceding the filing of this action. Neither the Husband nor the Wife are citizens of the United States.

7. **MINOR CHILD:** There is one minor child common to both parties and subject to this proceeding, to wit:

    S.K.   **FEMALE**   **BORN 2016**

There are no other minor children born of the marriage and none are expected.

8. **PARENTAL RESPONSIBILITY :** It would be detrimental for the parties to have shared parental responsibility and it is in the best interest of the parties' minor child that the Wife should have sole parental responsibility of the parties' minor child. It is in the best interest of the parties' minor child that the court order a parenting plan that provides the Wife with majority timesharing and the Husband with supervised timesharing both temporarily and on a permanent basis.

9. **CHILD SUPPORT:** Both parties are able-bodied and have an obligation to support the minor child as determined by Florida's child support guidelines, section 61.30 both temporarily and permanently. In addition, the Husband should have income imputed to him prior to the determination of his child support obligation. The Wife requests that the Husband's child support obligation, retroactive support obligation, any arrearage obligation ordered by this Court to be paid by the Husband via income withholding order.

10. **MEDICAL INSURANCE FOR MINOR CHILD:** The minor child is in need of health, hospitalization, major medical, dental insurance, vision and/or medical reimbursement plan,

both temporarily and on a permanent basis. The parties should be required to share in the costs to provide health insurance for the minor child.

11.   **UNCOVERED MEDICAL, DENTAL & VISION EXPENSES:** The Parties should be required to contribute to the minor child's uncovered medical, dental and vision expenses that are reasonable and necessary based on their pro rata share of the Florida Child Support Guidelines.

12.   **COST OF EXTRA-CURRICULAR ACTIVITIES :** The Husband should be required to pay 100% of the cost of the minor child's extra-curricular activities on a temporary and permanent basis.

13.   **ALIMONY:** Wife is in need of temporary, transitional, rehabilitative, bridge-the-gap, permanent, durational and/or lump sum alimony. Husband has the ability to pay Wife alimony commensurate with the lifestyle the parties enjoyed during the marriage. Income should be imputed to the Husband prior to any determination of the Husband's ability to pay alimony to the Wife.

14.   **LIFE INSURANCE:** It is in the best interest of the minor child for the Court to enter an Order requiring the Husband to maintain a life insurance policy naming the Wife as the irrevocable beneficiary as and for security for her alimony and child support obligations. The Husband has the ability to pay the premiums associated with maintaining a life insurance policy.

15.   **DEPENDENCY EXEMPTION:** In order to maximize the funds available to support the minor child, the Wife is requiring that she be awarded the right to claim the child as dependent for tax purposes on a temporary as well as permanent basis. The Wife requests that the Husband be ordered to annually execute any and all documentation necessary to allow Wife to claim the child.

16.   **MARITAL RESIDENCE:** The parties jointly own the residence at 9601 Greenbank Dr., Riverview, FL 33569. The Wife is in need of exclusive use and possession of the marital residence and it is in the minor child's best interest that the Court awards the Wife exclusive and possession of the marital residence on a temporary as well as a permanent basis.

17.   **ASSETS:** During the marriage the parties incurred certain assets Wife seeks an unequal division of all said assets.

18.   **LIABILITIES:** During the marriage the parties incurred certain debts and liabilities and Wife seeks an equitable division of all said debts and liabilities, excluding any non-marital portion.

19.   **PERSONAL PROPERTY:** The parties possess jointly owned personal property in regard to which the rights of the parties should be adjudicated by this court. The court should equitably distribute said personal property between the parties awarding the Wife an unequal distribution.

20.   **APPOINTMENT OF FORENSIC ACCOUNTANT:** The Wife requests that a Certified Forensic Accountant be appointed in order to provide identification, classification, valuation and to prepare any equitable distribution chart of the parties assets and liabilities in order to assist the parties in resolving their disputes or, in necessary, for trial in this matter. Furthermore, the Wife requests that a Certified Forensic accountant be appointed in order to prepare a standard of living analysis for the purposes of Wife's claims for alimony. The Wife requests that the Court order same and that the Husband be financially responsible for the fees and costs associated with the Certified Forensic Accountant on a temporary as well as permanent basis.

21.   **TEMPORARY INJUNCTION:** The Wife requests this Court enter a Temporary Injunction to prevent the Husband from disposing or and/or selling marital assets through

expenditures unrelated to the Parties usual living expenses or by sales or transfers to third parties without the knowledge or consent of the Wife. The Wife would be immediately and irreparably injured by the Husband's disposing of marital assets, as once the assets have been disposed of or sold, they are no retrievable. The Wife is fearful that any transfers or sales could jeopardize the Parties' ability to settle the case and will make even more difficult the transfers necessary to restore the marital estate for purposes of equitable distribution. In addition, the Wife fears the Husband will use the funds to post bond for himself and his mother and father. The Wife fears the Husband and/or his parents will cause her and the minor child physical harm and the Husband has threatened to kill her and the minor child prior to killing himself.

22. **ATTORNEY'S FEES:** Wife has employed the firm of Terryn H. Bennett, P.A., to represent her in this action and has agreed to pay a reasonable attorney's fee, cost and suit money for this representation. Wife is financially unable to pay said attorney or the costs of this action. Husband is in a superior financial situation to that of Wife and and has the ability to pay Wife's reasonable attorney's fees and costs both temporarily and permanently. Income should be imputed to the Husband for the determination of his ability to pay the Wife's attorney's fees. In addition, should the Husband take legal action that is unreasonable and unnecessary, the Wife requests that this Court consider Section 61.16, Florida Statutes, Wrona v. Wrona, 592 So.2d 694 (Fla. 2nd DCA 1991), Rosen v. Rosen, 696 So.2d 697 (Fla. 2nd DCA 1997), Diaz v. Diaz, 727 So.2d 954 (Fla. 1st DCA 1998) and their progeny in determining the parties' responsibility for these fees.

COUNT II
PARTITION OF REAL PROPERTY

23. **Averment of above allegations:**

The Wife re-avers and re-affirms paragraphs one (1) through twenty-two (22) as set-forth above in this Petition for Dissolution of Marriage.

24. **Partition of Residential Real Property**

Pursuant to Florida Statute Chapter 64 Partition of Property, the Wife seeks partition of

the residential real property located at 9601 Greenbank Dr., Riverview, Fl 33569 Folio: 076738-

2410 a legal description is as follows:

Lot 26, Block 13, Riverglen Units 5,6, and 7 Phase 1, according to the map or plat thereof, as recorded in Plat Book 81, Page(s) 46, of the Public Records of Hillsborough County, Florida.

25. Venue

Pursuant to section 64.0222 Florida Statutes VENUE, Venue is proper in Hillsborough

County because the land which is the subject of this matter is located in Hillsborough County.

26. **Ownership of Property**

The Parties to this Partition action are the Wife, ███████ whose current physical

address is ███████████████████ and the Husband, ███████ who

currently resides at the Hillsborough County Jail both of which own an indivisible interest in the

residential real property herein.

27. **Major Repairs on Residential Real Property**:

Husband should be required to pay for all major repairs, if any are required, on the above

referenced residential real property to ready said real property for partition on a temporary basis

and prior to close of escrow of the sale. Major repairs are defined as those in excess of $50.00.

28. **Mortgage Payments & Related Costs to Residential Real Property**:

Husband should be financially responsible to pay the mortgage payment, home equity

loan (if applicable) principle and interest, real property taxes, homeowners insurance, utilities

and maintenance on the above referenced residential real property, both temporarily and until the sale of same. The Court should determine the Parties entitlement for tax purposes to the mortgage interest, property tax deduction and related deductions and expenses of the residential real property on a temporary as well as permanent basis.

29. **Interest in Real Property:**

To the best of Wife's knowledge, no other person has or claims any interest in the property, other than the holder of the mortgage.

30. **Attorney's Fees & Costs:**

The Wife will necessarily expend costs and is obligated to pay the undersigned counsel a reasonable attorney's fee for services and costs rendered in this action and for this Partition count. The Wife has the financial need and the Husband has the financial ability to pay the Husband's attorney's fees and costs temporarily and on a permanent basis.

31. The residential real property listed herein is indivisible without irreparable harm to the interested Parties.

WHEREFORE, the Wife respectfully requests this court:

a. That pursuant to a Final Judgment of Dissolution of Marriage be entered dissolving the marriage.

b. That this Court makes an equitable distribution all the marital portion of all assets, real property, personal property, both tangible and intangible, excluding any non-marital portion and awarding the Wife an unequal distribution.

c. That this court makes an equitable distribution of all liabilities which were acquired during the marriage, excluding any non-marital portion and any unequal distribution requested by the Wife.

d.   That this court awards the Wife sole parental responsibility for the minor child both on a temporary and permanent basis.

e.   That this court awards the Wife majority time sharing with the minor child and limit the Husband to supervised timesharing both on a temporary and permanent basis.

f.   That this court determines the Parties' child support obligations in light of the timesharing schedule on a temporary as well as permanent basis after imputing income to the Husband. That this court enters an order for the Husband to pay child support, retroactive support, arrears and any fees and costs via an Income Withholding Order through the State of Florida Disbursement Unit on a temporary as well as permanent basis.

g.   That the Court awards the Wife temporary, transitional, rehabilitative, bridge-the gap, permanent, durational and/or lump sum alimony paid through an income withholding order if appropriate.

h.   Order that the Husband maintain health, dental and vision insurance on the minor child both temporarily and on a permanent basis and on the Wife temporarily during the pendency of this case and the equivalent coverage through COBRA both temporarily and on a permanent basis.

i.   Require that the parties share in reasonable and necessary uncovered costs associated with the medical, dental and vision insurance on the minor child based on their pro rata percentage on both a temporarily and on a permanent basis.

j.   Grant the Wife exclusive us and possession of the marital residence, both temporarily and on a permanent basis.

k.   Grant a temporary injunction in order to maintain the status quo of the marital assets.

l.   Order the Husband to maintain a life insurance policy unencumbered on his life naming the Wife as irrevocable beneficiary in a sufficient amount to secure future payments of child support and alimony both temporarily and on a permanent basis.

m.   Enter an order such that the Wife shall be entitled to claim the minor child for tax purposes each year until such time as the minor child no longer qualifies.

n.   That the Court awards the Wife attorney's fees, costs and suit money and expert fees both temporarily and on a permanent basis.

o.   That this Court grants such other and further relief as it deems just and proper.

p.   Partition the real property herein.

q.   Require the Husband to pay all major repairs to the above referenced residential real property, both temporarily and on a permanent basis.

r.   Require the Husband to pay the expenses of the mortgage payments, principle and interest, home equity loan payments, real property taxes, utilities and homeowners insurance on the above referenced residential real property on a temporary basis until the sale of the marital residence.

t.   For such other relief this Court shall deem just and proper.

COUNT THREE

ASSAULT WITH A DEADLY WEAPON (Principal)

32.   **GENERAL ALLEGATIONS:**

The Wife re-avers and re-affirms paragraphs one (1) through thirty-one (31) as set-forth above in this Petition for Dissolution of Marriage.

33.   This is an action for damages in excess of Fifteen Thousand ($15,000.00) Dollars.

34. That at all times material hereto, the Plaintiff, ███████, herein "Wife" was over the age of eighteen, a resident of Hillsborough county, and is otherwise sui juris.

35. That at all times material hereto, the Defendant, ███████, herein "Husband" was over the age of eighteen, a resident of Hillsborough County, and is other sui juris.

36. The Court has jurisdiction.

37. Venue is proper as that the residence of the Plaintiff and Defendant is in Hillsborough County.

SUPPORTING FACTS:

38. The Husband had physically abused the Wife for four years including but not limited to: he had hit her, kicked her, pulled her hair, dragged her from room to room by her hair.

39. As a result of the Husband's abuse, the Wife had separated from the Husband in June, 2017.

40. The Husband promised to change and so she returned to the marital home on or about August 25, 2017.

41. The Husband's parents were staying in the marital home.

42. On September 1, 2017, only six days after returning to the marital home, the Husband and Wife were involved in a verbal argument where the Husband was verbally abused the Wife.

43. The Husband intentionally struck the Wife against her will with an open hand, repeatedly and forcefully.

44. The Husband then began to throw the Wife's belonging and her purse.

45. The Husband's Father and Mother also joined the Husband in striking the Wife.

46. During the incident the Wife was holding the minor child in her arms and the child was struck in the face.

47.   The Husband took the Wife's phone and hid it with the intention to prevent her from contacting law enforcement and the Husband kept the keys to her vehicle.

48.   The Wife attempted to flee and the Husband intentionally blocked her exit and the Husband's father threatened her with a knife.

49.   The Wife feared that the Husband's father was going to kill her.

50.   The Husband then dragged the Wife into their shared bedroom against her will and continued to strike her.

51.   The Husband and his Father and Mother secured the door with the intent to prevent the Wife from leaving or contacting law enforcement.

52.   The Husband told the Wife that if she called law enforcement he would cut himself and his father with the knife and falsely accuse her of causing the injuries.

53.   The Husband also told her that in the time it took for law enforcement to arrive he would kill her, the child and himself.

54.   As a result of the violent attack of the Husband and his family the Wife suffered multiple bruises to her face and body.

55.   As a direct and proximate result of the Husband's Assault with a Deadly Weapon, she has suffered damages, including but not limited to: emotional harm, and economic harm. The Wife has also incurred and continues to incur attorney's fees and costs as a result of Husband's actions.

56.   The Wife demands Judgment against the Husband in excess of $15,000 (fifteen thousand dollars).

57.   The Wife will be requesting leave to amend for punitive damages.

58.   The Wife demands jury trial.

WHEREFORE, the Wife requests this honorable Court grant the following relief:

a. That this Court award compensatory damages in favor of the Wife, ██████ ██████, in an amount in excess of $250,000.

b. That this court award pre-judgment interests against the Husband.

c. That this Court award judgment against the Husband of Wife's reasonable and necessary attorney's fees, expenses and costs;

d. For such other and further relief as this Court deems just and equitable.

COUNT FOUR

BATTERY

59. **GENERAL ALLEGATIONS:**

The Wife re-avers and re-affirms paragraphs one (1) through fifty-eight (58) as set-forth above in this Petition for Dissolution of Marriage and Count Three for Assault.

60. This is an action for damages in excess of Fifteen Thousand ($15,000.00) Dollars.

61. That at all times material hereto, the Plaintiff, ██████████ herein "Wife" was over the age of eighteen, a resident of Hillsborough county, and is otherwise sui juris.

62. That at all times material hereto, the Defendant, ██████████ herein "Husband" was over the age of eighteen, a resident of Hillsborough County, and is other sui juris.

63. The Court has jurisdiction.

64. Venue is proper as that the residence of the Plaintiff and Defendant is in Hillsborough County.

65. As a direct and proximate result of the Husband's Battery of the Wife, she has suffered damages, including but not limited to: emotional harm, and economic harm. The Wife has also incurred and continues to incur attorney's fees and costs as a result of Husband's actions.

66. The Wife demands Judgment against the Husband in excess of $15,000 (fifteen thousand dollars).

67. The Wife will be requesting leave to amend for punitive damages.

68. The Wife demands jury trial.

    WHEREFORE, the Wife requests this honorable Court grant the following relief:

    a.   That this Court award compensatory damages in favor of the Wife, ███ ███, in an amount in excess of $250,000.

    b.   That this court award pre-judgment interests against the Husband.

    c.   That this Court award judgment against the Husband of Wife's reasonable and necessary attorney's fees, expenses and costs;

    d.   For such other and further relief as this Court deems just and equitable.

COUNT FIVE

FALSE IMPRISONMENT

69. **GENERAL ALLEGATIONS:**

    The Wife re-avers and re-affirms paragraphs one (1) through sixty-eight (68) as set-forth above in this Petition for Dissolution of Marriage and Count Three for Assault and Count Four for Battery.

70. This is an action for damages in excess of Fifteen Thousand ($15,000.00) Dollars.

71. That at all times material hereto, the Plaintiff, ███████ herein "Wife" was over the age of eighteen, a resident of Hillsborough county, and is otherwise sui juris.

72. That at all times material hereto, the Defendant, ███████ I, herein "Husband" was over the age of eighteen, a resident of Hillsborough County, and is other sui juris.

73. The Court has jurisdiction.

74. Venue is proper as that the residence of the Plaintiff and Defendant is in Hillsborough County.

75. As a direct and proximate result of the Husband's False Imprisonment of the Wife, she has suffered damages, including but not limited to: emotional harm, and economic harm. The Wife has also incurred and continues to incur attorney's fees and costs as a result of Husband's actions.

76. The Wife demands Judgment against the Husband in excess of $15,000 (fifteen thousand dollars).

77. The Wife will be requesting leave to amend for punitive damages.

78. The Wife demands jury trial.

      WHEREFORE, the Wife requests this honorable Court grant the following relief:

  a. That this Court award compensatory damages in favor of the Wife, ███████ ████ in an amount in excess of $250,000.

  b. That this court award pre-judgment interests against the Husband.

  c. That this Court award judgment against the Husband of Wife's reasonable and necessary attorney's fees, expenses and costs;

  d. For such other and further relief as this Court deems just and equitable.

COUNT SIX

INTENTIONAL INFLICTION OF EMOTIONAL DISTRESS

79. **GENERAL ALLEGATIONS:**

The Wife re-avers and re-affirms paragraphs one (1) through seventy-eight (78) as set-forth above in this Petition for Dissolution of Marriage and Count Three for Assault and Count Four for Battery and Count V for False Imprisonment.

80. This is an action for damages in excess of Fifteen Thousand ($15,000.00) Dollars.

81. That at all times material hereto, the Plaintiff, **SILKY GAIND**, herein "Wife" was over the age of eighteen, a resident of Hillsborough county, and is otherwise sui juris.

82. That at all times material hereto, the Defendant ████████ herein "Husband" was over the age of eighteen, a resident of Hillsborough County, and is other sui juris.

83. The Court has jurisdiction.

84. Venue is proper as that the residence of the Plaintiff and Defendant is in Hillsborough County.

85. The Husband knew or should have known that the Wife would suffer severe emotional distress from the physical and mental abuse, for the injuries to the minor child, from the assault with a deadly weapon and imminent threats of death, from being intentionally confined and from having her telephone and car keys taken from her so she could not contact law enforcement.

86. The Husband's conduct alone and as a principal in the crimes by his parents were outrageous and went beyond all bounds of decency and should be regarded as odious and utterly intolerable in a civilized community.

87. As a result of the intentional outrageous conduct of the Husband the Wife suffered severe emotional distress.

88. The Wife demands Judgment against the Husband in excess of $15,000 (fifteen thousand dollars).

89. The Wife will be requesting leave to amend for punitive damages.

90. The Wife demands jury trial.

WHEREFORE, the Wife requests this honorable Court grant the following relief:

a. That this Court award compensatory damages in favor of the Wife, ██████ ██████ in an amount in excess of $250,000.

b. That this court award pre-judgment interests against the Husband.

c. That this Court award judgment against the Husband of Wife's reasonable and necessary attorney's fees, expenses and costs;

d. For such other and further relief as this Court deems just and equitable.

Sept 11, 2017
_____
DATED

Terryn H Bennett
_____
TERRYN H. BENNETT, ESQ.
Attorney for the Wife
E-mail: terryn@terrynbennettlaw.com
FBN: 978700
TERRYN H. BENNETT, P.A.
2309 South MacDill Ave. Suite 105
Tampa, Florida 33629
(813) 251-0011 telephone

EXHIBIT #6

APPLICANT'S DAUGHTER'S BIRTH CERTIFICATE

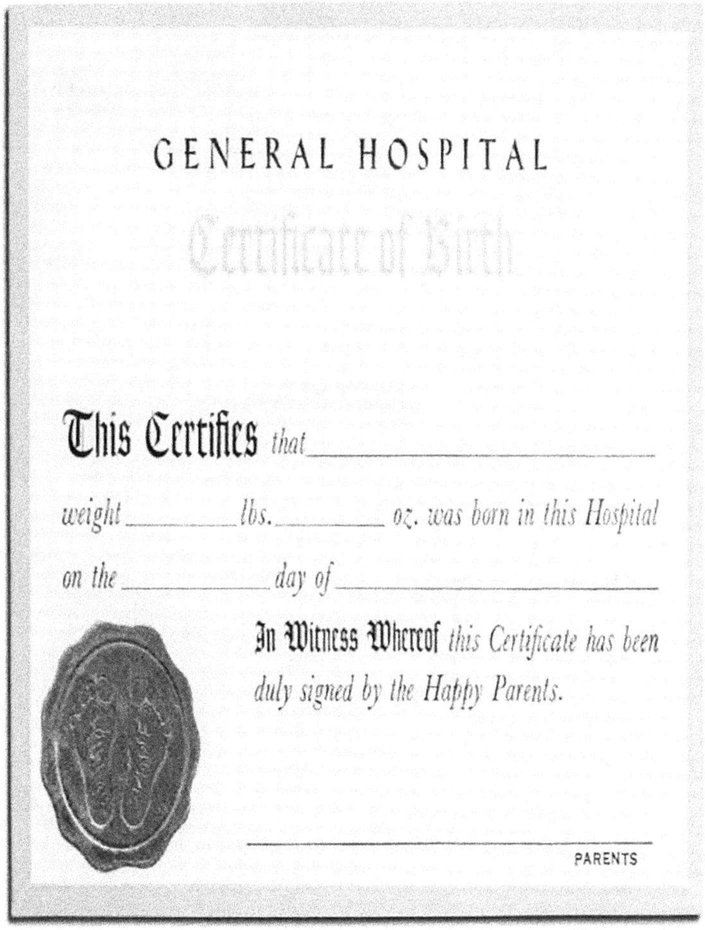

GENERAL HOSPITAL

Certificate of Birth

This Certifies *that*_____

*weight*_____*lbs.*_____*oz. was born in this Hospital*

*on the*_____*day of*_____

In Witness Whereof *this Certificate has been duly signed by the Happy Parents.*

_____
PARENTS

BUREAU of VITAL STATISTICS

CERTIFICATION OF BIRTH

STATE FILE NUMBER: 109-2016-212364   DATE FILED: December 13, 2016

CHILD'S INFORMATION

NAME:

DATE OF BIRTH: December 13, 2016   TIME OF BIRTH (24 HOUR):   0250

SEX: FEMALE   BIRTH WEIGHT: 8 LBS 6 OZ

PLACE OF BIRTH: HOSPITAL
                 ST JOSEPHS HOSPITAL - SOUTH
CITY, COUNTY OF BIRTH: RIVERVIEW, HILLSBOROUGH COUNTY

MOTHER'S/PARENT'S INFORMATION

NAME:

DATE OF BIRTH: November 28, 1983

BIRTHPLACE: INDIA

FATHER'S/PARENT'S INFORMATION

NAME:

DATE OF BIRTH: April 29, 1984

BIRTHPLACE: INDIA

DATE ISSUED: January 4, 2017

, State Registrar   REQ: 2017695853

34856015

CERTIFICATION OF VITAL RECORD

Florida HEALTH

EXHIBIT #7

APPLICANT'S MASTER OF SCIENCE IN FINANCE DEGREE

Illinois Institute of Technology

By authority of the Board of Trustees, and upon the recommendation of the faculty of the

Stuart School of Business

Illinois Institute of Technology hereby confers upon

the degree of

Master of Science in Finance

with all the rights, privileges, and honors thereunto appertaining

Awarded at Chicago, in the State of Illinois

December 20, 2010

Chairman of the Board of Trustees

Provost

John L. Anderson
President

Dean

EXHIBIT #8

HILLSBOROUGH COUNTY SHERIFF'S ARREST/INCIDENT REPORT

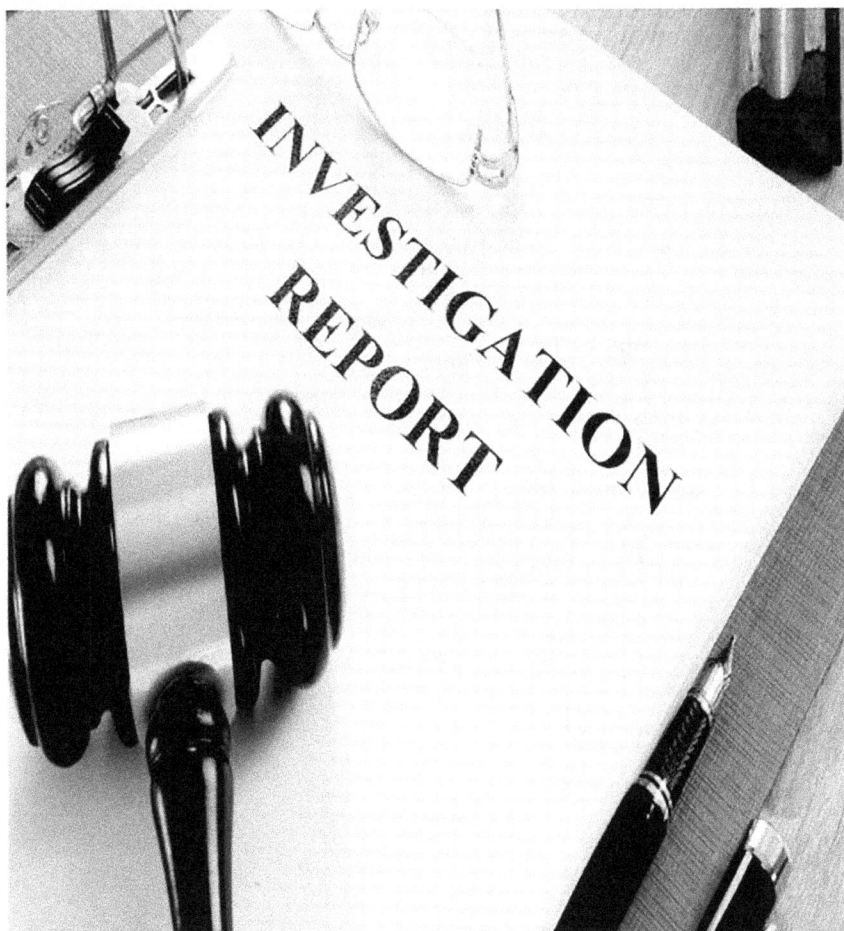

General Offense Information

Operational status: **CLEARED BY ARREST**
Reported on: **Sep-02-2017 (Sat.) 702**
Occurred between: **Sep-01-2017 (Fri.) 2100** and **Sep-02-2017 (Sat.) 625**
Approved on: **Sep-02-2017 (Sat.)** by: **2632 - Waytovich, David**
Report submitted by: **155757 - Tiburcio, Ismael**
Org unit: **D4 Day B JULIET Squad**
Address: ▓▓▓▓▓▓▓▓
      Municipality: **HILLSBOROUGH COUNTY**
      District: **D4** Beat: **J02** Grid: **HS4007**
Felony/Misdemeanor: **FELONY**
Special study: **Persons - Domestic Violence**
Family violence: **Yes**

Offenses (Completed/Attempted)

Offense: # 1 **ASSAULT-3 AGGRAVATED ASSAULT - COMPLETED**
Location: **Residence/Home (Mobile homes, apartments, condos, nursing homes)**
Offender suspected of using: **Not Applicable**
Weapon type: **Knife/Cutting Instrument (Ax,Screwdriver,Switchblade,Etc)**
Bias: **None (no bias)**
Offense: # 2 **KIDNAP-1 KIDNAPPING - COMPLETED**
Location: **Residence/Home (Mobile homes, apartments, condos, nursing homes)**
Offender suspected of using: **Not Applicable**
Bias: **None (no bias)**
Offense: # 3 **BATTERY-6 CHILD ABUSE - ALL OTHER - COMPLETED**
Location: **Residence/Home (Mobile homes, apartments, condos, nursing homes)**
Offender suspected of using: **Not Applicable**
Bias: **None (no bias)**

Related Attachment(s) - MRE Attachments

Attachment Description: STATEMENTS
Reference Number:

Hillsborough County Sheriff's Office STATEMENT	☐ Confidential Page 1 of 4	Case No. 17-628731			
Name of Person giving Statement:		Race W	Sex F	Age 35	DOB 11/28/19__

01	DAY Before yesterday, my Husband, his father
02	& mother, all humiliated me for 2 hours.
03	Then next day I was so sad & depressed,
04	I cried all night. They all insulted me, my
05	family and mentally harassed me. I
06	woke up did my office work & around
07	6:00pm I went to mall & b came back
08	at 9:00pm in the house. my husband
09	his father and mother all started scolding
10	me of coming late. They use abusive
11	language like bitch, fucker. Then I went
12	to the kitchen to prepare the food for my
13	daughter & I want to take butter from
14	the fridge. My husband don't like me to
15	use my hands to take the butter. He
16	told me to use the knife to take butter.
17	I refused him, he got mad & then he
18	with his full force take the butter. He started
19	insulting me in front of his parents. Then
20	he came & hit me over the face. I had

Signed this 2 day of September, 2017 at 1130 hours.

Subject: Gillje___

Deputy: A. Kasperske 4219) 18 675

Witness: _____
Witness: _____

I200 Rev 07/09

Hillsborough County Sheriff's Office STATEMENT	□ Confidential Page 2 of 4	1. Case No. 17-628731			
Name of Person giving Statement:		Race	Sex	Age	DOB
		W	F	33	11/28/1983
Location at which Statement is taken:					

```
01  my daughter in my hand. He a. She
02  also got hit over her face. Then I went
           second time
03  to our room + told him to calm down.
04  Again we had a an argument and he told
05  me to leave the house. He started
06  throwing my things, my clothes, my
07  handbag out (it then) he started using
08  bad language like you fucker, motherfucker
09  bitch (in our native language). His father
10  + mother they were provoking him. Then
11  his father hit me very hard on my face.
12  I tried to run away. (My husband grabbed
      pushing also slapped me
13  me over the door. And then his father
14  came with a knife to to kill me. It
15  I did pee in my pants (clothes) all
16  over. his father were mad at me
        I was so scared.
17  + came to smash my face so many
18  times he hit my face so many times.
19  Then my husband grabbed in (bedroom
                    dragged (s) me
20  try to hold me with his mother
```

Signed this 02 day of September , 2017 at 1130 hours.

Subject: Sily e d

Deputy: A. Karpenske #1 243578 ATK

Witness: _____

Witness: _____

3200 Rev. 03/09

Hillsborough County Sheriff's Office **STATEMENT**	☐ Confidential Page 3 of 4	1. Case No. 17-628731			
Name of Person giving Statement: ▇▇▇▇▇▇		Race W	Sex F	Age 35	DOB 11/28/123
Location at which Statement is taken: ▇▇▇▇▇▇					

```
01  and hit me so on my face so that
02  I should not call and his mother slapped
03  me too. My husband took my phone
04  and car keys. All three of them didnot
05  let me go outside. They were threatened
06  me if I call the police, they will also
07  cut themselves to show the police
08  that I did cut them also. They all
09  physically & mentally harassed me
10  my child is so scared after this all
11  this violence. My father-in-law
12  threatened me with a knife to kill
13  me, my husband stopped him. & my
14  husband cleaned all the pee &
15  then put my things back again to
16  finish the evidence just in case I run
17  and call the police. Then he was telling
18  me if you call the police our relationship
19  will end so don't call them for our
20  baby future. He cannot told me this will
```

Signed this 2 day of September, 2017 at 1130 hours.

Subject: ▇▇▇▇▇

Deputy: A. Kudgerski #2145?8   AMK   Witness: _____

Witness: _____

Hillsborough County Sheriff's Office STATEMENT	☐ Confidential	I. Case No.
Name of Person giving Statement:	Page 4 of 4	17 628 731

Race	Sex	Age	DOB
U	F	33	11/28/1983

Location at which statement is taken:

```
01  not happen again. I woke up in
02  the middle of night so many times
03  to I was totally broken. Then
04  police knocked the door.
05  I was physically and mentally abused
06  They all harassed me.
07  My husband physically abused me in
08  the past also so many times.
09  This happened earlier also so many
10  times. He don't know how to respect
11  his wife. He slept around also with
12  woman. His father + mother slapped
13  me also. I am emotionally, physically
14  + mentally drained. All the family was
15  over me. I was getting I want to
16  go outside + call the police my husband
17  were holding hard and tried to stop me
18  and I got bruises all over. He threatened
19  me if I call the police, it will take long min for the
20  police to come and till that time he will kill me +
```

Signed this 2 day of September, 2017 at 1130 hours. himself

Subject: Silky e

Deputy: A. Kniperske #24578

Witness: _____
Witness: _____

3200 Rev. 00/06

Related Attachment(s) - Waiver/Affidavit

Attachment Description:
Reference Number:

Hillsborough County Sheriff's Office **WAIVERS / AFFIDAVITS**	☐ Confidential Page ___ of ___	Case No. ___

Type of Incident:

I, (Name of person signing): _____ the undersigned

☐ Missing Person / Juvenile Runaway Affidavit

I, [kx] certify that _____ has been missing since _____

I am the ☐ Parent ☐ Family Member ☐ Legal Guardian ☐ Physician and/or other authorization source of the above person

The above listed person is missing due to ☐ Runaway ☐ Unknown Circumstances ☐ Physical/Mental Disability

I give my permission to release dental records or any other medical records on the above missing person. I further agree to notify the Hillsborough County Sheriff's Office immediately upon receiving any information concerning the above named missing person.

☐ Consent to Search/Waiver of Search Warrant for Oral Swab/DNA

I, [kx] do hereby consent that the below listed Hillsborough County Sheriff's Law Enforcement Official collect a mouth swab specimen from me for investigative purposes. I have been fully informed that this specimen will be analyzed and compared as evidence, and I further agree that this evidence can and will be used at trial in any matter of which I may stand accused. I have been fully informed and I agree that the results of any DNA analysis may be entered into a DNA database. I fully understand my constitutional rights in regard to this search and it is my intention to fully and completely waive such rights by this consent. I give this consent freely and voluntarily, without compulsion or threat of any kind.

☐ Request for Non-Law Enforcement Assistance

I, [kx] hereby request assistance from a Deputy Sheriff in a matter not related to law enforcement activity. I understand that said Deputy Sheriff is not a qualified service technician. I will not hold the Hillsborough County Sheriff's Office responsible for any damage arising out of the assistance provided. I am the owner, or I am authorized to act on behalf of the owner of the vehicle or property for which I am requesting assistance.

☐ Vehicle Loss or Damage Release Affidavit

I, [kx] give my permission, in lieu of impounding by the Hillsborough County Sheriff's Office, for the

Year	Make	Model	Style

Color Top/Bottom	Vehicle Identification Number (VIN)		License	State

that I have been operating to

☐ remain at: _____

☐ be released to: _____

This decision was made by me after the deputy listed below explained the possibility of damage or loss. Being aware of this by affixing my signature to this form, I release and hold harmless the Hillsborough County Sheriff's Office of any and all responsibility for damage or loss which may occur as a result of the release of this vehicle as aforesaid.

☐ Bloodborne Pathogen Warning

I, [kx], do certify that I have been duly warned that the property being released to me,

_____ (Describe: Residence, Vehicle, Personal Items)

is blood stained, thereby posing risk of serious infection or death; and further, that I have been directed to contact the Hillsborough County Health Department, Environmental Health Unit at 272-5200, for further information. Being aware of this by affixing my signature to this form, I release and hold harmless the Hillsborough County Sheriff's Office of any and all responsibility for any injury which may occur as a result of the release of this property.

Signed this ___ day of ___ 20 ___ at ___ hours	
Subject: _____	Witness: _____
Deputy: _____	Witness: _____

Related Attachment(s) - Cost Calculator

Attachment Description: ████
Reference Number:

Investigative Cost Calculator
HCSO

Date:	09/02/2017			Report Number:	17-628731
Def Last Name:	Kalsi	Def First Name:	Jasbir Singh	Def DOB:	05/18/1950

Item	Description	Personnel On Scene	Hourly Rate	Hours On Scene	Amount
1	Deputy	1	$34.85	4	$139.40
2	Corporal	1	$43.24	4	$172.96
3	Deputy	1	$24.88	4	$99.52
			Total Agency Investigative Cost		$411.88

Page 1 of 2

Page 2 of 2

Related Attachment(s) - Cost Calculator

Attachment Description: ▇▇▇▇
Reference Number:

Investigative Cost Calculator
HCSO

Date: 09/02/2017   Report Number: 17-628731

Def Last Name:	Kalsi	Def First Name:	Devbir	Def DOB:	04/29/1984

Item	Description	Personnel On Scene	Hourly Rate	Hours On Scene	Amount
1	Deputy	1	$24.88	3	$74.64
2	Corporal	1	$40.00	3	$120.00
3	Deputy	1	$30.00	3	$90.00
4	Deputy	1	$30.00	1.5	$45.00
5	Deputy	1	$21.99	1.5	$32.98
	Total Agency Investigative Cost				**$362.63**

Page 1 of 2

Related Attachment(s) - Criminal Report Affidavit

Attachment Description: ▆▆▆▆
Reference Number:

CRIMINAL REPORT AFFIDAVIT/HILLSBOROUGH COUNTY, FLORIDA

○ Supplemental Page   ○ Plant City Courthouse   ○ Notice To Appear   CRA #: HS17025762

● Fel ○ Misd ○ (APAD) Adult Pre-Arrest Div ○ Traffic ○ Tampa Ord ○ Juv Dailing ○ MAP   Booking #: 13012110

Arrest Type: ● FC ○ Warrant ○ FC VOP/VOCC   Request: ○ Warrant ○ SAO Review Direct File ○ JUV Pick-Up Order

Court Case #
Family #
SOID #

Agency: ● HCSO ○ TPD ○ PCPD ○ TTPD ○ FHP ○ Other: Report #: 17-628731   Report Written ● Yes ○ No

Offense Location: 9601 GREENBANK DR, RIVERVIEW, FL 33569   Offense Date: 09/01/2017   Offense Time: 2100

Arrest Location: 9601 GREENBANK DR, RIVERVIEW, FL 33569   Arrest Date: 09/02/2017   Arrest Time: 0909

Defendant: Last Name ▆▆▆   First Name ▆▆▆   Middle Name ▆▆▆   ○ Gang Name:

Race	Gender	DOB	DL#	State	POB (City, State)
White	● M ○ F	04/29/1984	K420177841490	FL	INDIA

Address Street: 9601 GREENBANK DR   City: RIVERVIEW   State: FL   Zip: 33569

School (JUV):   Parent/Guardian (JUV):

CO-Defendant: Last Name	First Name	Middle Name	Race	Gender	DOB
▆▆▆	▆▆▆	SINGH	W	● M ○ F	05/18/1950
			W	○ M ● F	11/02/1955

Statute	Level	Degree	Charge	Count	Citation #	DV
784.041(1)	Fel	T	BATTERY COMMIT FELONY BATTERY	1		●
787.02(1)(a)	Fel	T	KIDNAP-FALSE IMPRISONMENT ADULT	1		●
914.22(1)	Fel	T	OBSTRUCTING JUSTICE HARASSING IN 3RD DEGREE FELONY PROCEEDING	1		●
827.03(2)(c)	Fel	T	CRUELTY TOWARD CHILD ABUSE CHILD WITHOUT GREAT BODILY HARM	1		●

The undersigned swears there are reasonable grounds to believe that the above named defendant in Hillsborough County, Florida, did:
On 09-01-2017, at approximately 2100 hours, at 9601 Greenbank Dr, the defendant and victim were involved in a verbal argument. The argument turned physical when the defendant struck the victim against her will with an open hand, repeatedly and forcefully. As the victim attempted to defend herself, the co-defendants also engaged in striking the victim. As a result of the strikes, the victim suffered multiple bruises to her face, neck and torso. During the incident, the victim was holding her nine (9) month old child in her arms. As a result of the strikes, the child was accidentally struck in face so the defendant took the child from the mother and put her in a separate room. The defendant also took the victims phone and hid it with the intent to prevent her from contacting emergency services. After the initial incident, the defendant dragged the victim into their shared bedroom against her will. The defendant and co-defendants secured the door with the intent to prevent the victim from leaving or contacting Law Enforcement.

The victim and the defendant are married with a child in common. The co-defendants are the biological parents of the defendant. The victim identified the defendant and co-defendants as the persons who committed the crimes. The defendant identified himself verbally and was verified via valid Florida State Driver's License.

I attest, to Florida Statute §92.525 and under penalties of perjury, I declare that I have read the foregoing document and the facts stated in it are true to the best of my knowledge. For Notices to Appear, I also certify that a complete list of witnesses and evidence known to me is attached.

Affiant:	Officer #	Dist: 04	SWORN TO AND SUBSCRIBED BEFORE ME THIS DATE	Officer #
DEP A Karpenske Digitally signed on 2017.09.02 11:30:33	249578	SQD: D4406	CPL O Waytovich Digitally signed on 2017.09.02 11:32:14	2632

Judgment requested against defendant for agency investigative cost per Florida Statute 938.27: $352.63

Arresting Agency
(SERVICE OF COURT DOCUMENTS may be served on the State Attorney's office at MailProcessingStaff@sao13th.com)
Page 1 of 2

Agency Report #	17-628731	CRIMINAL REPORT AFFIDAVIT/ HILLSBOROUGH COUNTY, FLORIDA	CRA #:	HS17026762

Victim	Last Name: CAIRD	First: SILKY	M:	Race: W	Gender: ○ M ⦿ F	DOB: 11/28/1983
Address:		City: RIVERVIEW	State: FL	Zip: 33569	Primary Phil: (229) 637-3100	
Sworn: ⦿ Yes ○ No	Email				Vine: ⦿ Yes ○ No	
Victim	Last Name: KALSI	First: SAIRA	M:	Race: W	Gender: ○ M ⦿ F	DOB: 12/13/2016
Address:		City: RIVERVIEW	State: FL	Zip: 33569	Primary Phil:	
Sworn: ○ Yes ⦿ No	Email				Vine: ○ Yes ⦿ No	

Arresting Agency
(SERVICE OF COURT DOCUMENTS may be served on the State Attorney's office at !MailProcessingStaff@sao13th.com)
Page 2 of 2

For: SA0047   Printed On: Oct-05-2017 (Thu.)   Page 13 of 48

72 | P a g e

Related Attachment(s) - Criminal Report Affidavit

Attachment Description: **KALSI**

Reference Number:

CRIMINAL REPORT AFFIDAVIT/HILLSBOROUGH COUNTY, FLORIDA

○ Supplemental Page	○ Plant City Courthouse	○ Notice To Appear	CRA #:	HS17026766

○ Fel ○ Misd ○ (APAD) Adult Pre-Arrest Div ○ Traffic ○ Tampa Ord ○ Juv Del Ord ○ MM   Booking #: 12032338

Arrest Type: ● PC ○ Warrant ○ PC VOP/VOCC Request: ○ Warrant ○ SAO Review Direct File ○ JUV Pick-Up Order

Court Case #   Family #   SOID #

Agency:	● HCSO ○ TPD ○ PCPD ○ TTPD ○ FHP	Report #	17-628731	Report Written
○ Other:				● Yes ○ No

Offense Location:	9601 GREENBANK DR, RIVERVIEW, FL 33569	Offense Date:	09/01/2017	Offense Time:	2100

Arrest Location:	9601 GREENBANK DR, RIVERVIEW, FL 33569	Arrest Date:	09/02/2017	Arrest Time:	0909

Defendant:	Last Name	First Name	Middle Name	○ Gang Name:

Race White	Gender ● M ○ F	DOB 05/18/1950	DL#	State	POB (City, State) INDIA

Address Street:		City	PUNJAB	State:	Zip: 141003

School (JUV)	Parent/Guardian (JUV)

CO-Defendant: Last Name	First Name	Middle Name	Race	Gender	DOB
		SINGH	W	● M ○ F	04/29/1984
			W	○ M ● F	02/11/1955

Statute	Level	Degree	Charge	Count	Citation #	DV
827.03(2)(c)	Fel	T	CRUELTY TOWARD CHILD ABUSE CHILD WITHOUT GREAT BODILY HARM Active encouragement of any person to commit an act that results or could reasonably be expected to result in physical or mental injury to a child.	1		●
784.021(1)(a)	Fel	T	AGGRAV ASSLT - WEAPON W DEADLY WEAPON WITHOUT INTENT TO KILL	1		●
914.22(3)	Fel	T	OBSTRUCTING JUSTICE HARASSING IN 3RD DEGREE FELONY PROCEEDING	1		●
787.02(1)(a)	Fel	T	KIDNAP-FALSE IMPRISONMENT ADULT	1		●

The undersigned swears there are reasonable grounds to believe that the above named defendant in Hillsborough County, Florida, did:
On the above-listed date and time at 9601 Greenbank Drive Riverview, the defendant, Jasbir Singh Kalsi, and co-defendants Devbir Singh Kalsi and Bhupinder Kalsi did strike the victim's face with a opened hand. The defendant, Jasbir Singh Kalsi then obtained a kitchen knife and threatened to stab the victim with the knife. The defendant's actions placed the victim in an imminent fear of great bodily harm. The defendant, Jasbir Singh Kalsi, and co-defendants, Devbir Singh Kalsi and Bhupinder Kalsi held the victim against her will inside her room preventing the victim to call law enforcement for help by removing her phone from her possession. The victim's child was in the victim's arms during the incident and was also placed in danger of injury. The defendant, Jasbir Singh Kalsi, and co-defendants, Devbir Singh Kalsi and Bhupinder Kalsi with their active encouragement to commit an act of violence against the victim could reasonably be expected to result in physical or mental injury to a child. The victim identified her father in law, Jasbir Singh Kalsi to be the person who threatened her with the knife and forcefully slapped her repeatedly against her will. The defendant, Jasbir Singh Kalsi identified himself via his Republic Of India Passport number K2171414. The victim, Silky Garod, and co-defendants, Devbir Singh Kalsi are husband and wife with a child in common. The defendant, Jasbir Singh Kalsi and co-defendants Bhupinder Kalsi are the victims in laws.

Pursuant to Florida Statute 92.525 and under penalties of perjury, I declare that I have read the foregoing document and the facts stated in it are true to the best of my knowledge. For Notices to Appear, I also certify that a complete list of witnesses and evidence known to me is attached.

Affiant		Officer #	DIST.	D4	SWORN TO AND SUBSCRIBED BEFORE ME THIS DATE	Officer #
DEP J Tiburcio		155757	SQD:	D4406	CPL D Waytovich	2632
Digitally signed on 2017.09.02 11:27:06					Digitally signed on 2017.09.02 11:27:59	

Judgment requested against defendant for agency investigative cost per Florida Statute 938.27: $411.88

Arresting Agency

(SERVICE OF COURT DOCUMENTS may be served on the State Attorney's office at MailProcessingStaff@sao13th.com)

Page 1 of 2

Agency Report #	17-628731	CRIMINAL REPORT AFFIDAVIT/ HILLSBOROUGH COUNTY, FLORIDA	CRA #:	HS17026766

Victim	Last Name: ▆▆	First: ▆▆	M:	Race: W	Gender: ○ M ◉ F	DOB: 11/28/1983
Address: ▆▆▆▆▆		City: RIVERVIEW	State: FL	Zip: 33569	Primary Ph#: (229) 637-5300	
Sworn: ◉ Yes ○ No	Email:				Vine: ◉ Yes ○ No	
Victim	Last Name: ▆▆	First: ▆▆	M:	Race: W	Gender: ○ M ◉ F	DOB: 12/13/2016
Address: ▆▆▆▆▆		City: RIVERVIEW	State: FL	Zip: 33569	Primary Ph#:	
Sworn: ○ Yes ◉ No	Email:				Vine: ◉ Yes ○ No	

Arresting Agency

(SERVICE OF COURT DOCUMENTS may be served on the State Attorney's office at fMailProcessingStaff@sao13th.com)

Page 2 of 2

Related Attachment(s) - Cost Calculator

Attachment Description: █████████
Reference Number:

Investigative Cost Calculator
HCSO

Date: 09/02/2017   Report Number: **17-628731**

Def Last Name: ████   Def First Name: ████   Def DOB: 11/02/1955

Item	Description	Personnel On Scene	Hourly Rate	Hours On Scene	Amount
1	Deputy	1	$24.88	3	$74.64
2	Corporal	1	$40.00	3	$120.00
3	Deputy	1	$30.00	3	$90.00
4	Deputy	1	$30.00	1.5	$45.00
5	Deputy	1	$21.99	1.5	$32.98
	Total Agency Investigative Cost				**$362.63**

Page 1 of 2

Page 2 of 2

Related Attachment(s) - Criminal Report Affidavit

Attachment Description: ████████
Reference Number:

CRIMINAL REPORT AFFIDAVIT/HILLSBOROUGH COUNTY, FLORIDA

○ Supplemental Page   ○ Plant City Courthouse   ○ Notice To Appear   CRA #: HS17026774

○ Fel ○ Misd ○ (APAD) Adult Pre-Arrest Div ○ Traffic ○ Tampa Ord ○ Juv Delinq ○ IAAP   Booking #: 12032346

Arrest Type: ● PC ○ Warrant ○ PC VOP/VOCC   Request: ○ Warrant ○ SAO Review Direct File ○ JUV Pick-Up Order

Court Case #	Family #	SOID #

Agency: ● HCSO ○ TPD ○ PCPD ○ TTPD ○ FHP ○ Other:	Report # 17-628731	Report Written ● Yes ○ No

Offense Location: 9601 GREENBANK DR, RIVERVIEW, FL 33569	Offense Date: 09/01/2017	Offense Time: 2100
Arrest Location: 9601 GREENBANK DR, RIVERVIEW, FL 33569	Arrest Date: 09/02/2017	Arrest Time: 0909

Defendant: Last Name	First Name	Middle Name	○ Gang Name:

Race White	Gender ○ M ● F	DOB 11/02/1955	DL# NA	State	POB (City, State) INDIA

Address Street ████████	City MODEL TOWN, LUDHIANA	State:	Zip: 141003

School (JUV)	Parent/Guardian (JUV)

No Co-defendants Found

Statute	Level	Degree	Charge	Count	Citation #	DV
784.03(1)(a)2	Misd	F	BATTERY CAUSE BODILY HARM	1		●
39.205(1)	Fel	T	PUBLIC ORDER CRIMES FAIL REPRT SUSP CHILD ABUSE ABANDON NEGLEC	1		○

The undersigned swears there are reasonable grounds to believe that the above named defendant in Hillsborough County, Florida, did:
On 09-01-2017, at approximately 2100 hours, at 9601 Greenbank Dr, the victim and the co-defendant, Devbir Kalsi, were involved in a verbal altercation. The altercation turned physical and the defendant involved herself by striking the victim on her head and back with an open hand against the victim's will. As a result of the strikes, the victim suffered multiple bruises to her face, neck and torso. During the altercation, the victim was holding her child, and the child was inadvertently struck by the co-defendant. The defendant was present for the offense and failed to notify Law Enforcement or Emergency Medical Services.

The defendant is the Mother-in-law of the victim. The victim identified the defendant and co-defendants as the persons who committed this crimes. The defendant identified herself verbally and as confirmed by her official Passport.

Pursuant to Florida Statute 92.525 and under penalties of perjury, I declare that I have read the foregoing document and the facts stated in it are true to the best of my knowledge. For fictions to Agencies, I also certify that a complete list of witnesses and evidence known to me is attached.

Affiant: DEP A Karpenske Digitally signed on 2017.09.02 12:50:19	Officer # 249578	Dist: D4	Sqd: D4406	SWORN TO AND SUBSCRIBED BEFORE ME THIS DATE CPL D Waytovich Digitally signed on 2017.09.02 13:23:01	Officer # 2032

Judgment requested against defendant for agency investigative cost per Florida Statute 938.27: $362.63

Victim: Last Name: ████	First: ████	M:	Race: W	Gender: ○ M ● F	DOB: 11/28/1983
Address: ████	City: RIVERVIEW	State: FL	Zip: 33569	Primary Ph#: (224) 637-5100	
Sworn: ● Yes ○ No Email:				Vine: ● Yes ○ No	

Victim: Last Name: ████	First: ████	M:	Race: W	Gender: ○ M ● F	DOB: 12/11/2016
Address:	City: RIVERVIEW	State: FL	Zip: 33569	Primary Ph#:	
Sworn: ○ Yes ● No Email:				Vine: ○ Yes ● No	

Arresting Agency
(SERVICE OF COURT DOCUMENTS may be served on the State Attorney's office at !MailProcessingStaff@sao13th.com)
Page 1 of 1

Related Attachment(s) - SAO Letters

Attachment Description:
Reference Number:

State Attorney

ANDREW H. WARREN
Thirteenth Judicial Circuit
419 N. Pierce Street
Tampa, Florida 33602-4022
(813) 272-5400

STATE OF FLORIDA   CASE NUMBER: 2017-CF-013320

VS   BOOKING NUMBER: 17-032346

[redacted]

NOTICE OF CASE STATUS

Case Filing Decision: FILED CIRCUIT COURT

Agency Report Number: 2017-00628731 HCSO

Lead LEO: Deputy ANDREW T KARPENSKE DPSD4 D4406

SEP 2 2 2017

Case Decision Date: _____

New Case Number (if applicable): _2017-CF-013214-D003_

    Withdraw Pick-Up Order (Juvenile upgrade only): Yes

ASA Comments: _____
_____
_____
_____

JESSICA W O'CONNOR
Assistant State Attorney

Note: Notice JUVENILE CLERK OF COURT on Juvenile upgrade only
cc: LEO
     (}DJJ (if Juvenile)
     File

/dss

2017-043516/2017-CF-013214
Page 1 of 1
Notice of Case Status

Related Attachment(s) - SAO Letters

Attachment Description:
Reference Number:

State Attorney

ANDREW H. WARREN
Thirteenth Judicial Circuit
419 N. Pierce Street
Tampa, Florida 33602-4022
(813) 272-5400

STATE OF FLORIDA   CASE NUMBER: 2017-CF-013315

VS   BOOKING NUMBER: 17-013338

▆▆▆▆▆▆▆▆▆   **NOTICE OF CASE STATUS**

Case Filing Decision: FILED CIRCUIT COURT

Agency Report Number: 2017-00628731 HCSO

Lead LEO: Deputy ISMAEL TIBURCIO DFSD# D4406

SEP 2 2 2017

Case Decision Date: _____

New Case Number (if applicable): _2017-CF-013214-D002_

        Withdraw Pick-Up Order (Juvenile upgrade only): Yes

ASA Comments: _____

_____

_____

JESSICA M O'CONNOR
Assistant State Attorney

Note: Notice JUVENILE CLERK OF COURT on Juvenile upgrade only
cc: LEO
        []DJJ (if Juvenile)
        File

/das

2017-043515/2017-CF-013214
Page 1 of 1
Notice of Case Status

Related Attachment(s) - SAO Letters

Attachment Description:
Reference Number:

State Attorney
ANDREW H. WARREN
Thirteenth Judicial Circuit
419 N. Pierce Street
Tampa, Florida 33602-4022
(813) 272-5400

STATE OF FLORIDA   CASE NUMBER: 2017-CF-013214

VS   BOOKING NUMBER: 17-032339

[redacted]

NOTICE OF CASE STATUS

Case Filing Decision: FILED CIRCUIT COURT

Agency Report Number: 2017-00628731 HCSO

Lead LEO: Deputy ANDREW T KARPENSKE DPSD4 D4405

Case Decision Date: ___SEP 2 2 2017___

New Case Number (if applicable): _____

    Withdraw Pick-Up Order (Juvenile upgrade only): Yes

ASA Comments: _____

_____

_____

JESSICA W O'CONNOR
Assistant State Attorney

Note: Notice JUVENILE CLERK OF COURT on Juvenile upgrade only
cc: LEO
    []DJJ (if Juvenile)
    File

/dss

2017-043316/2017-CF-013214
Page 1 of 1
Notice of Case Status

Related Event(s)

CP	HS2017-628731
AB	HS2017-17032338
AB	HS2017-17032339
AB	HS2017-17032346

Related Person(s)

1. Victim # 1 - ██████████

(Case Specific Information)

Sex: **FEMALE**
Race: **WHITE**
Date of birth: **Nov-28-1983**
Address: ██████████████
      Municipality: **RIVERVIEW**, Florida **33569**
      District: **D4** Beat: **J02** Grid: **HS4007**

Phone Numbers
    Cellular: **(224) 637-5100**

Particulars

Place of birth: **India or Sikkim**
Citizenship: **America, United States of**
Marital status: **Married**
Ethnicity: **Not of Hispanic Origin**
Language(s) spoken: **English, Other**
Height: **5'04**
Disability: **No**
Build: **Thin** Complexion: **Light Brown**
Handed: **Right Handed**
Eye color: **Brown**
Hair color: **Black**
Hair style: **Medium (Shoulder Length)**
Facial hair color: **Other**
Facial hair style: **None**

Master Name Index Reference

Name: ██████████
Sex: **FEMALE**
Race: **UNKNOWN**
Date of birth: **Nov-28-1983**
Ethnicity: **Not of Hispanic Origin**
, **Florida**
Phone numbers
Cellular: **(224) 637-5100**

Home: (813)
Business: (813)

Linkage factors

Resident status : **Resident**
Age range : **30-49 Years**
Access to firearm : **No**
Victim of :
ASSAULT- 3 AGGRAVATED ASSAULT - COMPLETED
BATTERY- 6 CHILD ABUSE - ALL OTHER - COMPLETED
KIDNAP- 1 KIDNAPPING - COMPLETED

Victim's Relationship to Offender : **Victim Was In-law**
Person's role : **Arrestee #2**
Person's name : ▮▮▮▮▮▮▮▮▮▮▮(DOB: May-18-1950)

Victim's Relationship to Offender : **Victim Was Spouse**
Person's role : **Arrestee #3**
Person's name : ▮▮▮▮▮▮▮▮▮ (DOB: Apr-29-1984)

Victim's Relationship to Offender : **Victim Was In-law**
Person's role : **Arrestee #1**
Person's name : ▮▮▮▮▮▮▮▮ (DOB: Nov-02-1955)

Case Specific Clothing Details

Dress: **Colored / Sundress**

2. Arrestee # 1 - ▮▮▮▮▮▮▮▮▮▮

(Case Specific Information)

Sex: **FEMALE**
Race: **WHITE**
Date of birth: **Nov-02-1955**
Address: ▮▮▮▮▮▮▮▮
    Municipality: **LUDHIANA , India or Sikkim**
Phone Numbers
    Home: **000-**

Particulars

Place of birth: **India or Sikkim**
Marital status: **Married**
Ethnicity: **Not of Hispanic Origin**
Height: **5'03** Weight: **135 lbs.**
Build: **Thin** Complexion: **Light Brown**
Handed: **Right Handed**
Eye color: **Brown**
Hair color: **Gray or Partially Gray/Salt and Pepper**
Hair style: **Medium (Shoulder Length)**

Master Name Index Reference

Name: ███████████

Sex: **FEMALE**

Race: **WHITE**

Date of birth: **Nov-02-1955**

Ethnicity: **Not of Hispanic Origin**

Address: ███████████

    Municipality: **LUDHIANA , India or Sikkim**

Phone numbers

Home: 000-

Charge Summary

Charge # 1

Offense date: **Sep-02-2017 (Sat.)**

Offense : **Adult in Home Fails to Report Child Abuse W/I Home**

Charge statute: **F3**

Domestic Violence: **No**

Bond: **100000.00**

Court: **31O**

Charge # 2

Offense date: **Sep-02-2017 (Sat.)**

Offense : **BATTERY DOMESTIC VIOLENCE**

Charge statute: **M1**

Domestic Violence: **No**

Bond: **10000.00**

Court: **31O**

Linkage factors

Resident status : **Non-Resident**

Age range : **50-64 Years**

Access to firearm : **No**

Armed with : **Unarmed**

Offense: **ASSAULT- 3 AGGRAVATED ASSAULT - COMPLETED**

Arrest date: **Sep-02-2017 (Sat.)**

Arrest type: **Onview (Taken into custody without a warrant or previous report)**

3. Arrestee # 2 - ███████████

(Case Specific Information)

Sex: **MALE**

Race: **WHITE**

Date of birth: **May-18-1950**

Address: ███████████

    Municipality: **LUDHIANA , India or Sikkim   14100-**

Particulars

Height: **5'5** Weight: **168 lbs.**
Build: **Thin** Complexion: **Light Brown**
Eye color: **Brown**
Hair color: **Gray or Partially Gray/Salt and Pepper**
Hair style: **Ponytail**
Facial hair color: **Gray or Partially Gray**
Facial hair style: **Goatee**

Master Name Index Reference

Name: ▮▮▮▮▮▮▮▮▮▮▮▮▮
Sex: **MALE**
Race: **WHITE**
Date of birth: **May-18-1950**
Ethnicity: **Not of Hispanic Origin**
Address: ▮▮▮▮▮▮▮▮▮
  Municipality: **PUNJAB , Florida 14100**
Phone numbers
Home: ▮▮▮▮▮▮▮

Charge Summary

Charge # 1
  Offense date: **Sep-02-2017 (Sat.)**
  Offense : **CHILD ABUSE**
  Charge statute: **F3**
  Domestic Violence: **No**
  Bond: **0.00**
  Court: **31O**

Charge # 2
  Offense date: **Sep-02-2017 (Sat.)**
  Offense : **FALSE IMPRISONMENT**
  Charge statute: **F3**
  Domestic Violence: **No**
  Bond: **0.00**
  Court: **31O**

Charge # 3
  Offense date: **Sep-02-2017 (Sat.)**
  Offense : **HARASSING A WITNESS**
  Charge statute: **F3**
  Domestic Violence: **No**
  Bond: **0.00**
  Court: **31O**

Charge # 4
  Offense date: **Sep-02-2017 (Sat.)**

Offense : AGGRAVATED ASSAULT WITH DEADLY WEAPON
Charge statute: F3 784.021(1)(a)
Domestic Violence: No
Bond: 0.00
Court: 31O

Linkage factors

Resident status : Non-Resident
Age range : 65-98 Years
Access to firearm : No
Armed with : Unarmed
Offense: ASSAULT- 3 AGGRAVATED ASSAULT - COMPLETED
Arrest date: Sep-02-2017 (Sat.)

4. Arrestee # 3 - █████████████████

(Case Specific Information)

Sex: MALE
Race: WHITE
Date of birth: Apr-29-1984
Address: █████████████████████
        Municipality: RIVERVIEW , Florida 33569
        District: D4 Beat: J02 Grid: HS4007

Particulars

Place of birth: India or Sikkim
Citizenship: Other
Marital status: Married
Language(s) spoken: English, Other
Height: 6'00 Weight: 180 lbs.
Disability: No
Build: Thin   Complexion: Light Brown
Eye color: Brown
Hair color: Black
Hair style: Crew Cut, Short

Master Name Index Reference

Name: ████████████████████
Sex: MALE
Race: WHITE
Date of birth: Apr-29-1984
Ethnicity: Not of Hispanic Origin
Address: █████████████
        Municipality: RIVERVIEW , Florida 33569
        District: D4 Beat: J02 Grid: HS4007
Phone numbers

Home: **(708) 714-0588**

Charge Summary

Charge # 1

Offense date: Sep-02-2017 (Sat.)
Offense : **CHILD ABUSE**
Charge statute: **F3**
Docket #: **17-CF-013214-A**
Domestic Violence: No
Bond: **0.00**
Court: **31O**

Charge # 2

Offense date: Sep-02-2017 (Sat.)
Offense : **FALSE IMPRISONMENT**
Charge statute: **F3**
Docket #: **17-CF-013214-A**
Domestic Violence: No
Bond: **0.00**
Court: **31O**

Charge # 3

Offense date: Sep-02-2017 (Sat.)
Offense : **FELONY BATTERY**
Charge statute: **F3**
Docket #: **17-CF-013214-A**
Domestic Violence: No
Bond: **0.00**
Court: **31O**

Charge # 4

Offense date: Sep-02-2017 (Sat.)
Offense : **HARASSING A WITNESS**
Charge statute: **FP**
Docket #: **17-CF-013214-A**
Domestic Violence: No
Bond: **0.00**
Court: **31O**

Linkage factors

Resident status : **Resident**
Age range : **30-49 Years**
Access to firearm : **No**
Armed with : **Unarmed**
Offense: **ASSAULT- 3 AGGRAVATED ASSAULT - COMPLETED**
Arrest date: **Sep-02-2017 (Sat.)**

Arrest type: **Onview (Taken into custody without a warrant or previous report)**

5. NeighSrvy # 1 - ████████████████

(Case Specific Information)

Sex: **FEMALE**
Race: **WHITE**
Date of birth: **Mar-17-1940**
Address: ████████████████
      Municipality: **RIVERVIEW , Florida 33569**
      District: **D4** Beat: **J02** Grid: **HS4007**

Phone Numbers
    Home:
    Cellular: ████████████

Particulars

Place of birth: **Pennsylvania**
Citizenship: **America, United States of**
Marital status: **Married**
Ethnicity: **Not of Hispanic Origin**
Language(s) spoken: **English**
Height: **5'00** Weight: **110 lbs.**
Disability: **No**
Build: **Thin**   Complexion: **Light**
Eye color: **Brown**
Hair color: **Red or Auburn**
Hair style: **Short**

Master Name Index Reference

Name: ████████████████
Sex: **FEMALE**
Race: **WHITE**
Date of birth: **Mar-17-1940**
Ethnicity: **Not of Hispanic Origin**
Address: ████████████████
      Municipality: **RIVERVIEW , Florida 33569**
      District: **D4** Beat: **J04** Grid: **HS3780**

Phone numbers
Home: **(813) 672-8415**
Cellular: **(813) 431-8691**

Linkage factors

Resident status : **Resident**
Age range : **65-98 Years**
Access to firearm : **No**

6. VictimJUV # 2 - ████████████████

(Case Specific Information)

Sex: **FEMALE**
Race: **WHITE**
Date of birth: **Dec-13-2016**
Address: ████████████

    Municipality: **RIVERVIEW , Florida 33569**
    District: **D4** Beat: **J02** Grid: **HS4007**

Particulars

Place of birth: **Florida**

Master Name Index Reference

Name: ████████████
Sex: **FEMALE**
Race: **WHITE**
Date of birth: **Dec-13-2016**
Address: ████████████

    Municipality: **RIVERVIEW , Florida 33569**
    District: **D4** Beat: **J02** Grid: **HS4007**

Linkage factors

Resident status : **Resident**
Age range : **0-1 Year**
Access to firearm : **No**
Victim of :
BATTERY- 6 CHILD ABUSE - ALL OTHER - COMPLETED

Victim's Relationship to Offender : **Victim Was Child**
Person's role : **Arrestee #3**
Person's name ████████████ (DOB: Apr-29-1984)

Victim's Relationship to Offender : **Victim Was Grandchild**
Person's role : **Arrestee #1**
Person's name : ████████████ (DOB: Nov-02-1955)

Victim's Relationship to Offender : **Victim Was Grandchild**
Person's role : **Arrestee #2**
Person's name : ████████████ (DOB: May-18-1950)

Related Text Page(s)

Document: INVESTIGATION
Author: 155757 - ███████
Subject: INVESTIGATION
Related date/time: Sep-02-2017 (Sat.) 900

On 09-02-17 at approximately 0702 hours, I responded to ███████
Drive regarding a Welfare Check/Contact Message call. The complainant
advised the Communication's Center Call Taker that allegedly
his sister, Silky Gaind (victim), called her parents in India and advised
she was being beaten and held by her husband and his parents. The
complainant, Gaurad Gaind advised his sister called him and said to him
that her husband and in-laws are being abusive but won't report it and may
be scared to talk with law enforcement due to cultural traditions. Upon my
arrival, I determined there were persons inside the home but they all
refused to come to the door or acknowledge my presence.

I continued to knock when ███████ (victim) suddenly attempted to
open the door and in a state of shock, told me to save her and her
child. I pushed the door open and was immediately confronted by the
victim's husband Devbir Singh Kalsi (defendant) who attempted to push the
door back closed. I placed the husband in handcuffs for our safety. I was
then confronted by the husband's father Jasbir Singh Kalsi (Defendant) who
I placed in handcuffs for our safety.

I observed the victim, ███████ crying with her daughter Saira Kalsi
(nine months old) in her arms. I observed redness on the victim's neck
with a scratch on the left side of her face and bruises on her arms and
neck. I discovered Silky Gaind to have been severely beaten and bruised
over her entire body. Silky Gaind refused EMS.

I observed on Saira Kalsi a small contusion on her right cheek. Deputy M.
Massimei ABN: 2699 took digital photographs of the scene, knife, victim, and
her injuries. Deputy M. Massimei also obtained a written consent to search
her residence, see his supplement. I provided Silky Gaind with a
Hillsborough County Sheriff's Office (HCSO) case number and a Victim's
Rights Pamphlet. I explained to Silky Gaind the process of obtaining a
Domestic Violence Injunction. I also explained to Silky Graind the Spring
Shelter for victims of domestic violence. I read Jasbir Singh Kalsi his
Miranda Rights, from an State Attorney's Office(SAO) card dated July/2007.
Jasbir Singh Kalsi invoked his rights and no further questions were asked.

I read Devbir Singh Kalsi his Miranda Rights, from from an SAO card dated

July/2007 issued Miranda Rights card dated July 2007. Devbir Singh Kalsi invoked his rights and no further questions were asked. I read Bhupinder Kalsi her Miranda Rights, from from an SAO card dated July/2007. Bhupinder Kalsi invoked her rights and no further questions were asked.

The substantive evidence of the physical abuse that I obtained from my interview and observations from █████████ indicated the physical beatings and abuse has been ongoing for an extended period of time. My further investigation revealed that Devmir Kalsi contacted his parents regarding his wife being disobedient and they came from India to counsel and discipline her. In addition to the beatings Silky Gaind had already suffered from her husband, his parents then participated in holding her and her child against their will, holding a knife to her throat, taking her phone so she could not call 911, and assisted in additional physical beatings. Master Corporal Waytovich #2632 notified CID Detective C. Parsons ABN: 226877 of the event. I called the Florida Abuse Hotline and officer Juanita # 379 stated they will initiate a report with an immediate response. Master Corporal Waytovich made contact with ICE SSA Molina and advised him of this incident. SSA Molina advised an ICE hold would be placed on all three arrested foreign nationals.

HCSO Child Protective Investigator A. Grimmett ABN: 254139 and Child Protective Investigator N. Bennett ABN: 256167 responded to the scene and conducted their investigation. I completed a Criminal Report Affidavit on Jasbir Singh Kalsi charging him with Aggravated Assault with Deadly Weapon, False Imprisonment, Child Abuse, Denying Access to 911, and Battery Domestic Violence. Jasbir Singh Kalsi was transported to Central Booking at the Orient Road Jail. The Hillsborough County Sheriff's Office (HCSO) Jail Division 1- Central Booking SGT D. Bednarski ABN: 4727 was notified of the defendant's foreign national arrest status.

Deputy A. Karpenske ABN: 249578 completed the Criminal Report Affidavits on Defendant, Bhupinder Kalsi and Defendant, Devbir Singh Kalsi which both were transported to the Orient Road Jail, see his supplement. This ends my involvement in this incident.

Related Text Page(s)

Document: **INTERVIEW-VICTIM**
Author: 249578 - █████████████
Related date/time: **Sep-02-2017 (Sat.) 1602**

███████████ advised the following under verbal oath:

She came home from the mall last night (09-01-2017) at approximately 9:00 P.M.. As soon as she got home, her husband, Devbir Kalsi, and in-laws, Jasbir and Bhupinder Kalsi, started yelling at her for coming home too late. She went to the kitchen to prepare a meal for her daughter and her husband became even more upset because she used her fingers. She was holding her daughter as he was yelling at her. He then slapped her twice in the face and also accidentally hit their daughter.

She then tried to go to the bedroom and told her husband he needed to calm down. He followed her towards the bedroom and became even more mad. He continued to yell and scream at her and slap her. Her father-in-law, Jasbir Kalsi, tried to attack her with a steak knife. She thought he was going to kill her. She was so scared that she "peed her pants". Devbir Kalsi took the knife away from his father.

Devbir Kalsi then dragged her by her arms into their bedroom and continued to slap her on her head and back. Bhupinder Kalsi and Jasbir Kalsi also came into the bedroom and they were all hitting and slapping her. Devbir Kalsi took her cell phone away and hid her car keys.

They locked her in the bedroom so she could not escape or call 911.

Devbir cleaned up the "pee" and the other mess that was made during the incident.

She was afraid to call 911 but she text her brother to let him know that she was being abused.

This has been an ongoing issue for more than two (2) years.

Her in-laws were in town visiting from India.

Related Text Page(s)

Document: **INTERVIEW-VICTIM**
Author: **155757 - Tiburcio, Ismael**
Subject: **GAIND SILKY**
Related date/time: **Sep-02-2017 (Sat.) 1626**

The victim, ███████ related the following Under Oath:

She stated that on 09/01/17 at approximately 2100 hours she returned
home from the gym and was with their daughter. She stated that her husband
Devbir Singh Kalsi was very angry while waiting for her. She stated that
her husband slapped her several times in the face while holding her
daughter. She stated that her husband's father Jasbir Singh Kalsi was in
the kitchen and grabbed a kitchen knife and pointed at her neck. She stated
that she was afraid for her life and the life of her daughter.

She stated that her husband then pushed her into the master bedroom and
continued to hit her in her arms and torso. She stated that her husband's
mother Bhupinder Kalsi entered her room and slapped her face several times.
She stated that Devbir Singh Kalsi took her cell phone preventing her to
call 911 and seek help. She stated that all three were preventing her to
seek help and to exit the residence.

She stated that the beating from her husband has been occuring for
several years, but she was afraid to report the issue to the authorities
due to the Indian traditions. She stated that she called her brother and he
called the Hillsborough County Sheriff's Office.

Related Text Page(s)

Document: **SUPPLEMENTAL INVESTIGATION**
Author: **253963** - ███████
Related date/time: **Sep-02-2017 (Sat.) 845**

On 09/02/17, at approximately 0742 hours, I responded to 9601 Greenbank Dr in reference to a Domestic Battery Call. Upon my arrival, I made contact with ████████ (victim).

I observed ████████ to have severe bruising in different stages of severity. I observed bruises on both of her arms, her face, her neck, and her breasts. All of the bruises appeared to be in different stages of healing.

I escorted ████████ to a private area, so a female deputy could take the photographs. I took digital photographs of ████████ and later uploaded them into the Veripic System.

I conducted a neighborhood survey at the following locations:
████████ - Interviewed Lola Martinez.
████████ - No answer at door.
████████ - No answer at door.

This concludes my involvement with this investigation. I have no further information to provide at this time.

HRE Attachments:
NONE

Related Text Page(s)

Document: **SUPPLEMENTAL INVESTIGATION**
Author: **249578** - ▓▓▓▓▓▓▓▓▓▓
Related date/time: **Sep-02-2017 (Sat.) 1258**

On 09-02-2017, at approximately 0733 hours, I responded to 9601 Greenbank Dr, within the Riverglenn subdivision to assist Deputy I. Tiburcio (ABN:155757) with his investigation. I noted that the original call for service was entered as a Welfare Check in reference to possible Domestic Violence. Upon my arrival, I observed Deputy Tiburcio in contact with an adult female who was holding a young child and standing on the front porch of the residence. I later learned the adult female was Silky Gaind (Victim 1) and the child was Saira Kalsi (Victim 2).

Inside the residence, I observed two adult males detained in handcuffs sitting at the dining room table and an adult female standing in the kitchen. I learned that the adult males were Devbir Kalsi (Arrestee), husband of the victim, and his father Jasbir Kalsi (Arrestee) and the female was Bhupinder Kalsi (Arrestee). I noted that Bhupinder Kalsi is the mother of Devbir Kalsi and wife of Jasbir Kalsi.

I secured Devbir Kalsi in the rear of my marked patrol vehicle. I learned from Deputy Tiburcio that Devbir Kalsi declined to provide a statement after being read his Miranda warnings. I did not attempt to conduct any interviews with Devbir Kalsi.

I met with Silky Gaind and obtained a verbal and written statement (see interview). I impounded the statement at the Evidence Control Section. I provided Silky Gaind with a Victim's Advocacy pamphlet and discussed, at length, the information and contact numbers that it contains. I also discussed the availability of a Domestic Violence Shelter, specifically The Spring.

Silky Gaind advised there was possible evidence of her domestic violence stored on her cellular phone but was unable to display it at this time. I was also unable to locate photos or texts that were relevant to the incident. I set her cellular phone into "airplane mode" and impounded it at the Evidence Control Section.

I was directed by Deputy Tiburcio to a black handled steak knife, located on the kitchen counter of the residence. I noted the knife was allegedly involved in the incident. I impounded the knife at the Evidence Control Section.

I noted that Master Corporal D. Waytovich (ABN:2632) responded to the incident scene. Due to the arrestees' Non-Resident status, Master Corporal Waytovich contacted Agent Molina (#8736) of the U.S. Department of Homeland Security Immigration and Customs Enforcement (ICE) to advise them of the charges.

I completed an electronic Criminal Report Affidavit for Devbir Kalsi, charging him with Felony Battery, False Imprisonment, Witness Tampering, and Child Endangerment. I completed an electronic Criminal Report Affidavit for Bhupinder Kalsi, charging her with Simple Battery and Failure to Report Suspected Child Abuse/Endangerment.

I transported Devbir Kalsi to the Orient Road Jail without incident.

I notified Detention Sergeant D. Bednarski (ABN:4727) upon my arrival, per request of ICE Agent Molina and Master Corporal Waytovich.

This balance of my investigation is limited to the interview.

MRE Attachments:
Written Statement (COPY)

Related Text Page(s)

Document: **SUPPLEMENTAL INVESTIGATION**
Author: **2699 - Massimei, Michael**
Related date/time: **Sep-02-2017 (Sat.) 1507**

On 09/02/17 at 0735 hours, I arrived at ▒▒▒▒▒▒▒▒▒▒▒▒ and made contact with Deputy I. Tiburcio (ABN #155757), reference to a Domestic Violence call. I assisted with obtaining a signed Consent to Search form from ▒▒▒▒▒▒▒, who is one of the owners of the residence.

I used my issued Hillsborough County Sheriff's Office (HCSO) camera to photograph some of the injuries on ▒▒▒▒▒▒▒, the scene and the knife used in the incident. I later uploaded the photographs in the Veripic system at the HCSO District IV Office.

This concludes my involvement in this investigation.

MRE Attachments:
Consent to Search form

Related Text Page(s)

Document: **NEIGHBORHOOD SURVEY**
Author: **253963 - Basilone, Kenzie**
Subject: ███████████████
Related date/time: **Sep-02-2017 (Sat.) 1001**

Lola Martinez related the following:

She has never heard the family fighting before. They are all very friendly. She used to go over to the house and help out with the baby. She did not hear any yelling or fighting this morning.

Related Text Page(s)

Document: **EVIDENCE**
Author: **41999 - Roberts, Adam**
Subject: **FW: EVIDENCE CHECK OUT REQUEST - GO #**
Related date/time: **Sep-14-2017 (Thu.) 1105**

```
From:     Oliver Jason M
To:       EVIDENCE CHECK OUT REQUE
Subject:  FW: EVIDENCE CHECK OUT REQUEST - GO #
Date:     Thu. Sep 14, 2017 @ 10:53:26

######## ORIGINAL TEXT ########
#
From:     LaGasse Ryan R
To:       OLIVER JASON M
Subject:  EVIDENCE CHECK OUT REQUEST - GO #
Date:     Thu. Sep 14, 2017 @ 09:41:31


[I request the Evidence Control Section to provide the applying personnel with
the following evidence . The form is to be completed by the requesting employee
and sent in VMAIL to the Evidence Request handle (HEVIDR), if approval is
required by a supervisor send the VMAIL to them first.  Once approved, the
supervisor will forward the request via Vmail to Evidence Request.]


General Offense #  [2017]-[628731   ]          Purpose
Impounding Deputy :[249758  ]                  [   ]Court - Subpoena
Required
Requesting Deputy :[223294  ]                  [X ]Investigation
Court Date : [             ] Time: [        ]    [  ]Testing - FDLE
Pickup Date :[Sep-14-2017   ] Time: [0900  ]     [  ]Transfer to ATF
                                               [  ]Transfer to DEA
                                               [  ]Other (List Below)
                                               [                    ]


Prop #    Item(s)   All   Description
[639398  ] [1 -  ]   [     ] [PHONE                                    ]
[        ]  ] [      ]  [   ] [
]

[        ]  ] [      ]  [   ] [
]

[        ]  ] [      ]  [   ] [
]
```

```
[        ] [        ]  [    ] [
]

[        ] [        ]  [    ] [
]

[        ] [        ]  [    ] [
]

[        ] [        ]  [    ] [
]

[        ] [        ]  [    ] [
]

[        ] [        ]  [    ] [
]
```

```
To be completed by Supervisors ONLY
Supervisor                        Rank     ABN      Date
[   J. Oliver              ]      [  SGT  ][  4786  ][  09/14/17              ]
```

#

####### END OF ORIGINAL TEXT #######

GO# HS 2017-628731 CLEARED BY ARREST   ASSAULT-3 AGGRAVATED ASSAULT

Follow Up Report # HS 1

Follow Up Report # HS 1

Assignment Information

Assigned to: **223294 - LaGasse, Ryan**   Rank: **Detective**
Capacity: **Other Follow Up**   Org unit: **Violent Crimes Section**
Assigned on: **Sep-13-2017 (Wed.) 1031**   by: **4786 - Oliver, Jason**
Report due on: **Oct-04-2017 (Wed.)**

Submission Information

Submitted on: **Oct-03-2017 (Tue.) 1247**
Checked by: **119227 - Loy, Joshua**
Approved on: **Oct-03-2017 (Tue.)**   by: **119227 - Loy, Joshua**
Follow Up Conclusion
Follow Up concluded: **Yes**

Narrative Text Report # 1

Document: **DETECTIVE FOLLOW UP**
Author: **223294 - LaGasse, Ryan**
Related date/time: **Sep-14-2017 (Thu.)**

I received this case for review and investigative leads while working as a detective assigned to the Criminal Investigations Division in the Violent Crimes Section. During my review of the case, I learned the victim's cell phone, may have items of evidentiary value on it regarding the sequence of events in this investigation.

On 09/14/17, I retrieved the victim's phone from the HCSO evidence section via a property release form.

On 09/14/17, I responded to 9601 Greenbank Drive where I met with ▮▮▮▮ and her brother. Both were still extremely distraught and fearful of the family members who had been arrested. I handed Silky her phone, per her request, and she began charging it immediately as she wanted to speak to her parents in India.

▮▮▮▮ and her brother repeatedly asked about how long the family members would be incarcerated and told me how much fear they were in if they were to be released. Silky advised she would email any pertinent evidence from her phone once it becomes charged enough to turn on. I did not remain at the residence more than fifteen (15) minutes as they were both very shaky and I did not want to put them under any additional duress. I explained to them the process of the investigation and left them with my contact information. ▮▮▮▮ talked about fleeing the United States and travel to India to be safe from the incarcerated family members.

On 09/14/17, I received an email from ▮▮▮▮ where she attached a folder with photographs and an audio file. The audio file consisted of a conversation I am unable to understand due to the language in which it is spoken in.

On 09/21/17, I received an additional email from Silky Gaind with several photographs. The photographs consist of Silky and injuries she incurred. The time-line of these injuries in all photographs are unknown as I have not been able to make contact with Silky since my original contact with her on 09/14/17.

I have attached the photographs and audio file to the report.

On 10/03/17, I responded to Silky's residence and was unable to make contact with her or anyone else at the residence.

On 10/03/17, I emailed Silky in order to obtain her brother's information and have yet to hear back from her.

I request this case remain active pending further contact with Silky in order to obtain information on her brother and the dates/times of the photographs she sent to me.

Clearance Information

Agency: **Hillsborough County**
Cleared status: **Adult Arrest - Not Applicable**
Cleared on: **Sep-02-2017 (Sat.)**
Complainant/Victim notified: **No**

Related Property Report(s)

Report Information

Property Report #: 639398
Property case status: **EVIDENCE**
Submitted on: **Sep-02-2017 (Sat.)** by: **Karpenske, Andrew**
Authority for disposal: **Tiburcio, Ismael** Org unit: **D4 Day B JULIET Squad**
Related:
Offense: GO HS 2017- 628731
Location: ▮▮▮▮▮▮▮▮
Related items: **3**

Articles

Status: **EVIDENCE**   Tag #: **HS639398- 1**
Article: **DCELLPH- DATA PROCESSING EQUIPMENT**
Make: **SAMSUN**
Model: **GALAXY S6 EDGE+**   # of pieces:
Serial # 1: **R38G8016R8K**   OAN:
Value: **$0.00**   Color: **Silver/Aluminum**
Description: **GALAZY CELL PHONE (VICTIMS)**
Recovered date: -   Recovered value: **$0.00**
Current Location: **INVESTIGATION**

Articles

Status: **EVIDENCE**   Tag #: **HS639398- 2**
Article: **EBLADE- EQUIPMENT, MEASURING DEVICES, AND TOOLS**
Make: **NO BRA**
Serial # 1: **UNKNOWN**   OAN:
Value: **$0.00**   Color: **Black, Silver/Aluminum**
Description: **STEAK KNIFE**
Recovered date: -   Recovered value: **$0.00**
Current Location: **W1 GEN/01/K/07/H**

Articles

Status: **EVIDENCE**   Tag #: **HS639398- 3**
Article: **YDOCUME- OTHER ITEMS (MISCELLANEOUS)**
Make: **NO BRA**
Model: # of pieces: **4**
Serial # 1: **UNKNOWN**   OAN:
Value: **$0.00**   Color: **White**
Description: **DV VICTIM WRITTEN STATEMENT**
Recovered date: -   Recovered value: **$0.00**
Current Location: **W1 GEN/01/K/07/H**

Flags = d (disposed) x (x-reference) n (entered on NCIC) *e (evidence)

Related Arrest Report: AB# 2017-17032338

Arrestee: ▮▮▮▮▮▮▮▮▮▮▮▮▮
Date of birth: May-18-1950
Related CD#: 806161

Arrest Information

Status: **Probable Cause**
Reason for arrest: **Probable Cause**
Arrest date: **Sep-02-2017** (Sat.) 909
Rush file required: No
Booked into cell: No
Arrest agency: **HILLSBOROUGH COUNTY SHERIFF'S OFFICE**
Arresting officers: 155757 - Tiburcio, Ismael
Summary of facts: **CHILD ABUSE**

Arrest location

SODA zone: No Drug free zone: No

Additional Arrest Information

Case Screened: No
Notify victim on release: No
Juvenile: No
Armed with: **Unarmed**
Diversion recommended: No
Interpreter needed: No
Rights given: No
Marital status: **Married**
Mental exam required: No
Statement taken: No
Fingerprinted: No Photo taken: No
CD updated: No
Family notified: No
Lawyer called: No
Meal given: No Coffee given: No
Detained: No

Related Arrest Report: AB# 2017-17032339

Arrestee: ▮▮▮▮▮▮▮▮▮▮
Date of birth: **Apr-29-1984**
Related CD#: **806162**

Arrest Information

Status: **Probable Cause**
Reason for arrest: **Probable Cause**
Arrest date: **Sep-02-2017 (Sat.) 909**
Rush file required: **No**
Booked into cell: **No**
Arrest agency: **HILLSBOROUGH COUNTY SHERIFF'S OFFICE**
Arresting officers: **249578 - Karpenske, Andrew**
Summary of facts: **HARASSING A WITNESS**

Arrest location

SODA zone: **No** Drug free zone: **No**

Additional Arrest Information

Case Screened: **No**
Notify victim on release: **No**
Juvenile: **No**
Armed with: **Unarmed**
Diversion recommended: **No**
Interpreter needed: **No**
Rights given: **No**
Marital status: **Married**
Mental exam required: **No**
Statement taken: **No**
Fingerprinted: **No** Photo taken: **No**
CD updated: **No**
Family notified: **No**
Lawyer called: **No**
Meal given: **No** Coffee given: **No**
Arrestee's occupation: **ID DEPT**
Detained: **No**

Related Arrest Report: AB# 2017-17032346

Arrestee: █████████████
Date of birth: Nov-02-1955
Related CD#: 806163

Arrest Information

Status: **Probable Cause**
Reason for arrest: **Probable Cause**
Arrest date: **Sep-02-2017 (Sat.) 909**
Rush file required: No
Booked into cell: No
Arrest agency: **HILLSBOROUGH COUNTY SHERIFF'S OFFICE**
Arresting officers: **249578 - Karpenske, Andrew**
Summary of facts: **FAILURE TO REPORT CHILD ABUSE**

Arrest location

SODA zone: No Drug free zone: No

Additional Arrest Information

Case Screened: No
Notify victim on release: No
Juvenile: **No**
Armed with: **Unarmed**
Diversion recommended: No
Interpreter needed: No
Rights given: **No**
Marital status: **Married**
Mental exam required: No
Statement taken: No
Fingerprinted: No Photo taken: No
CD updated: No
Family notified: No
Lawyer called: No
Meal given: No Coffee given: No
Detained: No

*** END OF HARDCOPY ***

EXHIBIT #9

FINAL JUDGEMENT OF INJUNCTION FOR PROTECTION AGAINST
DOMESTIC VIOLENCE AGAINST APPLICANT'S HUSBAND AND IN-LAWS

IN THE CIRCUIT COURT OF THE THIRTEENTH JUDICIAL CIRCUIT,
IN AND FOR HILLSBOROUGH COUNTY, FLORIDA

████████████

PETITIONER

Vs

████████████

RESPONDENT

CASE NO: 17-DR-013876

Division G

FINAL JUDGMENT OF INJUNCTION FOR PROTECTION AGAINST DOMESTIC VIOLENCE WITH MINOR CHILD(REN) (AFTER NOTICE)

The Petition for Injunction for Protection Against Domestic Violence under section 741.30, Florida Statutes, and other papers filed in this Court have been reviewed. The Court has jurisdiction of the parties and the subject matter.

It is intended that this protection order meet the requirements of 18 U.S.C. Section 2265 and therefore intended that it be accorded full faith and credit by the court of another state or Indian tribe and enforced as if it were the order of the enforcing state or of the Indian tribe.

HEARING

This cause came before the Court for a hearing to determine whether an Injunction for Protection Against Domestic Violence in this case should be ☒ issued ☐ modified ☐ extended.

The hearing was attended by ☒ Petitioner   ☒ Respondent
                         ☒ Petitioner's Counsel   ☒ Respondent's Counsel

FINDINGS

On **01/10/2018**, a notice of this hearing was served on Respondent together with a copy of Petitioner's petition to this Court and the temporary injunction, if issued. Service was within the time required by Florida law, and Respondent was afforded an opportunity to be heard.

After hearing the testimony of each party present and of any witnesses, or upon consent of Respondent, the Court finds, based on the specific facts of this case, that Petitioner is a victim of domestic violence or has reasonable cause to believe that he/she is in imminent danger of becoming a victim of domestic violence by Respondent.

INJUNCTION AND TERMS

This injunction shall be in full force and effect until ☐ further order of the Court ☒ _March 23, 2021_. This injunction is valid and enforceable in all counties of the State of Florida. The terms of this injunction may not be changed by either party alone or by both parties together. Only the Court may modify the terms of this injunction. Either party may ask the Court to change or end this injunction at any time.

Florida Supreme Court Approved Family Law Form 12.980(d)(1), Final Judgment of Injunction for Protection Against Domestic Violence with Minor Child(ren) (After Notice) (06/12)   Page 1 of 10

Any violation of this injunction, whether or not at the invitation of Petitioner or anyone else, may subject Respondent to civil or indirect criminal contempt proceedings, including the imposition of a fine or imprisonment. Certain willful violations of the terms of this injunction, such as: refusing to vacate the dwelling that the parties share; going to or being within 500 feet of Petitioner's residence, going to Petitioner's place of employment, school, or other place prohibited in this injunction; telephoning, contacting or communicating with Petitioner if prohibited by this injunction; knowingly or intentionally coming within 100 feet of Petitioner's motor vehicle, whether or not it is occupied; defacing or destroying Petitioner's personal property; refusing to surrender firearms or ammunition if ordered to do so by the court; or committing an act of domestic violence against Petitioner constitutes a misdemeanor of the first degree punishable by up to one year in jail, as provided by sections 775.082 and 775.083, Florida Statutes. In addition, it is a federal criminal felony offense, punishable by up to life imprisonment, depending on the nature of the violation, to cross state lines or enter Indian country for the purpose of engaging in conduct that is prohibited in this injunction. 18 U.S.C. Section 2262.

ORDERED and ADJUDGED:

Violence Prohibited. Respondent shall not commit, or cause any other person to commit, any acts of domestic violence against Petitioner. Domestic violence includes: assault, aggravated assault, battery, aggravated battery, sexual assault, sexual battery, stalking, aggravated stalking, kidnapping, false imprisonment, or any other criminal offense resulting in physical injury or death to Petitioner or any of Petitioner's family or household members. Respondent shall not commit any other violation of the injunction through an intentional unlawful threat, word or act to do violence to the Petitioner.

No Contact. Respondent shall have no contact with the Petitioner unless otherwise provided in this section, or unless paragraphs 13 through 19 below provide for contact connected with the temporary parenting plan and temporary time-sharing with respect to the minor child(ren).

a. Unless otherwise provided herein, Respondent shall have no contact with Petitioner. Respondent shall not directly or indirectly contact Petitioner in person, by mail, e-mail, fax, telephone, through another person, or in any other manner. Further, Respondent shall not contact or have any third party contact anyone connected with Petitioner's employment or school to inquire about Petitioner or to send any messages to Petitioner. Unless otherwise provided herein, **Respondent shall not go to, in, or within 500 feet of:** Petitioner's current residence <u>Confidential Address</u>

or any residence to which Petitioner may move; Petitioner's current or any subsequent place of employment or place where Petitioner attends school or the following other places (if requested by Petitioner) where Petitioner or Petitioner's minor child(ren) go often:

_____

_____

Respondent may not knowingly come within 100 feet of Petitioner's automobile at any time.

b. ___ Other provisions regarding contact: _____

_____

3. Firearms. Unless paragraph a. is initialed below, Respondent shall not have in his or her

Florida Supreme Court Approved Family Law Form 12.980(d)(1), Final Judgment of Injunction for Protection Against Domestic Violence with Minor Child(ren) (After Notice) (06/12)   Page 2 of 10

110 | P a g e

care, custody, possession or control any firearm or ammunition. **It is a violation of section 790.233, Florida Statutes, and a first degree misdemeanor, for the respondent to have in his or her care, custody, possession or control any firearm or ammunition.**

[Initial if applies; write N/A if not applicable]

a. _____ Respondent is a state or local officer as defined in section 943.10(14), Florida Statutes, who holds an active certification, who receives or possesses a firearm or ammunition for use in performing official duties on behalf of the officer's employing agency and is not prohibited by the court from having in his or her care, custody, possession or control a firearm or ammunition. The officer's employing agency may prohibit the officer from having in his or her care, custody, possession or control a firearm or ammunition.

b. ✓ Respondent shall surrender any firearms and ammunition in the Respondent's possession to the Hillsborough County Sheriff's Office.

c. _____ Other directives relating to firearms and ammunition: _____

_____

NOTE: RESPONDENT IS ADVISED THAT IT IS A FEDERAL CRIMINAL FELONY OFFENSE TO SHIP OR TRANSPORT IN INTERSTATE OR FOREIGN COMMERCE, OR POSSESS IN OR AFFECTING COMMERCE, ANY FIREARM OR AMMUNITION; OR TO RECEIVE ANY FIREARM OR AMMUNITION WHICH HAS BEEN SHIPPED OR TRANSPORTED IN INTERSTATE OR FOREIGN COMMERCE WHILE SUBJECT TO SUCH AN INJUNCTION. 18 U.S.C. SECTION 922(g)(8).

4. **Evaluation/Counseling.**

[Check all that apply; write N/A if does not apply]

a. The Court finds that Respondent has:
   i. **N/A** willfully violated the ex parte injunction;
   ii. **N/A** been convicted of, had adjudication withheld on, or pled nolo contendere to a crime involving violence or a threat of violence; and/or
   iii. **N/A** in this state or any other state, had at any time a prior injunction for protection entered against the respondent after a hearing with notice.

Note: If Respondent meets any of the above enumerated criteria, the Court must order the Respondent to attend a batterers' intervention program unless it makes written factual findings stating why such a program would not be appropriate. See Section 741.30(6)(e), Florida Statutes.

b. Within ☐ 10 days ☐ _____days, (but no more than 10 days) of the date of this injunction, Respondent shall enroll in and thereafter without delay complete the following, and Respondent shall provide proof of such enrollment to the Clerk of Circuit Court within ☐ 30 days or ☐ days, (but no more than 30 days) of the date of this injunction:

   i. _____A certified batterers' intervention program from a list of programs to be provided by the Court or any entity designated by the Court. Respondent shall also successfully complete any substance abuse or mental health evaluation that the assessing program counselor deems necessary as a predicate to completion of the batterers' intervention program.

   ii. _____A substance abuse evaluation at:_____ or a similarly qualified facility and any substance abuse treatment recommended by that evaluation.

   iii. _____A mental health evaluation by a licensed mental health professional at: _____

Florida Supreme Court Approved Family Law Form 12.980(d)(1), Final Judgment of Injunction for Protection Against Domestic Violence with Minor Child(ren) (After Notice) (06/12)   Page 3 of 10

111 | P a g e

_____or any other similarly qualified facility and any mental health treatment recommended by that evaluation.

    iv. _____Other: DOMESTIC VIOLENCE ASSESSMENT at _____
_____, and must complete any recommended treatment.

    c. _____Although Respondent meets the statutory mandate of attendance at a batterers' intervention program, the Court makes the following written findings as to why the condition of batterers intervention program would be inappropriate: _____
_____

    d. <u>N/A</u> Petitioner is referred to a certified domestic violence center and is provided with a list of certified domestic violence centers in this circuit, which Petitioner may contact.

5. **Mailing Address.** Respondent shall notify the Clerk of the Court of any change in his or her mailing address within 10 days of the change. All further papers (excluding pleadings requiring personal service) shall be served by mail to Respondent's last known address. Such service by mail shall be complete upon mailing. Rule 12.080, Fla.Fam.L.R.P., section 741.30, Florida Statutes.

6. **Other provisions necessary to protect Petitioner from domestic violence:**
_____**RESPONDENT SHALL STAY**_____
_____**500 FEET AWAY FROM**_____
_____**THE PETITIONER.**_____

TEMPORARY EXCLUSIVE USE AND POSSESSION OF HOME

[Initial if applies; write N/A if not applicable]

7. <u>N/A</u> **Possession of the Home.** ☐ Petitioner ☐ Respondent shall have temporary exclusive use and possession of the dwelling located at: _____
_____

8. _____**Transfer of Possession of the Home.** A law enforcement officer with jurisdiction over the home shall accompany ☐ Petitioner ☐ Respondent to the home, and shall place ☐ Petitioner ☐ Respondent in possession of the home.

9. _____**Personal Items.** ☐ Petitioner ☐ Respondent, **in the presence of a law enforcement officer,** may return to the premises described above ( ) on _____, at _____ a.m./p.m., or ☐ at a time arranged with the law enforcement department with jurisdiction over the home, accompanied by a law enforcement officer only, for the purpose of obtaining his or her clothing and items of personal health and hygiene and tools of the trade. A law enforcement officer with jurisdiction over the premises shall go with ☐ Petitioner ☐ Respondent to the home and stand by to insure that he/she vacates the premises with only his/her personal clothing, toiletries, tools of the trade, and any items listed in paragraph 10 below. The law enforcement agency shall not be responsible for storing or transporting any property. **IF THE RESPONDENT IS NOT AWARDED POSSESSION OF THE HOME AND GOES TO THE HOME WITHOUT A LAW ENFORCEMENT OFFICER, IT IS A VIOLATION OF THIS INJUNCTION.**

10. <u>N/A</u> The following other personal possessions may also be removed from the premises at this

Florida Supreme Court Approved Family Law Form 12.980(d)(1), Final Judgment of Injunction for Protection Against Domestic Violence with Minor Child(ren) (After Notice) (06/12)   Page 4 of 10

time: _____

11. **N/A** Other: _____

TEMPORARY PARENTING PLAN AND TIME- SHARING WITH MINOR CHILD(REN)

12. **Jurisdiction.** [Initial one only.]

    ✓ Jurisdiction to determine issues relating to parenting plan and time-sharing with respect to any minor child(ren) listed in paragraph 13 below is proper under the Uniform Child Custody Jurisdiction and Enforcement Act (UCCJEA).

    Jurisdiction is exclusive to the dependency court, and accordingly no order is made herein. (Case Number ___17-DP- 880___ .)

13. **Temporary Parenting Plan for Minor Child(ren).** Except for that time-sharing (if any) specified for the other parent in paragraph 14, below, ☐ **Petitioner** ☐ **Respondent** shall on a temporary basis have 100% of the time-sharing with the parties' minor child(ren) listed below and shall have sole decision-making responsibility until further court order:

Name	Birth date
███████████	12/13/2016

When requested by the parent to whom the majority of overnight time-sharing with the child(ren) is awarded on a temporary basis herein, in this case the ☐ Petitioner ☐ Respondent, law enforcement officers shall use any and all reasonable and necessary force to physically deliver the minor child(ren) listed above to the parent to whom the majority of overnight time-sharing with the child(ren) is awarded on a temporary basis herein. The other parent shall not take the child(ren) from the parent to whom the majority of overnight time-sharing with the child(ren) is awarded on a temporary basis herein or any child care provider or other person entrusted by the parent to whom the majority of overnight time-sharing with the child(ren) is awarded on a temporary basis herein with the care of the child(ren).

14. **Temporary Parenting Plan with Time-Sharing for Minor Child(ren).** The Petitioner and Respondent shall have time-sharing with the minor child(ren) on the following schedule:

[Initial one only]

    a. _____ ☐ Petitioner ☐ Respondent shall have 100% of time-sharing and ☐ Petitioner ☐ Respondent shall have 0% of time sharing with the child(ren) until further order of the Court. Until further order of the Court, all parenting decisions shall be made by the parent with 100% of the time-sharing.

    b. _____ ☐ Petitioner ☐ Respondent shall have time-sharing from _____ a.m./p.m. to _____ a.m./p.m on the following day(s) _____ The other parent will have the remaining time-sharing. _____

    c. _____ Other _____

Florida Supreme Court Approved Family Law Form 12.980(d)(1), Final Judgment of Injunction for Protection Against Domestic Violence with Minor Child(ren) (After Notice) (06/12)   Page 5 of 10

113 | P a g e

15. **Limitations on Time-Sharing** The time-sharing specified in paragraph 14, above, for ☐ Petitioner ☐ Respondent with the child(ren) shall be:_____
[Initial all that apply; write N/A if does not apply]

    a. _____ unsupervised.

    b. _____ supervised by the following specified responsible adult:_____.

    c. _____ at a supervised visitation center located at: **CHILDREN'S JUSTICE CENTER, 700 EAST TWIGGS STREET, SUITE 102, TAMPA, FL 33602; (813) 272-7179** and shall be subject to the available times and rules of the supervised visitation center. The cost associated with the services of the supervised visitation center shall be paid by ☐ parent to whom the majority of overnight time-sharing with the child(ren) is awarded on a temporary basis herein ☐ other parent ☐ both:_____.

    If specified, the level of supervision shall be:_____
_____
_____

16. **Arrangements for Time-Sharing with Minor Child(ren).**
[Initial all that apply; write N/A if does not apply]

    a. _____ A responsible person shall coordinate the time-sharing arrangements with respect to the minor child(ren).

    If specified, the responsible person shall be: {name} _____

    b. _____ Other conditions for time-sharing arrangements as follows: _____
_____
_____

17. **Exchange of Minor Child(ren).**
[Initial all that apply; write N/A if does not apply]

    a. _____ The parties shall exchange the child(ren) at ☐ school or daycare, or ☐ at the following location(s): _____

    b. _____ A responsible person shall conduct all exchanges of the child(ren). The ☐ Petitioner ☐ Respondent shall not be present during the exchange. If specified, the responsible person shall be: {name}_____

    c. _____ Other conditions for exchange as follows: _____
_____
_____

18. **Other Additional Provisions Relating to the Minor Child(ren).** _____

    NEITHER PARTY SHALL REMOVE THE CHILD(REN)
    FROM THE JURISDICTION OF THE COURT FOR
    MORE THAN 48 HOURS.

Florida Supreme Court Approved Family Law Form 12.980(d)(1), Final Judgment of Injunction for Protection Against Domestic Violence with Minor Child(ren) (After Notice) (06/12)   Page 6 of 10

114 | P a g e

TEMPORARY SUPPORT

19. Temporary Alimony.
[Initial all that apply; write N/A if does not apply]

    a. <u>N/A</u> The court finds that there is a need for temporary alimony and that [ ] Petitioner [ ] Respondent (hereinafter Obligor) has the present ability to pay alimony and shall pay temporary alimony to [ ] Petitioner [ ] Respondent (hereinafter Obligee) in the amount of $____ per month, payable [ ] in accordance with Obligor's employer's payroll cycle, and in any event, at least once a month [ ] other *(explain)* ____ beginning *(date)* ____ . This alimony shall continue until modified by court order, until a final judgment of dissolution of marriage is entered, until Obligee dies, until this injunction expires, or until *(date)*, whichever occurs first.

    b. <u>N/A</u> [ ] Petitioner [ ] Respondent shall be required to maintain health insurance coverage for the other party. Any uncovered medical costs for the party awarded alimony shall be assessed as follows:

    c. <u>N/A</u> Other provisions relating to alimony:

20. Temporary Child Support.
[Initial all that apply; write N/A if does not apply]

    a. ____ The Court finds that there is a need for temporary child support and that ☐ Petitioner ☐ Respondent (hereinafter Obligor) has the present ability to pay child support. The amounts in the Child Support Guidelines Worksheet, Florida Family Law Form 12.902(e), filed by ☐ Petitioner ☐ Respondent are correct **OR** the Court makes the following findings: The Petitioner's net monthly income is $_____ . (Child Support Guidelines ____%). The Respondent's net monthly income is $_____ , (Child Support Guidelines ____%). Monthly child care costs are $ _____ . Monthly health/dental insurance costs are $_____ .

    b. ____ **Amount.** Obligor shall pay temporary child support in the amount of $ ____ , per month payable ☐ in accordance with Obligor's employer's payroll cycle, and in any event at least once a month ☐ other _____ beginning *(date)* _____ , and continuing until further order of the court, or until *(date/event)* _____ ,*(explain)* _____
_____ .If the child support ordered deviates from the guidelines by more than 5%, the factual findings which support that deviation are: _____
_____

    c. <u>N/A</u> ( ) Petitioner ( ) Respondent shall be required to maintain ( ) health ( ) dental insurance coverage for the parties' minor child(ren) so long as reasonably available. **OR** ( ) Health ( ) dental insurance is not reasonably available at this time.

    d. <u>N/A</u> Any reasonable and necessary **uninsured medical/dental/prescription drug costs** for the minor child(ren) shall be assessed as follows:

    e. <u>N/A</u> Florida Supreme Court Approved Family Law Form 12.902(j), **Notice of Social Security Number**, is incorporated herein by reference.

    f. <u>N/A</u> Other provisions relating to child support:

Florida Supreme Court Approved Family Law Form 12.980(d)(1), Final Judgment of Injunction for Protection Against Domestic Violence with Minor Child(ren) (After Notice) (06/12)   Page 7 of 10

115 | P a g e

21. **Method of Payment.**
[Initial one only]

    a. __N/A__ Obligor shall pay any temporary child support/alimony ordered through income deduction, and such support shall be paid to the state disbursement unit. Obligor is individually responsible for paying this support obligation in the event that all or any portion of said support is not deducted from Obligor's income. Obligor shall also pay the applicable state disbursement unit service charge. Until child support/alimony payments are deducted from Obligor's paycheck pursuant to the Income Deduction Order, Obligor is responsible for making timely payments directly to the state disbursement unit.

    b. _____ Temporary child support/alimony shall be paid through the state disbursement unit in the office of the Hillsborough County Clerk of Circuit Court. Obligor shall also pay the applicable state disbursement unit service charge. Income deduction is not in the best interests of the child(ren) because:_____

    c. __N/A__ Other provisions relating to method of payment: _____
_____

OTHER SPECIAL PROVISIONS

(This section to be used for inclusion of local provisions approved by the chief judge as provided in Florida Family Law Rule 12.610.)

DIRECTIONS TO LAW ENFORCEMENT OFFICER IN ENFORCING THIS INJUNCTION
(Provisions in this injunction that do not include a line for the judge to either initial or write N/A are considered mandatory provisions and should be interpreted to be part of this injunction.)

1. **This injunction is valid in all counties of the State of Florida.** Violation of this injunction should be reported to the appropriate law enforcement agency. Law enforcement officers of the jurisdiction in which a violation of this injunction occurs shall enforce the provisions of this injunction and are authorized to arrest without warrant pursuant to section 901.15, Florida Statutes, for any violation of its provisions, except those regarding child support and/or alimony, which constitutes a criminal act under section 741.31, Florida Statutes. **When inconsistent with this order, any subsequent court order issued under Chapter 61 or Chapter 39, Florida Statutes, shall take precedence over this order on all matters relating to property division, alimony, parental responsibility, parenting plan, time-sharing , child custody, or child support.**

2. THIS INJUNCTION IS ENFORCEABLE IN ALL COUNTIES OF FLORIDA, AND LAW ENFORCEMENT OFFICERS MAY EFFECT ARRESTS PURSUANT TO SECTION 901.15(6), FLORIDA STATUTES. The arresting agent shall notify the State Attorney's Office immediately after arrest.

3. **Reporting alleged violations.** If Respondent violates the terms of this injunction and there has not been an arrest, Petitioner may contact the Clerk of the Circuit Court of the county in which the violation occurred and complete an affidavit in support of the violation, or Petitioner may contact the State Attorney's office for assistance in filing an action for indirect civil contempt or indirect criminal contempt. Upon receiving such a report, the State Attorney is hereby appointed to prosecute such violations by indirect criminal contempt proceedings, or the State Attorney may decide to file a criminal charge, if warranted by the evidence.

4. **Respondent, upon service of this injunction, shall be deemed to have knowledge of and to be

Florida Supreme Court Approved Family Law Form 12.980(d)(1), Final Judgment of Injunction for Protection Against Domestic Violence with Minor Child(ren) (After Notice) (06/12)   Page 8 of 10

116 | P a g e

bound by all matters occurring at the hearing and on the face of this injunction.

5. The temporary injunction, if any, entered in this case is extended until such time as service of this injunction is effected upon Respondent.

6. THIS IS A "CUSTODY ORDER" FOR PURPOSES OF THE UCCJEA AND ALL STATUTES MAKING IT A CRIME TO INTERFERE WITH CUSTODY UNDER CHAPTER 787 OF FLORIDA STATUTES AND OTHER SIMILAR STATUTES.

ORDERED _March 23, 2018_ @ _10:24_ (a.m.) p.m.

_____
CIRCUIT JUDGE

COPIES TO:
Sheriff of Hillsborough County
Petitioner (or his or her attorney):

☐ by U. S. Mail
☒ by hand delivery in open court (Petitioner must acknowledge
receipt in writing on the face of the original order - see below.)
Respondent (or his or her attorney):
☐ forwarded to sheriff for service
☒ by hand delivery in open court (Respondent must
acknowledge receipt in writing on the face of the original order
see below.)
☐ by certified mail (may only be used when Respondent is
present at the hearing and Respondent fails or refuses to
acknowledge the receipt of a certified copy of this injunction.)

☐ State Attorney's Office
☐ Batterer's intervention program (if ordered)
☐ Central Governmental Depository (if ordered)
☐ Department of Revenue
☐ Other _____

I CERTIFY the foregoing is a true copy of the original as it appears on file in the office of the Clerk of the Circuit
Court of Hillsborough County, Florida, and that I have furnished copies of this order as indicated above.

CLERK OF THE CIRCUIT COURT

(SEAL)

By _____
Deputy Clerk

ACKNOWLEDGMENT

██████████████ , acknowledge receipt of a certified copy of this Injunction for Protection.

Petitioner _____

ACKNOWLEDGMENT

██████████████ , acknowledge receipt of a certified copy of this Injunction for Protection

Respondent _____

Florida Supreme Court Approved Family Law Form 12.980(d)(1), Final Judgment of Injunction for Protection Against Domestic
Violence with Minor Child(ren) (After Notice) (06/12)   Page 10 of 10

IN THE CIRCUIT COURT OF THE THIRTEENTH JUDICIAL CIRCUIT,
IN AND FOR HILLSBOROUGH COUNTY, FLORIDA

███████████
PETITIONER

Vs

CASE NO: 17-DR-015182

Division G

JASBIR KALSI
RESPONDENT

FINAL JUDGMENT OF INJUNCTION FOR PROTECTION AGAINST DOMESTIC VIOLENCE WITHOUT MINOR CHILD(REN) (AFTER NOTICE)

The Petition for Injunction for Protection Against Domestic Violence under section 741.30, Florida Statutes, and other papers filed in this Court have been reviewed. The Court has jurisdiction of the parties and the subject matter.

It is intended that this protection order meet the requirements of 18 U.S.C. ' 2265 and therefore intended that it be accorded full faith and credit by the court of another state or Indian tribe and enforced as if it were the order of the enforcing state or of the Indian tribe.

HEARING
AGREED

This cause came before the Court for a hearing to determine whether an Injunction for Protection Against Domestic Violence in this case should be ☒ issued ☐ modified ☐ extended.

The hearing was attended by ☒ Petitioner ☐ Respondent presence waived by counsel.
☑ Petitioner's Counsel ☑ Respondent's Counsel

FINDINGS

On **01/10/2018**, a notice of this hearing was served on Respondent together with a copy of Petitioner=s petition to this Court and the temporary injunction, if issued. Service was within the time required by Florida law, and Respondent was afforded an opportunity to be heard.

After hearing the testimony of each party present and of any witnesses, or upon consent of Respondent, the Court finds, based on the specific facts of this case, that Petitioner is a victim of domestic violence or has reasonable cause to believe that he/she is in imminent danger of becoming a victim of domestic violence by Respondent.

INJUNCTION AND TERMS

This injunction shall be in full force and effect until ☐ further order of the Court ☑ March 23, 2021. This injunction is valid and enforceable in all counties of the State of Florida. The terms of this injunction may not be changed by either party alone or by both parties together. Only the Court may modify the terms of this injunction. Either party may ask the Court to change or end this injunction at any time.

Any violation of this injunction, whether or not at the invitation of Petitioner or anyone else, may subject Respondent to civil or indirect criminal contempt proceedings, including the imposition of a fine or imprisonment. Certain willful violations of the terms of this injunction, such as: refusing to vacate the dwelling that the parties share; going to or being within 500 feet of Petitioner's residence, going to Petitioner=s place of employment, school, or other place prohibited in this injunction; telephoning, contacting or communicating with Petitioner if prohibited by this injunction; knowingly or intentionally coming within 100 feet of Petitioner=s motor vehicle, whether or not it is occupied; defacing or destroying Petitioner=s personal property; refusing to surrender firearms or ammunition if ordered to do so by the court; or committing an act of domestic violence against Petitioner constitutes a misdemeanor of the first degree punishable by up to one year in jail, as provided by sections 775.082 and 775.083, Florida Statutes. In addition, it is a federal criminal felony offense, punishable by up to life imprisonment, depending on the nature of the violation, to cross state lines or enter Indian country for the purpose of engaging in conduct that is prohibited in this injunction. 18 U.S.C. ' 2262.

ORDERED and ADJUDGED:

1. **Violence Prohibited.** Respondent shall not commit, or cause any other person to commit, any acts of domestic violence against Petitioner. Domestic violence includes: assault, aggravated assault, battery, aggravated battery, sexual assault, sexual battery, stalking, aggravated stalking, kidnaping, false imprisonment, or any other criminal offense resulting in physical injury or death to Petitioner or any of Petitioner's family or household members. Respondent shall not commit any other violation of the injunction through an intentional unlawful threat, word or act to do violence to the Petitioner.

2. **No Contact.** Respondent shall have no contact with the Petitioner unless otherwise provided in this section.

a. Unless otherwise provided herein, Respondent shall have no contact with Petitioner. Respondent shall not directly or indirectly contact Petitioner in person, by mail, e-mail, fax, telephone, through another person, or in any other manner. Further, Respondent shall not contact or have any third party contact anyone connected with Petitioner's employment or school to inquire about Petitioner or to send any messages to Petitioner. Unless otherwise provided herein, **Respondent shall not go to, in, or within 500 feet of:** Petitioner's current residence <u>Confidential Address</u>

_____ or any residence to which Petitioner may move; Petitioner's current or any subsequent place of employment or place where Petitioner attends school or the following other places (if requested by Petitioner) where Petitioner or Petitioner's minor child(ren) go often:

_____
_____
_____

Respondent may not knowingly come within 100 feet of Petitioner's automobile at any time.

b. _____ Other provisions regarding contact: _____
_____

3. **Firearms.** Unless paragraph a. is initialed below, Respondent shall not have in his or her care, custody, possession or control any firearm or ammunition. It is a violation of section 790.233, Florida Statutes, and a first degree misdemeanor, for the respondent to have in his or her care, custody, possession or control any firearm or ammunition.

Florida Supreme Court Approved Family Law Form 12.980(c)(2), Final Judgment of Injunction for Protection Against Domestic Violence without Minor Child(ren) (After Notice) (06/12)   Page 2 of 7

120 | P a g e

[Initial if applies; write N/A if not applicable]

a. __N/A__ Respondent is a state or local officer as defined in section 943.10(14), Florida Statutes, who holds an active certification, who receives or possesses a firearm or ammunition for use in performing official duties on behalf of the officer=s employing agency and is not prohibited by the court from having in his or her care, custody, possession or control a firearm or ammunition. The officer's employing agency may prohibit the officer from having in his or her care, custody, possession or control a firearm or ammunition.

b. __✓__ Respondent shall surrender any firearms and ammunition in the Respondent's possession to the Hillsborough County Sheriff's Office.

c. Other directives relating to firearms and ammunition:_____

_____

NOTE: RESPONDENT IS ADVISED THAT IT IS A FEDERAL CRIMINAL FELONY OFFENSE TO SHIP OR TRANSPORT IN INTERSTATE OR FOREIGN COMMERCE, OR POSSESS IN OR AFFECTING COMMERCE, ANY FIREARM OR AMMUNITION; OR TO RECEIVE ANY FIREARM OR AMMUNITION WHICH HAS BEEN SHIPPED OR TRANSPORTED IN INTERSTATE OR FOREIGN COMMERCE WHILE SUBJECT TO SUCH AN INJUNCTION. 18 U.S.C. ' 922(g)(8).

4. Evaluation/Counseling.

[Initial all that apply; write N/A if does not apply]

a. The Court finds that Respondent has:

    i. __N/A__ willfully violated the ex parte injunction;

    ii. __N/A__ been convicted of, had adjudication withheld on, or pled nolo contendere to a crime involving violence or a threat of violence; and/or

    iii. __N/A__ in this state or any other state, had at any time a prior injunction for protection entered against the respondent after a hearing with notice.

Note: If respondent meets any of the above enumerated criteria, the Court must order the Respondent to attend a batterers' intervention program unless it makes written factual findings stating why such a program would not be appropriate. See ' 741.30(6)(e), Florida Statutes.

b. Within ☐ 10 days ☐ _____ days, (but no more than 10 days) of the date of this injunction, Respondent shall enroll in and thereafter without delay complete the following, and Respondent shall provide proof of such enrollment to the Clerk of Circuit Court within ☐ 30 days or ☐ _____ days, (but no more than 30 days) of the date of this injunction:

    i. _____ A certified batterers' intervention program from a list of programs to be provided by the Court or any entity designated by the Court. Respondent shall also successfully complete any substance abuse or mental health evaluation that the assessing program counselor deems necessary as a predicate to completion of the batterers' intervention program.

    ii. _____ A substance abuse evaluation at:_____ or a similarly qualified facility and any substance abuse treatment recommended by that evaluation.

    iii. _____ A mental health evaluation by a licensed mental health professional at: _____ _____ or any other similarly qualified facility and any mental health treatment recommended by that evaluation.

    iv. _____ Other: DOMESTIC VIOLENCE ASSESSMENT at _____ _____, and must complete any recommended treatment.

c. _____ Although Respondent meets the statutory mandate of attendance at a batterers' intervention program, the Court makes the following written findings as to why the condition

Florida Supreme Court Approved Family Law Form 12.980(c)(2), Final Judgment of Injunction for Protection Against Domestic Violence without Minor Child(ren) (After Notice) (06/12)   Page 3 of 7

121 | P a g e

of batterers intervention program would be inappropriate: _____

    d.   **N/A** Petitioner is referred to a certified domestic violence center and is provided with a list of certified domestic violence centers in this circuit, which Petitioner may contact.

5. **Mailing Address.** Respondent shall notify the Clerk of the Court of any change in his or her mailing address within 10 days of the change. All further papers (excluding pleadings requiring personal service) shall be served by mail to Respondent=s last known address. Such service by mail shall be complete upon mailing. Rule 12.080, Fla.Fam.L.R.P., section 741.30, Florida Statutes.

6. **Other provisions necessary to protect Petitioner from domestic violence:**
                                  RESPONDENT SHALL STAY
                              500   FEET AWAY FROM
                              THE PETITIONER.

TEMPORARY EXCLUSIVE USE AND POSSESSION OF HOME

[Initial if applies; write N/A if not applicable]

    7.   **N/A** **Possession of the Home.** ☐ Petitioner ☐ Respondent shall have temporary exclusive use and possession of the dwelling located at: _____
_____.

    8.   _____ **Transfer of Possession of the Home.** A law enforcement officer with jurisdiction over the home shall accompany ☐ Petitioner ☐ Respondent to the home, and shall place ☐ Petitioner ☐ Respondent in possession of the home.

    9.   _____ **Personal Items.** ☐ Petitioner ☐ Respondent, **in the presence of a law enforcement** officer, may return to the premises described above ( ) on _____, at _____ a.m./p.m., or ☐ at a time arranged with the law enforcement department with jurisdiction over the home, accompanied by a law enforcement officer only, for the purpose of obtaining his or her clothing and items of personal health and hygiene and tools of the trade. A law enforcement officer with jurisdiction over the premises shall go with ☐ Petitioner ☐ Respondent to the home and stand by to insure that he/she vacates the premises with only his/her personal clothing, toiletries, tools of the trade, and any items listed in paragraph 10 below. The law enforcement agency shall not be responsible for storing or transporting any property. **IF THE RESPONDENT IS NOT AWARDED POSSESSION OF THE HOME AND GOES TO THE HOME WITHOUT A LAW ENFORCEMENT OFFICER, IT IS A VIOLATION OF THIS INJUNCTION.**

  10. **N/A** The following other personal possessions may also be removed from the premises at this time: _____

  11. **N/A** Other: _____
_____
_____

12. Temporary Alimony.
[Initial all that apply; write N/A if does not apply]

   a. __N/A__ The court finds that there is a need for temporary alimony and that [   ] Petitioner [   ] Respondent (hereinafter Obligor) has the present ability to pay alimony and shall pay temporary alimony to [   ] Petitioner [   ] Respondent (hereinafter Obligee) in the amount of $_____ per month, payable [   ] in accordance with Obligor's employer's payroll cycle, and in any event, at least once a month [   ] other *(explain)* _____ beginning *(date)* _____. This alimony shall continue until modified by court order, until a final judgment of dissolution of marriage is entered, until Obligee dies, until this injunction expires, or until *(date)* _____, whichever occurs first.

   b. __N/A__ [   ] Petitioner [   ] Respondent shall be required to maintain health insurance coverage for the other party. Any uncovered medical costs for the party awarded alimony shall be assessed as follows:

   c. __N/A__ Other provisions relating to alimony:

13. Method of Payment.
[Initial one only]

   a. __N/A__ Obligor shall pay any temporary child support/alimony ordered through income deduction, and such support shall be paid to the state disbursement unit. Obligor is individually responsible for paying this support obligation in the event that all or any portion of said support is not deducted from Obligor's income. Obligor shall also pay the applicable state disbursement unit service charge. Until child support/alimony payments are deducted from Obligor's paycheck pursuant to the Income Deduction Order, Obligor is responsible for making timely payments directly to the state disbursement unit.

   b. __N/A__ Temporary child support/alimony shall be paid through the state disbursement unit in the office of the Hillsborough County Clerk of Circuit Court. Obligor shall also pay the applicable state disbursement unit service charge. Income deduction is not in the best interests of the child(ren) because:

   c. __N/A__ Other provisions relating to method of payment:

Florida Supreme Court Approved Family Law Form 12.980(c)(2), Final Judgment of Injunction for Protection Against Domestic Violence without Minor Child(ren) (After Notice) (06/12)   Page 5 of 7

123 | P a g e

OTHER SPECIAL PROVISIONS
(This section to be used for inclusion of local provisions approved by the chief judge as provided in Florida Family Law Rule 12.610.)

DIRECTIONS TO LAW ENFORCEMENT OFFICER IN ENFORCING THIS INJUNCTION
(Provisions in this injunction that do not include a line for the judge to either initial or write N/A are considered mandatory provisions and should be interpreted to be part of this injunction.)

1. **This injunction is valid in all counties of the State of Florida.** Violation of this injunction should be reported to the appropriate law enforcement agency. Law enforcement officers of the jurisdiction in which a violation of this injunction occurs shall enforce the provisions of this injunction and are authorized to arrest without warrant pursuant to section 901.15, Florida Statutes, for any violation of its provisions, except those regarding child support and/or alimony, which constitutes a criminal act under section 741.31, Florida Statutes. **When inconsistent with this order, any subsequent court order issued under Chapter 61, Florida Statutes, shall take precedence over this order on all matters relating to property division, alimony, child custody, or child support.**

2. **THIS INJUNCTION IS ENFORCEABLE IN ALL COUNTIES OF FLORIDA, AND LAW ENFORCEMENT OFFICERS MAY EFFECT ARRESTS PURSUANT TO SECTION 901.15(6), FLORIDA STATUTES.** The arresting agent shall notify the State Attorney's Office immediately after arrest.

3. **Reporting alleged violations.** If Respondent violates the terms of this injunction and there has not been an arrest, Petitioner may contact the Clerk of the Circuit Court of the county in which the violation occurred and complete an affidavit in support of the violation, or Petitioner may contact the State Attorney's office for assistance in filing an action for indirect civil contempt or indirect criminal contempt. Upon receiving such a report, the State Attorney is hereby appointed to prosecute such violations by indirect criminal contempt proceedings, or the State Attorney may decide to file a criminal charge, if warranted by the evidence.

4. Respondent, upon service of this injunction, shall be deemed to have knowledge of and to be bound by all matters occurring at the hearing and on the face of this injunction.

5. The temporary injunction, if any, entered in this case is extended until such time as service of this injunction is effected upon Respondent.

ORDERED _March 23, 2016_ @ _10:26_ (a.m.) p.m. _[signature]_

_____
CIRCUIT JUDGE

Florida Supreme Court Approved Family Law Form 12.980(c)(2), Final Judgment of Injunction for Protection Against Domestic Violence without Minor Child(ren) (After Notice) (06/12)   Page 6 of 7

124 | P a g e

COPIES TO:
Sheriff of Hillsborough County
Petitioner (or his or her attorney):

☐ by U. S. Mail
☒ by hand delivery in open court (Petitioner must acknowledge receipt in writing on the face of the original order - see below.)
Respondent (or his or her attorney):
☑ forwarded to sheriff for service
☐ by hand delivery in open court (Respondent must acknowledge receipt in writing on the face of the original order see below.)
☐ by certified mail (may only be used when Respondent is present at the hearing and Respondent fails or refuses to acknowledge the receipt of a certified copy of this injunction.)

☐ State Attorney's Office
☐ Batterer's intervention program (if ordered)
☐ Central Governmental Depository (if ordered)
☐ Department of Revenue
☐ Other_____

I CERTIFY the foregoing is a true copy of the original as it appears on file in the office of the Clerk of the Circuit Court of Hillsborough County, Florida, and that I have furnished copies of this order as indicated above.

CLERK OF THE CIRCUIT COURT

(SEAL)

By: _____
Deputy Clerk

ACKNOWLEDGMENT

I, ▮▮▮▮▮▮▮▮▮▮ ,acknowledge receipt of a certified copy of this Injunction for Protection.

Petitioner _____

ACKNOWLEDGMENT

I, ▮▮▮▮▮▮▮▮▮▮ , acknowledge receipt of a certified copy of this Injunction for Protection.

Respondent _____ Did not appear _____

Florida Supreme Court Approved Family Law Form 12.980(c)(2), Final Judgment of Injunction for Protection Against Domestic Violence without Minor Child(ren) (After Notice) (06/12)   Page 7 of 7

IN THE CIRCUIT COURT OF THE THIRTEENTH JUDICIAL CIRCUIT,
IN AND FOR HILLSBOROUGH COUNTY, FLORIDA

████████
PETITIONER

CASE NO: 17-DR-015198

Vs

Division G

FILED
CLERK OF CIRCUIT COURT
3/23/18
10:30
HILLSBOROUGH CNTY, FL
FAMILY LAW

████████
RESPONDENT

FINAL JUDGMENT OF INJUNCTION FOR PROTECTION AGAINST DOMESTIC VIOLENCE WITHOUT MINOR CHILD(REN) (AFTER NOTICE)

The Petition for Injunction for Protection Against Domestic Violence under section 741.30, Florida Statutes, and other papers filed in this Court have been reviewed. The Court has jurisdiction of the parties and the subject matter.

It is intended that this protection order meet the requirements of 18 U.S.C. ' 2265 and therefore intended that it be accorded full faith and credit by the court of another state or Indian tribe and enforced as if it were the order of the enforcing state or of the Indian tribe.

HEARING
AGREED

This cause came before the Court for a hearing to determine whether an Injunction for Protection Against Domestic Violence in this case should be ☒ issued ☐ modified ☐ extended.

The hearing was attended by   ☒ Petitioner   ☐ Respondent *presence waived by counsel*
                          ☑ Petitioner's Counsel   ☑ Respondent's Counsel

FINDINGS

On **01/10/2018**, a notice of this hearing was served on Respondent together with a copy of Petitioner=s petition to this Court and the temporary injunction, if issued. Service was within the time required by Florida law, and Respondent was afforded an opportunity to be heard.

After hearing the testimony of each party present and of any witnesses, or upon consent of Respondent, the Court finds, based on the specific facts of this case, that Petitioner is a victim of domestic violence or has reasonable cause to believe that he/she is in imminent danger of becoming a victim of domestic violence by Respondent.

INJUNCTION AND TERMS

This injunction shall be in full force and effect until ☐ further order of the Court ☑ *March 23, 2021* This injunction is valid and enforceable in all counties of the State of Florida. The terms of this injunction may not be changed by either party alone or by both parties together. Only the Court may modify the terms of this injunction. Either party may ask the Court to change or end this injunction at any time.

Florida Supreme Court Approved Family Law Form 12.980(c)(2), Final Judgment of Injunction for Protection Against Domestic Violence without Minor Child(ren) (After Notice) (06/12)   Page 1 of 7

Any violation of this injunction, whether or not at the invitation of Petitioner or anyone else, may subject Respondent to civil or indirect criminal contempt proceedings, including the imposition of a fine or imprisonment. Certain willful violations of the terms of this injunction, such as: refusing to vacate the dwelling that the parties share; going to or being within 500 feet of Petitioner's residence, going to Petitioner=s place of employment, school, or other place prohibited in this injunction; telephoning, contacting or communicating with Petitioner if prohibited by this injunction; knowingly or intentionally coming within 100 feet of Petitioner=s motor vehicle, whether or not it is occupied; defacing or destroying Petitioner=s personal property; refusing to surrender firearms or ammunition if ordered to do so by the court; or committing an act of domestic violence against Petitioner constitutes a misdemeanor of the first degree punishable by up to one year in jail, as provided by sections 775.082 and 775.083, Florida Statutes. In addition, it is a federal criminal felony offense, punishable by up to life imprisonment, depending on the nature of the violation, to cross state lines or enter Indian country for the purpose of engaging in conduct that is prohibited in this injunction. 18 U.S.C. ' 2262.

ORDERED and ADJUDGED:

1. Violence Prohibited. Respondent shall not commit, or cause any other person to commit, any acts of domestic violence against Petitioner. Domestic violence includes: assault, aggravated assault, battery, aggravated battery, sexual assault, sexual battery, stalking, aggravated stalking, kidnaping, false imprisonment, or any other criminal offense resulting in physical injury or death to Petitioner or any of Petitioner's family or household members. Respondent shall not commit any other violation of the injunction through an intentional unlawful threat, word or act to do violence to the Petitioner.

2. No Contact. Respondent shall have no contact with the Petitioner unless otherwise provided in this section.
   a. Unless otherwise provided herein, Respondent shall have no contact with Petitioner. Respondent shall not directly or indirectly contact Petitioner in person, by mail, e-mail, fax, telephone, through another person, or in any other manner. Further, Respondent shall not contact or have any third party contact anyone connected with Petitioner's employment or school to inquire about Petitioner or to send any messages to Petitioner. Unless otherwise provided herein, **Respondent shall not go to, in, or within 500 feet of:** Petitioner's current residence <u>Confidential Address</u>

   _____ or any residence to which Petitioner may move; Petitioner's current or any subsequent place of employment or place where Petitioner attends school or the following other places (if requested by Petitioner) where Petitioner or Petitioner's minor child(ren) go often:

   _____
   _____
   Respondent may not knowingly come within 100 feet of Petitioner's automobile at any time.

   b. _____ Other provisions regarding contact:_____
   _____

3. Firearms. Unless paragraph a. is initialed below, Respondent shall not have in his or her care, custody, possession or control any firearm or ammunition. It is a violation of section 790.233, Florida Statutes, and a first degree misdemeanor, for the respondent to have in his or her care, custody, possession or control any firearm or ammunition.

Florida Supreme Court Approved Family Law Form 12.980(c)(2), Final Judgment of Injunction for Protection Against Domestic Violence without Minor Child(ren) (After Notice) (06/12)   Page 2 of 7

127 | P a g e

[Initial if applies; write N/A if not applicable]

a. __N/A__ Respondent is a state or local officer as defined in section 943.10(14), Florida Statutes, who holds an active certification, who receives or possesses a firearm or ammunition for use in performing official duties on behalf of the officer=s employing agency and is not prohibited by the court from having in his or her care, custody, possession or control a firearm or ammunition. The officer's employing agency may prohibit the officer from having in his or her care, custody, possession or control a firearm or ammunition.

b. __✓__ Respondent shall surrender any firearms and ammunition in the Respondent's possession to the Hillsborough County Sheriff's Office.

c. Other directives relating to firearms and ammunition:_____

_____

NOTE: **RESPONDENT IS ADVISED THAT IT IS A FEDERAL CRIMINAL FELONY OFFENSE TO SHIP OR TRANSPORT IN INTERSTATE OR FOREIGN COMMERCE, OR POSSESS IN OR AFFECTING COMMERCE, ANY FIREARM OR AMMUNITION; OR TO RECEIVE ANY FIREARM OR AMMUNITION WHICH HAS BEEN SHIPPED OR TRANSPORTED IN INTERSTATE OR FOREIGN COMMERCE WHILE SUBJECT TO SUCH AN INJUNCTION. 18 U.S.C. ' 922(g)(8).**

4. **Evaluation/Counseling.**

[Initial all that apply; write N/A if does not apply]

a. The Court finds that Respondent has:
   i. __N/A__ willfully violated the ex parte injunction;
   ii. __N/A__ been convicted of, had adjudication withheld on, or pled nolo contendere to a crime involving violence or a threat of violence; and/or
   iii. __N/A__ in this state or any other state, had at any time a prior injunction for protection entered against the respondent after a hearing with notice.

   Note: If respondent meets any of the above enumerated criteria, the Court must order the Respondent to attend a batterers' intervention program unless it makes written factual findings stating why such a program would not be appropriate. See ' 741.30(6)(e), Florida Statutes.

b. Within ☐ 10 days ☐ _____ days, (but no more than 10 days) of the date of this injunction, Respondent shall enroll in and thereafter without delay complete the following, and Respondent shall provide proof of such enrollment to the Clerk of Circuit Court within ☐ 30 days or ☐ _____ days, (but no more than 30 days) of the date of this injunction:
   i. _____ A certified batterers' intervention program from a list of programs to be provided by the Court or any entity designated by the Court. Respondent shall also successfully complete any substance abuse or mental health evaluation that the assessing program counselor deems necessary as a predicate to completion of the batterers' intervention program.
   ii. _____ A substance abuse evaluation at:_____
   or a similarly qualified facility and any substance abuse treatment recommended by that evaluation.
   iii. _____ A mental health evaluation by a licensed mental health professional at: _____
   _____ or any other similarly qualified facility and any mental health treatment recommended by that evaluation.
   iv. _____ Other: DOMESTIC VIOLENCE ASSESSMENT at _____
   _____, and must complete any recommended treatment.

c. _____ Although Respondent meets the statutory mandate of attendance at a batterers' intervention program, the Court makes the following written findings as to why the condition

Florida Supreme Court Approved Family Law Form 12.980(c)(2), Final Judgment of Injunction for Protection Against Domestic Violence without Minor Child(ren) (After Notice) (06/12)   Page 3 of 7

128 | P a g e

of batterers intervention program would be inappropriate: _____
_____

d. __N/A__ Petitioner is referred to a certified domestic violence center and is provided with a list of certified domestic violence centers in this circuit, which Petitioner may contact.

5. __Mailing Address.__ Respondent shall notify the Clerk of the Court of any change in his or her mailing address within 10 days of the change. All further papers (excluding pleadings requiring personal service) shall be served by mail to Respondent=s last known address. Such service by mail shall be complete upon mailing. Rule 12.080, Fla.Fam.L.R.P., section 741.30, Florida Statutes.

6. __Other provisions necessary to protect Petitioner from domestic violence:__
_____
RESPONDENT SHALL STAY
500 FEET AWAY FROM
THE PETITIONER.
_____

TEMPORARY EXCLUSIVE USE AND POSSESSION OF HOME

[Initial if applies; write N/A if not applicable]

7. __N/A__ **Possession of the Home.** ☐ Petitioner ☐ Respondent shall have temporary exclusive use and possession of the dwelling located at: _____
_____ .

8. _____ **Transfer of Possession of the Home.** A law enforcement officer with jurisdiction over the home shall accompany ☐ Petitioner ☐ Respondent to the home, and shall place ☐ Petitioner ☐ Respondent in possession of the home.

9. _____ **Personal Items.** ☐ Petitioner ☐ Respondent, **in the presence of a law enforcement** officer, may return to the premises described above ( ) on _____, at _____ a.m./p.m., or ☐ at a time arranged with the law enforcement department with jurisdiction over the home, accompanied by a law enforcement officer only, for the purpose of obtaining his or her clothing and items of personal health and hygiene and tools of the trade. A law enforcement officer with jurisdiction over the premises shall go with ☐ Petitioner ☐ Respondent to the home and stand by to insure that he/she vacates the premises with only his/her personal clothing, toiletries, tools of the trade, and any items listed in paragraph 10 below. The law enforcement agency shall not be responsible for storing or transporting any property. **IF THE RESPONDENT IS NOT AWARDED POSSESSION OF THE HOME AND GOES TO THE HOME WITHOUT A LAW ENFORCEMENT OFFICER, IT IS A VIOLATION OF THIS INJUNCTION.**

10. __N/A__ The following other personal possessions may also be removed from the premises at this time: _____
_____

11. __N/A__ Other: _____
_____
_____

Florida Supreme Court Approved Family Law Form 12.980(c)(2), Final Judgment of Injunction for Protection Against Domestic Violence without Minor Child(ren) (After Notice) (05/12)   Page 4 of 7

129 | P a g e

12. Temporary Alimony.

[Initial all that apply; write N/A if does not apply]

    a.   **N/A** The court finds that there is a need for temporary alimony and that [ ] Petitioner [ ] Respondent (hereinafter Obligor) has the present ability to pay alimony and shall pay temporary alimony to [ ] Petitioner [ ] Respondent (hereinafter Obligee) in the amount of $_____ per month, payable [ ] in accordance with Obligor's employer's payroll cycle, and in any event, at least once a month [ ] other *{explain}* _____ beginning *{date}* _____. This alimony shall continue until modified by court order, until a final judgment of dissolution of marriage is entered, until Obligee dies, until this injunction expires, or until *{date}* _____, whichever occurs first.

    b.   **N/A** [ ] Petitioner [ ] Respondent shall be required to maintain health insurance coverage for the other party. Any uncovered medical costs for the party awarded alimony shall be assessed as follows:

    c.   **N/A** Other provisions relating to alimony:

13. Method of Payment.

[Initial one only]

    a.   **N/A** Obligor shall pay any temporary child support/alimony ordered through income deduction, and such support shall be paid to the state disbursement unit. Obligor is individually responsible for paying this support obligation in the event that all or any portion of said support is not deducted from Obligor's income. Obligor shall also pay the applicable state disbursement unit service charge. Until child support/alimony payments are deducted from Obligor's paycheck pursuant to the Income Deduction Order, Obligor is responsible for making timely payments directly to the state disbursement unit.

    b.   **N/A** Temporary child support/alimony shall be paid through the state disbursement unit in the office of the Hillsborough County Clerk of Circuit Court. Obligor shall also pay the applicable state disbursement unit service charge. Income deduction is **not** in the best interests of the child(ren) because:

    c.   **N/A** Other provisions relating to method of payment:

Florida Supreme Court Approved Family Law Form 12.980(c)(2), Final Judgment of Injunction for Protection Against Domestic Violence without Minor Child(ren) (After Notice) (06/12)   Page 5 of 7

130 | P a g e

OTHER SPECIAL PROVISIONS
(This section to be used for inclusion of local provisions approved by the chief judge as provided in Florida Family Law Rule 12.610.)

DIRECTIONS TO LAW ENFORCEMENT OFFICER IN ENFORCING THIS INJUNCTION
(Provisions in this injunction that do not include a line for the judge to either initial or write N/A are considered mandatory provisions and should be interpreted to be part of this injunction.)

1. This injunction is valid in all counties of the State of Florida. Violation of this injunction should be reported to the appropriate law enforcement agency. Law enforcement officers of the jurisdiction in which a violation of this injunction occurs shall enforce the provisions of this injunction and are authorized to arrest without warrant pursuant to section 901.15, Florida Statutes, for any violation of its provisions, except those regarding child support and/or alimony, which constitutes a criminal act under section 741.31, Florida Statutes. When inconsistent with this order, any subsequent court order issued under Chapter 61, Florida Statutes, shall take precedence over this order on all matters relating to property division, alimony, child custody, or child support.

2. THIS INJUNCTION IS ENFORCEABLE IN ALL COUNTIES OF FLORIDA, AND LAW ENFORCEMENT OFFICERS MAY EFFECT ARRESTS PURSUANT TO SECTION 901.15(6), FLORIDA STATUTES. The arresting agent shall notify the State Attorney's Office immediately after arrest.

3. Reporting alleged violations. If Respondent violates the terms of this injunction and there has not been an arrest, Petitioner may contact the Clerk of the Circuit Court of the county in which the violation occurred and complete an affidavit in support of the violation, or Petitioner may contact the State Attorney's office for assistance in filing an action for indirect civil contempt or indirect criminal contempt. Upon receiving such a report, the State Attorney is hereby appointed to prosecute such violations by indirect criminal contempt proceedings, or the State Attorney may decide to file a criminal charge, if warranted by the evidence.

4. Respondent, upon service of this injunction, shall be deemed to have knowledge of and to be bound by all matters occurring at the hearing and on the face of this injunction.

5. The temporary injunction, if any, entered in this case is extended until such time as service of this injunction is effected upon Respondent.

ORDERED _March 23 2018_ @ _10:27_ (a.m.)/p.m.

_____
CIRCUIT JUDGE

Florida Supreme Court Approved Family Law Form 12.980(c)(2), Final Judgment of Injunction for Protection Against Domestic Violence without Minor Child(ren) (After Notice) (05/12)   Page 6 of 7

131 | Page

COPIES TO:
Sheriff of Hillsborough County
Petitioner (or his or her attorney):

☐ by U. S. Mail
☒ by hand delivery in open court (Petitioner must acknowledge receipt in writing on the face of the original order - see below.)
Respondent (or his or her attorney):
☑ forwarded to sheriff for service
☐ by hand delivery in open court (Respondent must acknowledge receipt in writing on the face of the original order see below.)
☐ by certified mail (may only be used when Respondent is present at the hearing and Respondent fails or refuses to acknowledge the receipt of a certified copy of this injunction.)

☐ State Attorney's Office
☐ Batterer's intervention program (if ordered)
☐ Central Governmental Depository (if ordered)
☐ Department of Revenue
☐ Other_____

    I CERTIFY the foregoing is a true copy of the original as it appears on file in the office of the Clerk of the Circuit Court of Hillsborough County, Florida, and that I have furnished copies of this order as indicated above.

CLERK OF THE CIRCUIT COURT

(SEAL)

By_____
          Deputy Clerk

ACKNOWLEDGMENT

I, ███████████ , acknowledge receipt of a certified copy of this Injunction for Protection.

Petitioner _Silly a g_____

ACKNOWLEDGMENT

I, ███████████ , acknowledge receipt of a certified copy of this Injunction for Protection.

Respondent _Did Not Appear_____

Florida Supreme Court Approved Family Law Form 12.980(c)(2), Final Judgment of Injunction for Protection Against Domestic Violence without Minor Child(ren) (After Notice) (06/12)   Page 7 of 7

132 | P a g e

EXHIBIT #10

APPLICANT'S HUSBAND'S AND IN-LAW'S CONVICTION DOCUMENTS

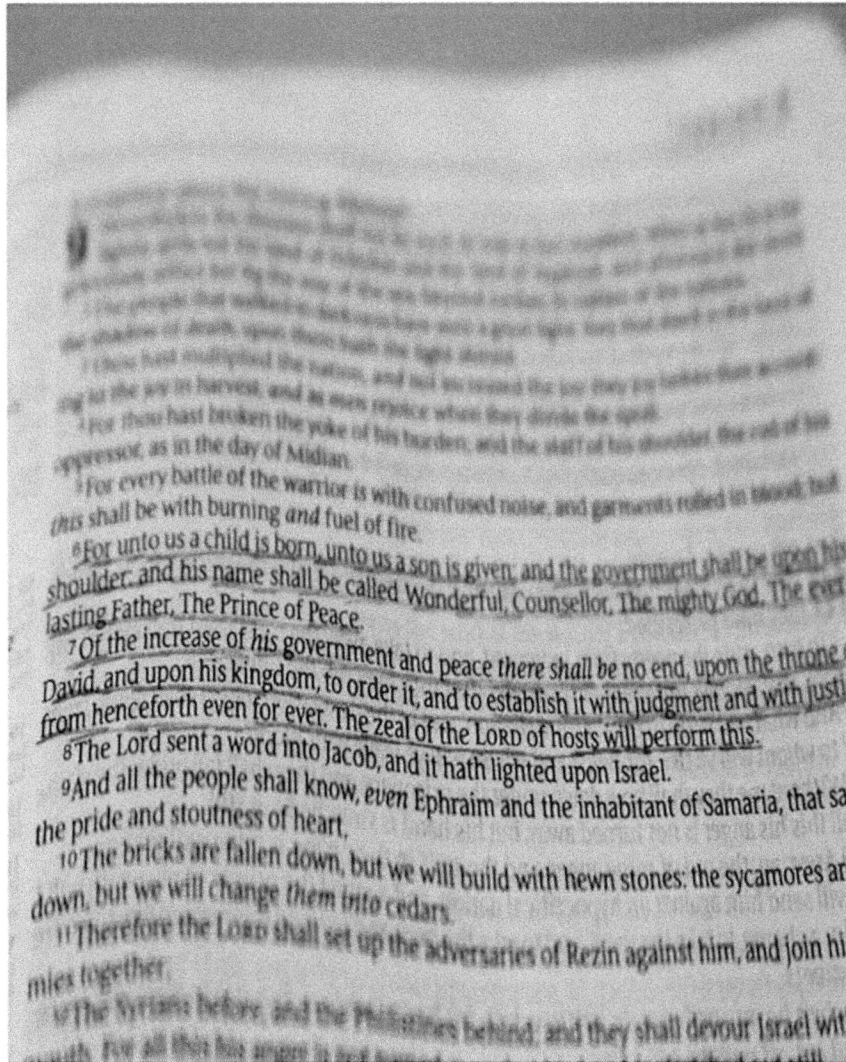

Case Information

Uniform Case Number: 292017CF013214000AHC

STATE OF FLORIDA VS KALSI, DEVBIR SINGH

Icon Keys   Summary   Parties   Events\Documents   Charges   Hearings   Financial   Bonds   Disposition

File Location

Case Information

Case Number \ Citation

Case Number: *17-CF-013214-A*

Citation Number:

Booking Numbers

Booking Numbers
2017-32339
17032339

Case Information

Case Category Description: *Criminal*

Case Type Description: *FELONY*

Case Sub Type Description:

Case Status: *CLOSED*

Case Filed On: *2017-09-02*

Financial Information

Balance Due: *$1,116.63*

Due Date: *07/13/2020*

Judge Assignment

Judge: *Nash, C. Christopher*

Division: *Division C*

Judge Assignment History ▾

Return to Search Results (/html/case/searchResults.html)

Case Information

Uniform Case Number: 292017CF013214000AHC

STATE OF FLORIDA VS ▮▮▮▮▮▮▮▮▮▮

🔑 Icon Keys 📗 Summary 👥 Parties 📄 Events/Documents 📃 Charges 📅 Hearings 💲 Financial 🔖 Bonds ⚖ Disposition

📁 File Location

Parties on the Case

Show [25] entries   [Column visibility] [Excel] [CSV]   Search: [   ]

Party Type	Name	Party Demographics	Attorney Name	Attorney Contact
Plaintiff	STATE OF FLORIDA 11 TAMPA, FL 33602		BROWN , CHRISTINE SHIVER	Telephone: 813-272-5400 419 N PIERCE ST TAMPA, FL 33602
Defendant	▮▮▮▮▮▮▮▮▮	Date of Birth: 04/29/1984 Height (inches): 71 Weight: 165 Race: White Gender: Male	HACKWORTH , JONATHAN	Telephone: 813-280-2911 HACKWORTH LAW 1818 N 15TH ST TAMPA, FL 33605
Defendant	▮▮▮▮▮▮▮▮▮	Date of Birth: 04/29/1984 Height (inches): 71 Weight: 165 Race: White Gender: Male	DEFENDER, PUBLIC	Telephone: 813-272-5980 PO BOX 172910 TAMPA, FL 33672

Showing 1 to 3 of 3 entries

Previous [1] Next

↩ Return to Search Results (/html/case/searchResults.html)

Case Information

Uniform Case Number: 292017CF013214000AHC

STATE OF FLORIDA VS ████████████████

Icon Keys | Summary | Parties | Events\Documents | Charges | Hearings | Financial | Bonds | Disposition

File Location

Charges

Show [25] entries

Column visibility | Excel | CSV

Search: [ ]

Select	Charge Number	Offense Description	Offense Date	Degree Description	Disposition
	4	784031-BATT1102 (MF) BATTERY DOMESTIC VIOLENCE	09/01/2017	FIRST DEGREE MISDEMEANOR	NT - ADJUDICATION WITHHELD

Arrest Information
  Arrest Date: 09/02/2017

Plea Information
| Date: 07/16/2018 | Plea: GUILTY |
| Date: 09/29/2017 | Plea: WRITTEN PLEA OF NOT GUILTY |

Prosecutor Information
| Date: 09/22/2017 | Description: FILED |

CriminalDispo Information
| Date: 07/16/2018 | Description: NT - ADJUDICATION WITHHELD | | Judge: Nash, Christopher C. |

Sentence Information
| Date: 07/16/2018 | Description: NT - ADJUDICATION WITHHELD | | Code: NTAW |

| | 1 | 787021-KIDN5003 (FT) FALSE IMPRISONMENT | 09/01/2017 | THIRD DEGREE FELONY | NT - ADJUDICATION WITHHELD |

Arrest Information
  Arrest Date: 09/02/2017

Plea Information
| Date: 07/16/2018 | Plea: GUILTY |
| Date: 09/29/2017 | Plea: WRITTEN PLEA OF NOT GUILTY |

Prosecutor Information
| Date: 09/22/2017 | Description: FILED |

CriminalDispo Information
| Date: 07/16/2018 | Description: NT - ADJUDICATION WITHHELD | | Judge: Nash, Christopher C. |

Sentence Information
| Date: 07/16/2018 | Description: NT - ADJUDICATION WITHHELD | | Code: NTAW |

| | 3 | 9142234E-TAMP2240 (FP) HARASSING A WITNESS | 09/01/2017 | FELONY PUNISHABLE BY LIFE | NT - NO INFORMATION FILED |

Arrest Information
  Arrest Date: 09/02/2017

Prosecutor Information
| Date: 09/22/2017 | Description: NO INFORMATION FILED |

CriminalDispo Information
| Date: 09/22/2017 | Description: NT - NO INFORMATION FILED | | Judge: Nash, |

| | 2 | 827031B2C-CHAB1602 (FT) CHILD ABUSE | 09/01/2017 | THIRD DEGREE FELONY | Christopher C.
NT - NO INFORMATION FILED |

Arrest Information
   Arrest Date: 09/02/2017
Prosecutor Information
   Date: 09/22/2017   Description: *NO INFORMATION FILED*
CriminalDispo Information
   Date: 09/22/2017   Description: *NT - NO INFORMATION FILED*   Judge: *Nash,*
Christopher C.

Showing 1 to 4 of 4 entries   Previous 1 Next

🔄 Return to Search Results (/html/case/searchResults.html)

Case Information

STATE OF FLORIDA VS ▮▮▮▮▮▮▮▮▮▮▮

🔑 Icon Keys   📖 Summary   👥 Parties   📄 Events/Documents   📋 Charges   📅 Hearings   💰 Financial   🔖 Bonds   ⚖ Disposition

📁 File Location

⚖ Disposition (Charge Sentence Information)

Show [25] entries

[Column visibility] [Excel] [CSV]

Search: [   ]

Document Index	Charge Number	Offense Date	Charge Offense Description	Degree Description	Citation Number
🔍	1	09/01/2017	787021-KIDN5003 (FT) FALSE IMPRISONMENT	THIRD DEGREE FELONY	

Sentence Information

Plea	07/16/2018	GUILTY		
Disposition	07/16/2018	NT - ADJUDICATION WITHHELD		
Sentence	07/16/2018	CRIMINAL		
		Community Service (Hours: 50, Comment: @ 5/MO)		
		State Probation (24 Mo)		
		Provisions		

- AUTOMATIC TERMINATION OF PROBATION WHEN CONDITIONS COMPLETE,
- COURT COSTS,
- NO CONTACT WITH VICTIM OR PROPERTY,
- OTHER COURT RESTRICTIONS,

Comment: COMPLETE ANGER MANAGEMENT, COM

Prosecutor:	BROWN CHRISTINE SHIVER
Defense:	HACKWORTH JONATHAN

Document Index	Charge Number	Offense Date	Charge Offense Description	Degree Description	Citation Number
🔍	4	09/01/2017	784031-BATT1102 (MF) BATTERY DOMESTIC VIOLENCE	FIRST DEGREE MISDEMEANOR	

Sentence Information

Plea	07/16/2018	GUILTY	
Disposition	07/16/2018	NT - ADJUDICATION WITHHELD	
Sentence	07/16/2018	CRIMINAL	
		Provisions	

- SENTENCED TO TIME SERVED - LENGTH UNSPECIFIED,

Showing 1 to 2 of 2 entries

Previous [1] Next

↩ Return to Search Results (/html/case/searchResults.html)

IN THE CIRCUIT COURT IN AND FOR HILLSBOROUGH COUNTY, STATE OF FLORIDA

CASE NO.   17-CF-013214-A

STATE OF FLORIDA

VS

Division   C

Offense Date: 9/1/2017

Case Number: 17-CF-013214-A

Defense   Case Number: 17-CF-013214-A
Address: HACKWORTH , JONATHAN
          HACKWORTH LAW
          1818 N 15TH ST
          TAMPA, FL 33605

JUDGMENT AND SENTENCE

The above named Defendant is now before the Court:

State:

Cnt	Charge Description	Lev Deg	Plea	Disp Date	Disposition
1	787021 FALSE IMPRISONMENT	F3	GUILTY	07/16/18	NT - ADJUDICATION WITHHELD
4	784031 BATTERY DOMESTIC VIOLENCE	M1	GUILTY	07/16/18	NT - ADJUDICATION WITHHELD

Ct.1 SENTENCE: CRIMINAL

Community Service (Hours: 50, Comment: @ 5/MO)
State Probation (24 Months)
Provisions
- COURT COSTS
- NO CONTACT WITH VICTIM
- COMPLETE ANGER MANAGEMENT
- COMPLETE DOMESTIC VIOLENCE COURSE
- ABIDE BY ALL TERMS OF INJUNCTION
- MAY TRAVEL OUT OF COUNTY (INTERNATIONAL FLIGHT)
- COURT PERMITS RETURN PASSPORT CURRENTLY WITH HCSO
- AUTOMATIC TERM ONCE PROOF OF RESIDENCY OF INDIA TO COURTS

Ct.4 SENTENCE: CRIMINAL

Provisions
- SENTENCED TO TIME SERVED - LENGTH UNSPECIFIED

Fees :
- $360.63   CR-8884 INVESTIGATION COST - HCSO 938.27   FS AUTH: 938.27
- $100.00   CR-2399 INVESTIGATIVE COSTS SAO REVENUE FS 938.27(8)   FS AUTH: 938.27(8)
- $11.00   CR-R201 COPY CHARGES   FS AUTH:
- $100.00   CR-8366 CFF CRIMES AGAINST MINORS -DOR-DCF GRANTS CHILD ADV   FS AUTH: 938.10(2)
- $50.00   CR-8450 DOR-DCF GRNT & DON -GRDN ADLITEM 938.10   FS AUTH: 938.10(2)
- $1.00   CR-R235 CRIMES AGAINST MINORS   FS AUTH: 938.10

- 17-CF-013214-A   Page 1 of 3   henry

07/25/2018 04:50:10 PM Electronically Filed: Hillsborough County/13th Judicial Circuit.   Page 1

139 | P a g e

- $6.00   CR-R206 WRITE/COPY/SIGN/SEAL   FS AUTH: 28.24(8)
- $1.00   FS AUTH: 938.05(1)(a)
- $50.00   CR-8081 CRIME PREVENTION   FS AUTH: 775.083(2)
- $65.00   CR-8097 ADDITIONAL COSTS (BOCC) - PROGRAMS   FS AUTH: 939.185(1)(a
- $49.00   CR-8311 FCCA CRIMES COMPENSATION TRUST FUND   FS AUTH: 938.03
- $17.00   CR-A362 CRIME STOPPERS TRUST FUND   FS AUTH: 938.06
- $200.00   CR-R252 ADDITIONAL COURT COST - CLERK - CIR CRIM   FS AUTH: 938.05(1)(a)
- $25.00   FS AUTH: 938.05(1)(a)
- $1.00   CR-R617 CRIMES COMPENSATION FEE 938.03   FS AUTH: 938.03
- $3.00   CR-RA20 CRIME STOPPERS TRUST FUND FEE   FS AUTH: 938.06
- $49.00   CR-2780 PD APP FEE - INDIGENT CRIMINAL TRUST FUND   FS AUTH: 27.52(1)(b)
- $0.80   CR-3991 PD APP FEE- INDIGENT CRIM TR FEE 2%- CLERKS OF CT TF   FS AUTH: 27.52(1)(b)
- $0.20   CR-4005 PD APP ADDL FEE - CLERK OF COURT T.F./DOR/GEN FUND   FS AUTH: 27.52(1)(b)
- $3.00   CR-R207 CERTIFYING CHARGE   FS AUTH: 28.24(3)
- $1.00   FS AUTH: 938.05(1)(a)
- $6.00   CR-R229 FELONY PREP FEE FOR CRIMINAL JUDGMENT - 28.24(8)   FS AUTH: FS 28.24(8)
- $1.00   CR-R229D FELONY PREP FEE FOR CRIMINAL JUDGMENT - 28.24(8)   FS AUTH: FS 28.24(8)
- $6.00   CR-R228 FELONY PREP FEE FOR CRIM SATISFACTION - 28.24(8)   FS AUTH: FS 28.24(8)
- $1.00   CR-R228D FELONY PREP FEE FOR CRIM SATISFACTION - 28.24(8)   FS AUTH: FS 28.24(8)
- $9.00   CR-1100J RECORDING FEE FOR CRIMINAL JUDGMENT 28.24(12)(a)(b)   FS AUTH: FS 28.24(12)(a)(b)
- $10.00   CR-1100S RECORDING FEE FOR CRIM SATISFACTION 28.24(12)(a)(b)   FS AUTH: FS 28.24(12)(a)(b)

Fee Total : $1126.63

**FEE TOTALS INCLUDE ALL OUTSTANDING FEES OWED ON THE CASE AT THE TIME OF THIS JUDGMENT, EXCEPT FOR COST OF SUPERVISION AND THE PROBATION SERVICE FEE. SEE ORDER OF PROBATION FOR DETAILS. THE ABOVE FEES INCLUDE THE ASSESSMENT OF JUDGMENT AND SATISFACTION FEES, AS APPLICABLE.

If you are a "qualifying offender" under section 943.325, Florida Statutes, you are required to submit a DNA sample in a manner consistent with Florida law.

The defendant SHALL pay all mandatory and discretionary costs, fines, fees, penalties, & surcharges applicable to this matter, per Florida Statutes and Hillsborough County Ordinances; as stated above.

Probation: If probation is ordered, the conditions of Probation will be provided to you on a separate written order prepared by the HCSO Probation Services or Florida Department of Corrections.

Jail: At the time of sentencing, if jail is ordered, the defendant may be taken into custody by the Sheriff of Hillsborough County, Florida or given a date to report for incarceration in the County Jail under supervision of the Board of Criminal Justice of Hillsborough County.

Judgment For Money Ordered To Be Paid: It is the order of the Court that a judgment is entered, on behalf of the Hillsborough County Clerk of Circuit and County Courts, on behalf of Hillsborough County, and on behalf of the State of Florida, on the money that is ordered to be paid as a result of the JUDGMENT AND SENTENCE to the charge(s) in this matter, FOR WHICH LET EXECUTION ISSUE.

17-CF-013214-A   Page 2 of 3   henry

07/25/2018 04:50:10 PM Electronically Filed: Hillsborough County/13th Judicial Circuit.   Page 2

140 | P a g e

Current Address of Lien Holder(s): State of Florida – **Payable to the: Clerk of the Circuit Court, PO Box 3360 – Tampa, FL 33601**

DONE AND ORDERED in open court in Tampa, Hillsborough County, Florida on, 7/16/2018.

17-CF-013214-A 7/25/2018 4:50:06 PM

17-CF-013214-A 7/25/2018 4:50:06 PM

Christopher C Nash, PRESIDING JUDGE

Florida Statute 28.246(6), authorizes unpaid balances to be referred to a collection agent. This will add additional penalties of up to 40% of the amount owed. Pursuant to Florida Statute 322.245(5)(a), the Clerk of Court may notify the Department of Highway Safety Motor Vehicles (DHSMV) of your failure to pay financial obligations related to criminal offenses which will result in the suspension of your driver's license. To avoid additional costs, please remit payment in full immediately.

CERTIFICATE OF SERVICE

I, PAT FRANK, Clerk of the Circuit and County Court of the County of Hillsborough, State of Florida, having by law the custody of the seal and all records, books, documents and papers of or appertaining to the County Court, do hereby certify that a true and correct copy of this document has been hand delivered, mailed or served electronically to the Office of the State Attorney, the Defense Attorney, and/or Defendant, if appearing Pro Se.

IN WITNESS WHEREOF, I have hereunto set my hand and seal of said County Court, this 30th day of July , 20 18

PAT FRANK

As Clerk of the Circuit and County Court

As Deputy Clerk
Paulette Wong

KALSI, DEVBIR SINGH - 17-CF-013214-A   Page 3 of 3   henry

07/25/2018 04:50:10 PM Electronically Filed: Hillsborough County/13th Judicial Circuit.   Page 3

141 | P a g e

STATE OF FLORIDA

VS.

CASE NUMBER: 17-CF-013214-A

FILED

████████████

JUL 16 2018

DEFENDANT

CLERK OF CIRCUIT COURT

FINGERPRINTS OF DEFENDANT

1. Right Thumb	2. Right Index	3. Right Middle	4. Right Ring	5. Right Little

6. Left Thumb	7. Left Index	8. Left Middle	9. Left Ring	10. Left Little

Fingerprints taken by: DEP R VADASZ 235199 _____ BAILIFF

NAME   TITLE

I HEREBY CERTIFY that the above and foregoing are the fingerprints of the defendant,

████████████ , and that they were placed thereon by the defendant in my

presence in open court this date.

DONE AND ORDERED in open court in Hillsborough County, Florida, this 16TH day of

JULY , 20 18 .

_____

JUDGE

07/25/2018 04:50:10 PM Electronically Filed: Hillsborough County/13th Judicial Circuit.   Page 4

STATE OF FLORIDA

-VS-

███████████████████
Defendant

IN THE THIRTEENTH JUDICIAL
CIRCUIT COURT, IN AND FOR
HILLSBOROUGH COUNTY

CASE NUMBER   17-CF-013214-A
DIVISION C
DC NUMBER   A10014

ORDER OF PROBATION

This cause coming before the Court to be heard, and you, the defendant, being now present before the court, and you having

☒   entered a plea of guilty to

Count 1   **FALSE IMPRISONMENT**

SECTION 2: ORDER WITHHOLDING ADJUDICATION

☒   Now, therefore, it is ordered and adjudged that the adjudication of guilt is hereby withheld and that you be placed on Probation for a period of 24 months under the supervision of the Department of Corrections, subject to Florida law.

IT IS FURTHER ORDERED that you shall comply with the following standard conditions of supervision as provided by Florida law:

(1) You will report to the probation officer as directed.

(2) You will pay the State of Florida the amount of $40.00 per month, as well as 4% surcharge, toward the cost of your supervision in accordance with s. 948.09, F.S., unless otherwise exempted in compliance with Florida Statutes.

(3) You will remain in a specified place. You will not change your residence or employment or leave the county of your residence without first procuring the consent of your officer.

(4) You will not possess, carry or own any firearm. You will not possess, carry, or own any weapon without first procuring the consent of your officer.

(5) You will live without violating any law. A conviction in a court of law is not necessary for such a violation of law to constitute a violation of your probation, community control, or any other form of court ordered supervision.

(6) You will not associate with any person engaged in any criminal activity.

(7) You will not use intoxicants to excess or possess any drugs or narcotics unless prescribed by a physician. Nor will you visit places where intoxicants, drugs or other dangerous substances are unlawfully sold, dispensed or used.

(8) You will work diligently at a lawful occupation, advise your employer of your probation status, and support any dependents to the best of your ability, as directed by your officer.

(9) You will promptly and truthfully answer all inquiries directed to you by the court or the officer, and allow your officer to visit in your home, at your employment site or elsewhere, and you will comply with all instructions your officer may give you.

(10) You will pay restitution, court costs, and/or fees in accordance with special conditions imposed or in accordance with the attached orders.

(11) You will submit to random testing as directed by your officer or the professional staff of the treatment center where you are receiving treatment to determine the presence or use of alcohol or controlled substances.

07/25/2018 06:10:38 PM Electronically Filed: Hillsborough County/13th Judicial Circuit.   Page 1

143 | P a g e

(12) You will submit a DNA sample, as directed by your officer, for DNA analysis as prescribed in ss. 943.325 and 948.014, F.S.

(13) You will submit to the taking of a digitized photograph by the department. This photograph may be displayed on the department's website while you are on supervision, unless exempt from disclosure due to requirements of s. 119.07, F.S.

(14) You will report in person within 72 hours of your release from incarceration to the probation office in Hillsborough County, Florida, unless otherwise instructed by the court or department. (This condition applies only if section 3 on the previous page is checked.) Otherwise, you must report immediately to the probation office located at 1313 N Tampa St Suite 124 Tampa, FL 33602.

SPECIAL CONDITIONS

☒   1. You will successfully complete 50 hours of community service at a rate of 5 hours per month, at a work site approved by your officer.
       Additional instructions ordered: _____

☒   2. You will have no contact (direct or indirect) with the victim or the victim's family during the period of supervision.

☒   3. You must successfully complete Anger Management / Batterer's Intervention Program, and be responsible for the payment of any costs incurred while receiving said treatment, unless waived. If convicted of a Domestic Violence offense, as defined in s. 741.28, F.S., you must attend and successfully complete a batterer's intervention program, unless otherwise directed by the court.
       Additional instructions ordered: _____

☒   4. The defendant can work off court costs by doing additional community service hours at the rate of $10.00 per hour.

☒   5. The defendant may travel out of the county for purposes of international flight.

☒   6. The defendant may automatically terminate probation once proof of residency in India is provided to the courts.

☒   7. The defendant is required to abide by all terms of the injunction.

Effective for offenders whose crime was committed on or after September 1, 2005, there is hereby imposed, in additional to any other provision in this section, mandatory electronic monitoring as a condition of supervision for those who:
- Are placed on supervision for a violation of chapter 794, s. 800.04(4), (5), or (6), s. 827.071, or s. 847.0145 and the unlawful sexual activity involved a victim 15 years of age or younger and the offender is 18 years of age or older; or
- Are designated as a sexual predator pursuant to s. 775.21; or
- Has previously been convicted of a violation of chapter 794, s. 800.04(4), (5), or (6), s. 827.071, or s. 847.0145 and the unlawful sexual activity involved a victim 15 years of age or younger and the offender is 18 years of age or older.

You are hereby placed on notice that should you violate your probation or community control, and the conditions set forth in s. 948.063(1) or (2) are satisfied, whether your probation or community control is revoked or not revoked, you shall be placed on electronic monitoring in accordance with F.S. 948.063.

Effective for offenders who are subject to supervision for a crime that was committed on or after May 26, 2010, and who has been convicted at any time of committing, or attempting, soliciting, or conspiring to commit, any of the criminal offenses listed in s. 943.0435(1)(h)1.a.(I), or a similar offense in another jurisdiction, against a victim who was under the age of 18 at the time of the offense; the following conditions are imposed in addition to all other conditions:

     (a) A prohibition on visiting schools, child care facilities, parks, and playgrounds, without prior approval from the offender's supervising officer. The court may also designate additional locations to protect a victim. The prohibition ordered under this paragraph does not prohibit the offender from visiting a school, child care facility, park, or playground for the sole purpose of attending a religious service as defined in s. 775.0861 or picking up or dropping off the offender's children or grandchildren at a child care facility or school.

     (b) A prohibition on distributing candy or other items to children on Halloween; wearing a Santa Claus costume, or other costume to appeal to children, on or preceding Christmas; wearing an Easter Bunny costume, or other costume to appeal to children, on or preceding Easter; entertaining at children's parties; or wearing a clown costume; without prior approval from the court.

Effective for offenders whose crime was committed on or after October 1, 2014, and who is placed on probation or community control for a violation of chapter 794, s. 800.04, s. 827.071, s. 847.0135(5), or s. 847.0145, in addition to all other conditions imposed, is prohibited from viewing, accessing, owning, or possessing any obscene, pornographic, or sexually stimulating visual or auditory material unless otherwise indicated in the treatment plan provided by a qualified practitioner in the sexual offender treatment program. Visual or auditory material includes, but is not limited to, telephone, electronic media, computer programs, and computer services.

YOU ARE HEREBY PLACED ON NOTICE that the court may at any time rescind or modify any of the conditions of your probation, or may extend the period of probation as authorized by law, or may discharge you from further supervision. If you violate any of the conditions of your probation, you may be arrested and the court may revoke your probation, adjudicate you guilty if adjudication of guilt was withheld, and impose any sentence that it might have imposed before placing you on probation or require you to serve the balance of the sentence.

IT IS FURTHER ORDERED that when you have been instructed as to the conditions of probation, you shall be released from custody if you are in custody, and if you are at liberty on bond, the sureties thereon shall stand discharged from liability. (This paragraph applies only if section 1 or section 2 is checked.)

IT IS FURTHER ORDERED that you pay:
Court Costs, Fees, and Fines, as imposed at sentencing, in the total amount of: $1116.63

Payments processed through the Department of Corrections will be assessed a 4% surcharge pursuant to s. 945.31, F.S.
Pursuant to s. 948.09, F.S., you will be assessed an amount of $2.00 per month for each month of supervision for the Training Trust Fund Surcharge.

☐ Court Costs/Fines Waived
☐ Court Costs/Fines in the amount of _____ converted to _____ community service hours
☐ Court Costs/Fines in the amount of _____ reduced to civil judgment.

SPECIFIC INSTRUCTIONS FOR PAYMENT: _____

IT IS FURTHER ORDERED that the clerk of this court file this order in the clerk's office and provide certified copies of same to the officer for use in compliance with the requirements of law.

    DONE AND ORDERED, on July 16, 2018

17-CF-013214-A 7/25/2018 6:10:35 PM

_____
Christopher C. Nash, Circuit Judge

I acknowledge receipt of a copy of this order and that the conditions have been explained to me and I agree to abide by them.

Date: _____

_____
Defendant

Instructed by: _____
    Supervising Officer

Page 3 of 3   Revised 07-01-2017

07/25/2018 06:10:38 PM Electronically Filed: Hillsborough County/13th Judicial Circuit.   Page 3

145 | P a g e

IN THE CIRCUIT COURT OF THE THIRTEENTH JUDICIAL CIRCUIT
EN LA CORTE DEL CIRCUITO DEL DECIMOTERCER CIRCUITO JUDICIAL
HILLSBOROUGH COUNTY, FLORIDA
ESTADO DE FLORIDA, EN Y PARA EL CONDADO DE HILLSBOROUGH
CRIMINAL JUSTICE DIVISION
DIVISIÓN DE JUSTICIA PENAL

STATE OF FLORIDA
ESTADO DE FLORIDA

CASE NO: 17-CF-13214
NO. DE CASO:

v.

DIVISION:
DIVISIÓN:

FILED

JUL 16 2018

CLERK OF CIRCUIT COURT

UNIFORM PLEA, ACKNOWLEDGMENT AND WAIVER OF RIGHTS FORM
FORMULARIO UNIFORME DE DECLARACIÓN, RECONOCIMIENTO Y RENUNCIA DE DERECHOS

CHARGE(S) CARGO(S)	MANDATORY MINIMUM PENA MÍNIMA OBLIGATORIA	MAXIMUM PENALTY PENA MÁXIMA
Battery Domestic Violence	Ø	364 days
False Imprisonment	Ø	5 yrs

For sections 1 and 2, check either "a" or "b." Para la sección 1 y 2, marque "a" o "b."

☑ 1(a)   I am pleading guilty, and acknowledge (my guilt)(I feel it is in my best interests to do so)
Me declaro culpable y reconozco (mi culpabilidad) (pienso que es lo que más me conviene hacer)

OR / O

☐ 1(b)   I am pleading *nolo contendere*, and acknowledge I feel it is in my best interest to do so.
Me declaro no me opongo, y reconozco que es lo que más me conviene hacer.

☐ 2(a)   I am pleading open to the Court and understand there is no agreement as to what sentence I will receive,
and the Court can sentence me within its discretion
Me declaro abiertamente ante el juez y entiendo que no existe ningún acuerdo relacionado con la
sentencia que voy a recibir y que el juez puede sentenciarme a su discreción

OR / O

☑ 2(b)   I am pleading pursuant to a plea agreement and the terms of that agreement are as follows:
Me declaro conforme a un acuerdo de declaración y los términos son los siguientes:

FSP _____Ø_____   Psychological evaluation and treatment if necessary _____Ø_____
Prisión Estatal de Florida   Evaluación psicológica y tratamiento (de ser necesario)

County Jail _____Ø_____   Probation 24 months   Specified Residency _____Ø_____
Cárcel del Condado   Probatoria   Residencia Específica

Page 1 of 4

- No Contact w/ Victim
- Anger Management Classes
- DV Classes

Community Control _____ 0
Reclusión Domiciliaria

Community Control II _____ 0
Reclusión domiciliaria II

Restitution to: _____ 0 ____ in the amount of ____ 0 ____ to be paid monthly @ ____ 0
Restitución a: _____ por la cantidad de. _____ para pagarse mensualmente a

Drug/Alcohol Evaluation (within 30 days) and treatment if necessary (counseling/urine screens) ____ 0
Evaluación de Alcohol/Drogas (dentro de 30 días) y tratamiento de ser necesario (con un consejero/exámenes de orina)

Community Service ____ 50 _____ Driver's License Revocation ____ 0
Servicio Comunitario _____ Revocación de Licencia de Conducir
at ____ 5 ____ hours per month _____ GED ____ 0
a _____ horas por mes _____ GED

Other: _Abide by all terms and conditions of the Orders_
Otros: _in place in refure to the Injunction and the TPR of no minor child,_ _Inv Cost._ _536.263_ _State shall not object to early termination upon proof of residency in India_ _return passport currently at HCSO to △_ _Free to travel out of county solely for purposes of International flight_

3. I understand if probation or community control is part of the plea agreement the court may impose any special conditions it believes it should but such special conditions will be orally pronounced by the Court at the time of sentencing. I understand the court may require me to pay up to $1 per month to "First Step of Hillsborough, Inc." as a special condition of probation or community control pursuant to section 948.039, Florida Statutes.
Entiendo que si la probatoria o la reclusión domiciliaria forman parte del acuerdo declaratorio, la corte podria imponer cualesquiera condiciones especiales que crea debe imponer, pero dichas condiciones especiales se pronunciarán oralmente por el juez en el momento de la sentencia. Entiendo que la corte me requerirá pagar hasta $1 por mes para "First Step of Hillsborough, Inc." como una condición especial de probatoria o reclusión domiciliaria de acuerdo a la sección 948.039, Estatutos de la Florida.

4. I understand I have a right to plead not guilty and the right to be tried by a jury to determine whether I am guilty or not guilty. I understand I have the right to be represented by an attorney at the trial and if I cannot afford one, the Court will appoint an attorney to represent me. I understand I have the right to compel the attendance of witnesses on my behalf, the right to confront and cross examine all witnesses testifying against me, and the right to remain silent. I understand if I plead guilty or nolo contendere there will be no trial and I waive all the rights that go along with a trial.
Entiendo que tengo el derecho de declararme no culpable y el derecho de ser juzgado por un jurado que decidiria si soy culpable o no. Entiendo que tengo el derecho de ser representado por un abogado para el juicio y que si no tengo los medios para contratar a uno, la corte nombrará un abogado para que me represente. Entiendo que tengo el derecho de obligar la comparecencia de testigos para que declaren a mi favor, el derecho de repreguntar a todos los testigos de cargo y el derecho de permanecer en silencio. Entiendo que si me declaro culpable o no me opongo, no habrá juicio y renuncio a todos los derechos propios de un juicio.

5. I understand I have the RIGHT TO APPEAL the judgment and sentence of the Court within thirty (30) days from the date of sentence. I understand if I wish to take an appeal and cannot afford an attorney to help me in my appeal, the Court will appoint an attorney to represent me for that purpose. I understand if I plead guilty or nolo contendere without reserving the right to appeal, I am waiving my rights to appeal all matters relating to the judgment including the issue of my guilt or innocence. I admit there is a factual basis for the charge(s) to which I am entering a plea.
Entiendo que tengo EL DERECHO APELAR el fallo y condena/sentencia de la corte dentro del término de treinta (30) días a partir de la fecha de la sentencia. Entiendo que si deseo apelar y no tengo los medios para contratar a un abogado para que me ayude en mi apelación, la corte nombrará a un abogado para que me represente con ese propósito. Entiendo que si me declaro culpable o no me opongo sin reservar mi derecho de apelar, estaré renunciando a mi derecho de apelar todos los asuntos propios de la sentencia, incluso lo relativo a mi culpabilidad o inocencia. Admito que hay fundamento para el (los) cargo (s) al (a los) cual (es) me estoy declarando.

6. I understand there are facts the State could use to prove the charge(s) against me.

Page 2 of 4

Entiendo que existen hechos que el Estado podría usar para probar el o los cargos en mi contra.

7.   I understand if I plead guilty or *nolo contendere* the judge may ask me questions about the charge(s) to which I have just pled and if I am untruthful, my answer(s) may later be used against me in a prosecution for perjury.
Entiendo que si me declaro culpable o no me opongo, el juez podría hacerme preguntas respecto al cargo al cual me acabo de declarar y que si falto a la verdad, mis respuestas podrían ser usadas en mi contra en un proceso por perjurio.

8.   I understand if I plead guilty or *nolo contendere* and am not a United States citizen, my plea may cause immigration problems, including DEPORTATION, exclusion and problems for adjustment of immigration status pursuant to the laws and regulations governing the United States Naturalization and Immigration Service.
Entiendo que si no soy ciudadano (a) de los Estados Unidos y me declaro culpable o no me opongo, esto podría ocasionarme problemas con inmigración, incluyendo DEPORTACIÓN, exclusión o problemas en mi modificación de estado migratorio, conforme a las leyes y reglamentos que gobiernan al Servicio de Naturalización e Inmigración de los Estados Unidos.

9.   I understand this plea could result in my driver's license being suspended or revoked if the charge(s) to which I am pleading is one where automatic, mandatory suspension or revocation is required by law.
Entiendo que esta declaración podría resultar en la suspensión o revocación de mi licencia de conducir si el cargo al cual me estoy declarando es un delito donde se requiere la suspensión o revocación automática obligatoria por la ley.

10.   I understand if I plead guilty or *nolo contendere* to a sexually violent offense or a sexually motivated offense, or if I have been previously convicted of such an offense, the plea may subject me to involuntary civil commitment as a sexually violent predator upon completion of any prison sentence or jail sentence on this or any other case.
Entiendo que si me declaro culpable o no me opongo a un delito sexual con violencia, o a un delito motivado sexualmente, o si previamente he sido condenado por dicho delito, esta declaración me sujetaría a un confinamiento involuntario civil como un depredador sexual violento una vez que haya concluido cualquier sentencia de prisión o cárcel en este o cualquier otro caso.

11.   I understand if I plead guilty or *nolo contendere* to a qualifying sexual offense, or if I have been previously convicted of such an offense or if I have been designated a sexual predator, I will be subject to mandatory electronic monitoring pursuant to section 948.30(3), Florida Statutes.
Entiendo que si me declaro culpable o no me opongo a un delito de categoría sexual, o si he sido condenado previamente por dicho delito, o se me ha catalogado como depredador sexual, estaré sujeto a un control electrónico obligatorio conforme a la sección 948.30 (3), de los Estatutos de la Florida.

12.   I understand my pleading guilty or *nolo contendere* will result in the Court imposing MANDATORY statutory costs. I also understand my plea may result in the Court imposing certain other costs and attorney's fees and I do not object to the imposition or amount of such costs and fees and I waive my right to a hearing on the imposition and amount of such costs and fees. I have had an opportunity to review the Uniform Order Assessing Costs, Fines & Surcharges with my attorney. I understand if I fail to pay the imposed costs and fees my driver's license may be suspended.
Entiendo que si me declaro culpable o no me opongo traerá como resultado que el juez imponga las costas OBLIGATORIAS de ley. Asimismo, entiendo que mi declaración podría hacer que el juez imponga ciertos costos y honorarios del abogado. No me opongo a la imposición o la cantidad de costos y honorarios y renuncio a mi derecho a una audiencia respecto a la imposición y la cantidad de costos y honorarios. He tenido la oportunidad de revisar con mi abogado, la Orden Uniforme de Imposición de Costas, Multas y sobrecargos. Entiendo que si no pago los costos y honorarios impuestos, mi licencia de conducir podría ser suspendida.

13.   I understand a conviction for an offense to which I am pleading guilty or *nolo contendere* may serve to enhance the sentence for any offense for which I may be convicted of in the future.
Entiendo que una condena por un delito al cual me estoy declarando culpable o no me opongo podría servir para aumentar la sentencia por cualquier delito por el cual se me podría condenar en el futuro.

14.   I am not under the influence of drugs, an alcoholic beverage or medication, but I am taking this medication.
_____
No me encuentro bajo los efectos de drogas ni bebidas alcohólicas, aunque estoy tomando este medicamento.

15.   I do not have any mental illness that would keep me from understanding this plea and its consequences.

Page 3 of 4

No padezco de ninguna enfermedad mental que podría impedirme entender esta declaración y sus consecuencias.

16. I certify that no one has threatened or coerced me in any way in order to get me to enter this plea, and I am pleading freely and voluntarily. Other than the terms of the plea negotiation as set forth above (if applicable), no one has promised me anything upon which I have relied in order to influence me to enter this plea.
Certifico que nadie me ha amenazado ni coaccionado de ninguna manera para que yo asiente esta declaración y me declaro libre y voluntariamente. Aparte del acuerdo declaratorio, como se estipula en el párrafo antes mencionado (si es aplicable), nadie me ha prometido nada en lo cual yo me he basado con el motivo de influenciarme para que yo asiente esta declaración.

17. I certify that I have discussed the charges with my attorney including the maximum possible and mandatory minimum (if any) penalties and possible defenses and am fully satisfied with the representation of my attorney. I understand by entering this plea there is no guarantee what gain time, if any, the Department of Corrections or any county jail may award me.
Certifico que he revisado los cargos con mi abogado, incluso las penas máximas posibles y mínimas obligatorias (si las hubiera) y defensas posibles y estoy completamente satisfecho con la representación de mi abogado. Entiendo que al asentar, esta declaración no hay garantía del tiempo ganado, de haberlo, que el Departamento de Corrección o cualquier cárcel del condado podrán conceder me.

18. I have reviewed my criminal punishment code scoresheet and it is correct.
He revisado mi hoja de puntuación y está correcta.

19. I have reviewed the standard terms of supervision and I understand I must follow them as well as any special conditions the court thinks are appropriate.
He revisado las condiciones generales de supervisión y entiendo que debo cumplirlas, así como cualesquiera otras condiciones que la corte considere apropiadas.

20. I understand no one, including my attorney, can accurately predict the actual time I will serve on a sentence and I may be required to serve the entire sentence.
Entiendo que nadie, incluyendo mi abogado, puede predecir con certeza el tiempo real que cumpliré por una sentencia y que podría requerirse
que cumpla la sentencia completa.

21. I certify that there are not any other witnesses I want my attorney to investigate or call, nor is there any other type of discovery or investigation I want my attorney to do prior to entering this plea.
Certifico que no hay otros testigos que quiero que mi abogado investigue o llame, ni tampoco existe otro tipo de prueba o investigación que quiero que mi abogado haga antes de asentar esta declaración.

22. I certify that no one, including my attorney, has made any promises concerning the jail credit or prison credit I am to receive other than the fact that I am going to receive credit for every day I actually spent incarcerated on this case.
Certifico que nadie, incluyendo mi abogado (a) me ha hecho ninguna promesa respecto al tiempo que será acreditado de la cárcel o prisión además del hecho que voy a recibir credito por cada día que realmente pasé encarcelado en este (os) caso (s).

_____   7/16/2018_____
Defendant / Acusado   Date / Fecha

STATEMENT OF ATTORNEY

I, as the attorney for the above Defendant, state that I have reviewed this plea form and the Uniform Order Assessing Costs, Fines & Surcharges with my client and it is my belief the Defendant fully understands their contents.

_____   7/16/2018_____
Attorney   Date   Revised 37/16

Jonathan Hawkins   Page 4 of 4

CASE NUMBER   2017-CF-013214
DIVISION

IN THE CIRCUIT COURT OF THE THIRTEENTH JUDICIAL CIRCUIT OF THE
STATE OF FLORIDA IN AND FOR HILLSBOROUGH COUNTY
CIRCUIT CRIMINAL DIVISION

——— **SEP 2 2 2017** ——— , SPRING Term, 2017

STATE OF FLORIDA

V

[REDACTED]

DIRECT AS TO COUNT ONE AS
TO DEFENDANT BHUPINDER
KALSI AND DIRECT AS TO
COUNT FOUR AS TO DFEFENDANT
JASBIR KALSI

INFORMATION FOR:

COUNT ONE
FALSE IMPRISONMENT
F.S. 787.02 (1)/787.02 (2)
(DEVBIR SINGH KALSI,
BHUPINDER KALSI)

COUNT TWO
ARMED FALSE
IMPRISONMENT
F.S. 787.02(1)/775.087(1)
(JASBIR SINGH KALSI)

COUNT THREE
AGGRAVATED ASSAULT
WITH DEADLY WEAPON
F.S. 784.021(1)(a)
(JASBIR SINGH KALSI)

COUNT FOUR
BATTERY
(DOMESTIC VIOLENCE)
F.S. 784.03(1)
(ALL DEFENDANTS)

2017-043516/2017-CF-013214
Page 1 of 6
Information
        INFORMATIONS-5024 2017-043516

IN THE NAME AND BY THE AUTHORITY OF THE STATE OF FLORIDA, ANDREW H. WARREN, STATE ATTORNEY OF THE THIRTEENTH JUDICIAL CIRCUIT IN AND FOR THE COUNTY OF HILLSBOROUGH, CHARGES THAT:

COUNT ONE

████████████████████████████████, between the 1st day of September, 2017, and the 2nd day of September, 2017, inclusive in the County of Hillsborough and State of Florida, did, without lawful authority, forcibly, by threat, or secretly confining, abduct, imprison, or restrain SILKY GAIND against her will.

COUNT TWO

JASBIR SINGH KALSI, between the 1st day of September, 2017, and the 2nd day of September, 2017, inclusive in the County of Hillsborough and State of Florida, did, without lawful authority, forcibly, by threat or secretly confining, abduct, imprison or restrain SILKY GAIND against her will, and during the commission of the offense JASBIR KALSI carried, displayed, used, threatened to use, or attempted to use a weapon, to-wit: knife.

COUNT THREE

████████████████ between the 1st day of September, 2017, and the 2nd day of September, 2017, inclusive in the County of Hillsborough and State of Florida, did intentionally and unlawfully threaten by word or act to do violence to the person of SILKY GAIND, coupled with an apparent ability to do so, and did an act creating a well-founded fear in the said SILKY GAIND that such violence was imminent, and in so doing did use a deadly weapon, to-wit: knife, without intent to kill ████████████

2017-043516/2017-CF-013214
Page 2 of 6

COUNT FOUR

███ between the 1st day of September, 2017, and the 2nd day of September, 2017, inclusive in the County of Hillsborough and State of Florida, did actually and intentionally touch or strike ███████ against the will of the said ████ ████ or did intentionally cause bodily harm to ████████. Contrary to the form of the statute in such cases made and provided, and against the peace and dignity of the State of Florida.

STATE OF FLORIDA
COUNTY OF HILLSBOROUGH

Personally appeared before me the undersigned Assistant State Attorney of the Thirteenth Judicial Circuit in and for Hillsborough County, Florida, who, being first duly sworn, says that this prosecution is set forth in the foregoing INFORMATION are based upon facts that have been sworn to as true by the material witness or witnesses for the offense and which, if true, would constitute the offense therein charged, and that the prosecution is being instituted in good faith.

Assistant State Attorney of the
Thirteenth Judicial Circuit in and
For Hillsborough County, Florida

Florida Bar # ___14597___

Sworn to and subscribed before me at Tampa, Florida

This ___22nd___ day of ___September___, 2017

Signature of Notary Public - State of Florida

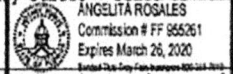

Print, Type or Stamp Commissioned Name of Notary
And Date Commission Expires

Personally known ___V___ or Produced Identification ____

_____
Type of Identification Produced

September 22, 2017
JESSICA W O'CONNOR/dss

MailProcessingStaff@saol3th.com

Parent

2017043516/2017-CF-013214-D001   DEVBIR SINGH KALSI   (Open)

Include N/A

Consolidate
2017-043698/2017-CF-013319-D001 KALSI, JASBIR SINGH   (Open)
2017-043689/2017-CF-013320-D001 KALSI, BHUPINDER   (Open)

DEFENDANT: ████████████████
DOB   : 04/29/1984
RACE   : White
GENDER   : Male
SSN   : N/A
DL#   : K420177841490-FL
HAIR   : N/A
EYES   : N/A
ADDRESS   : ████████████████████████

DEFENDANT: ████████████████
DOB   : 05/18/1950
RACE   : White
GENDER   : Male
SSN   : N/A
DL#   : N/A
HAIR   : Grey
EYES   : Brown
ADDRESS   : ████████████████████

DEFENDANT: ████████████████
DOB   : 11/02/1955
RACE   : White
GENDER   : Female
SSN   : N/A
DL#   : N/A
HAIR   : Grey
EYES   : Brown
ADDRESS   : ████████████████████████

Agency :   Hillsborough County Sheriffs Office 2017-00628731

2017-043516/2017-CF-013214
Page 5 of 6

COUNT ONE
FALSE IMPRISONMENT
F.S. 787.02 (1)/787.02 (2)
3RD DEGREE FELONY
(DEVBIR SINGH KALSI, BHUPINDER KALSI)
KIDN5003

COUNT TWO
ARMED FALSE
IMPRISONMENT
F.S. 787.02(1)/775.087(1)
2ND DEGREE FELONY
(JASBIR SINGH KALSI)
KIDN5005

COUNT THREE
AGGRAVATED ASSAULT
WITH DEADLY WEAPON
F.S. 784.021(1)(a)
3RD DEGREE FELONY
(JASBIR SINGH KALSI)
ASSA5005

COUNT FOUR
BATTERY
(DOMESTIC VIOLENCE)
F.S. 784.03(1)
1ST DEGREE MISDEMEANOR
(ALL DEFENDANTS)
BATT1102

State Attorney

ANDREW H. WARREN
Thirteenth Judicial Circuit
419 N. Pierce Street
Tampa, Florida 33602-4022
(813) 272-5400

<u>Notice to Clerk of Factors Relating to Division Assignment
in accordance with Circuit Criminal Administrative Order</u>

Date: September 22, 2017

To: Clerk of Court

From: SAO Personnel

Defendant's Name: ███████████

Case Number: 2017-CF-013214

Division Proposed by Clerk: C
Presumed Division per SAO Research: C

__X__ Case should be assigned to the Proposed Division that has already been assigned by the Clerk because none of the following exceptions apply.

--EXCEPTIONS--

In accordance with the current administrative order governing assignment of cases in the Circuit Criminal Division, please assign a division based on the following exceptions to the proposed division case assignment:

_____ Case meets the Drug Court criteria and therefore should be assigned to Division "Y."

_____ Case meets the Veterans Court criteria and therefore should be assigned to Division "V."

_____ Defendant has multiple proposed divisions. Earliest assigned proposed division is _____.

_____ Defendant has Pending Case with lowest pending case #: _____; Division _____.

_____ Co-Defendant has multiple proposed divisions. Earliest assigned proposed division is _____.

_____ Co-Defendant has Pending Case with lowest pending case #: _____; Division _____.

_____ Case is re-filed after SAO dismissed it. Original case assigned to Division _____.

Associated Cases: _____

2017-043516/2017-CF-013214
Page 1 of 1 Notice of Division

State Attorney

ANDREW H. WARREN
Thirteenth Judicial Circuit
419 N. Pierce Street
Tampa, Florida 33602-4022
(813) 272-5400

**Notice to Clerk of Factors Relating to Division Assignment
in accordance with Circuit Criminal Administrative Order**

Date: September 22, 2017

To: Clerk of Court

From: SAO Personnel

Defendant's Name: ███████████████

Case Number: 2017-CF-013319

Division Proposed by Clerk: I
Presumed Division per SAO Research: C

_____ Case should be assigned to the Proposed Division that has already been assigned by the Clerk because none of the following exceptions apply.

--EXCEPTIONS--

In accordance with the current administrative order governing assignment of cases in the Circuit Criminal Division, please assign a division based on the following exceptions to the proposed division case assignment:

_____ Case meets the Drug Court criteria and therefore should be assigned to Division "Y."

_____ Case meets the Veterans Court criteria and therefore should be assigned to Division "V."

_____ Defendant has multiple proposed divisions. Earliest assigned proposed division is _____.

_____ Defendant has Pending Case with lowest pending case #: _____; Division _____.

__X__ Co-Defendant has multiple proposed divisions. Earliest assigned proposed division is __C__.

_____ Co-Defendant has Pending Case with lowest pending case #: _____; Division _____.

_____ Case is re-filed after SAO dismissed it. Original case assigned to Division _____.

Associated Cases: _____

2017-043516/2017-CF-013214
Page 1 of 1 Notice of Division

State Attorney

ANDREW H. WARREN
Thirteenth Judicial Circuit
419 N. Pierce Street
Tampa, Florida 33602-4022
(813) 272-5400

<u>Notice to Clerk of Factors Relating to Division Assignment
in accordance with Circuit Criminal Administrative Order</u>

Date: September 22, 2017

To: Clerk of Court

From: SAO Personnel

Defendant's Name: ████████████

Case Number: 2017-CF-013320

Division Proposed by Clerk: C
Presumed Division per SAO Research: C

__X__ Case should be assigned to the Proposed Division that has already been assigned by the Clerk because none of the following exceptions apply.

---EXCEPTIONS--

In accordance with the current administrative order governing assignment of cases in the Circuit Criminal Division, please assign a division based on the following exceptions to the proposed division case assignment:

_____ Case meets the Drug Court criteria and therefore should be assigned to Division "Y."

_____ Case meets the Veterans Court criteria and therefore should be assigned to Division "V."

_____ Defendant has multiple proposed divisions. Earliest assigned proposed division is _____.

_____ Defendant has Pending Case with lowest pending case #: _____; Division _____.

_____ Co-Defendant has multiple proposed divisions. Earliest assigned proposed division is _____.

_____ Co-Defendant has Pending Case with lowest pending case #: _____; Division _____.

_____ Case is re-filed after SAO dismissed it. Original case assigned to Division _____.

Associated Cases: _____

2017-043516/2017-CF-013214
Page 1 of 1 Notice of Division

Case Information

Uniform Case Number: 292017CF013214000BHC

STATE OF FLORIDA VS ██████████

Icon Keys | Summary | Parties | Events/Documents | Charges | Hearings | Financial | Bonds | Disposition

File Location

Case Information

Case Number \ Citation

Case Number: 17-CF-013214-B

Citation Number:

Booking Numbers

Booking Numbers
2017-32338
17032338

Case Information

Case Category Description: Criminal

Case Type Description: FELONY

Case Sub Type Description:

Case Status: CLOSED

Case Filed On: 2017-09-22

Financial Information

Balance Due: $1,122.88

Due Date: 07/09/2020

Judge Assignment

Judge: Nash, C. Christopher

Division: Division C

Judge Assignment History ▾

Return to Search Results (/html/case/searchResults.html)

Case Information

Uniform Case Number: 292017CF013214000BHC

STATE OF FLORIDA VS KALSI, JASBIR SINGH

Icon Keys Summary Parties Events\Documents Charges Hearings Financial Bonds Disposition

File Location

Parties on the Case

Show 25 entries   Column visibility Excel CSV   Search:

Party Type	Name	Party Demographics	Attorney Name	Attorney Contact
Plaintiff	STATE OF FLORIDA 11 TAMPA, FL 33602		BROWN , CHRISTINE SHIVER	Telephone: 813-272-5400 419 N PIERCE ST TAMPA, FL 33602
Defendant	███████	Date of Birth: 05/18/1950 Height (inches): 68 Weight: 128 Race: White Gender: Male	HANLON , WILLIAM WOOTEN	Telephone: 813-228-7095 HANLON LAW 210 N PIERCE ST TAMPA, FL 33602
Defendant	███████	Date of Birth: 05/18/1950 Height (inches): 68 Weight: 128 Race: White Gender: Male	VASIGH , MAJID	Telephone: 813-800-1111 101 N 12TH ST UNIT 104 TAMPA, FL 33602

Showing 1 to 3 of 3 entries   Previous 1 Next

Return to Search Results (/html/case/searchResults.html)

© 2016 - Hillsborough County Clerk of the Circuit Court

Case Information

STATE OF FLORIDA VS ████████████

🔖 Icon Keys   📘 Summary   👥 Parties   📑 Events/Documents   📄 Charges   📅 Hearings   💲 Financial   🔗 Bonds   ⚖ Disposition

📁 File Location

Charges

Show 25 entries   [Column visibility] [Excel] [CSV]   Search: [_____]

Select	Charge Number	Offense Description	Offense Date	Degree Description	Disposition
	1	8270318 2C-CHAB1602 (FT) CHILD ABUSE	09/01/2017	THIRD DEGREE FELONY	NT - NO INFORMATION FILED

Arrest Information
Arrest Date: 09/02/2017
Prosecutor Information
Date: 09/22/2017   Description: NO INFORMATION FILED
CriminalDispo Information
Date: 09/22/2017   Description: NT - NO INFORMATION FILED   Judge: Nash, Christopher C.

| | 3 | 7840211A-ASSA5005 (FT) AGGRAVATED ASSAULT WITH DEADLY WEAPON | 09/01/2017 | THIRD DEGREE FELONY | NT - ADJUDGED GUILTY |

Arrest Information
Arrest Date: 09/02/2017
Plea Information
Date: 07/16/2018   Plea: GUILTY
Date: 09/19/2017   Plea: WRITTEN PLEA OF NOT GUILTY
Prosecutor Information
Date: 09/22/2017   Description: FILED
CriminalDispo Information
Date: 07/16/2018   Description: NT - ADJUDGED GUILTY   Judge: Nash, Christopher C.
Sentence Information
Date: 07/16/2018   Description: NT - ADJUDGED GUILTY   Code: ADJG

| | 5 | 9142234B-TAMP2210 (FT) HARASSING A WITNESS | 09/01/2017 | THIRD DEGREE FELONY | NT - NO INFORMATION FILED |

Arrest Information
Arrest Date: 09/02/2017
Prosecutor Information
Date: 09/22/2017   Description: NO INFORMATION FILED
CriminalDispo Information
Date: 09/22/2017   Description: NT - NO INFORMATION FILED   Judge: Nash, Christopher C.

| | 2 | 787021-KIDN5005 (FS) ARMED FALSE IMPRISONMENT | 09/01/2017 | SECOND DEGREE FELONY | NT - ADJUDGED GUILTY |

Arrest Information

Arrest Date: 09/02/2017

Plea Information

| Date: 07/16/2018 | Plea: GUILTY |
| Date: 09/19/2017 | Plea: WRITTEN PLEA OF NOT GUILTY |

Prosecutor Information

| Date: 09/22/2017 | Description: FILED |

CriminalDispo Information

| Date: 07/16/2018 | Description: NT - ADJUDGED GUILTY | | Judge: Nash, Christopher C. |

Sentence Information

| Date: 07/16/2018 | Description: NT - ADJUDGED GUILTY | | Code: ADJG |

| 4 | 784031-BATT1102 (MF) BATTERY DOMESTIC VIOLENCE | 09/01/2017 | FIRST DEGREE MISDEMEANOR | NT - ADJUDGED GUILTY |

Plea Information

| Date: 07/16/2018 | Plea: GUILTY |
| Date: 09/19/2017 | Plea: WRITTEN PLEA OF NOT GUILTY |

Prosecutor Information

| Date: 09/22/2017 | Description: FILED |

CriminalDispo Information

| Date: 07/16/2018 | Description: NT - ADJUDGED GUILTY | | Judge: Nash, Christopher C. |

Sentence Information

| Date: 07/16/2018 | Description: NT - ADJUDGED GUILTY | | Code: ADJG |

Showing 1 to 5 of 5 entries

Previous 1 Next

Return to Search Results (/html/case/searchResults.html)

Case Information

Uniform Case Number: 292017CF013214000BHC

STATE OF FLORIDA VS ████████

🔍 Icon Keys   📖 Summary   👥 Parties   📄 Events/Documents   ⚖ Charges   📅 Hearings   💲 Financial   🔗 Bonds   ⚖ Disposition

📁 File Location

⚖ Disposition (Charge Sentence Information)

Show `25` entries   Column visibility   Excel   CSV   Search:

Document Index	Charge Number	Offense Date	Charge Offense Description	Degree Description	Citation Number
	2	09/01/2017	787021-KIDN5006 (FS) ARMED FALSE IMPRISONMENT	SECOND DEGREE FELONY	

Sentence Information

Plea	07/16/2018		GUILTY		
Disposition	07/16/2018		NT - ADJUDGED GUILTY		
Sentence	07/16/2018		CRIMINAL		
			Community Service (Hours: 50. Comment: @ 5/MO)		Sentence
			State Probation (24 Mo)		Status (EACH
			Provisions		COUNT

- AUTOMATIC TERMINATION OF PROBATION WHEN CONDITIONS COMPLETE,
- COURT COSTS,
- NO CONTACT WITH VICTIM OR PROPERTY,
- OTHER COURT RESTRICTIONS,

Comment: COURT PERMITS RETURN PASSPORT

CONCURRENT)

Prosecutor:	BROWN CHRISTINE SHIVER
Defense	VASIGH MAJID

	3	09/01/2017	7840211A-ASSA5005 (FT) AGGRAVATED ASSAULT WITH DEADLY WEAPON	THIRD DEGREE FELONY	

Sentence Information

Plea	07/16/2018		GUILTY		
Disposition	07/16/2018		NT - ADJUDGED GUILTY		
Sentence	07/16/2018		CRIMINAL		
			Community Service (Hours: 50, Comment: @ 5/MO)		Sentence
			State Probation (24 Mo)		Status (EACH
			Provisions		COUNT

- AUTOMATIC TERMINATION OF PROBATION WHEN CONDITIONS COMPLETE,
- COURT COSTS,
- NO CONTACT WITH VICTIM OR PROPERTY,
- OTHER COURT RESTRICTIONS,

Comment: COURT PERMITS RETURN PASSPORT

CONCURRENT)

Prosecutor:	BROWN CHRISTINE SHIVER
Defense	VASIGH MAJID

	4	09/01/2017	784031-BATT1102 (MF) BATTERY DOMESTIC VIOLENCE	FIRST DEGREE MISDEMEANOR	

Sentence Information

Plea	07/16/2018		GUILTY		
Disposition	07/16/2018		NT - ADJUDGED GUILTY		
Sentence	07/16/2018		CRIMINAL		
			Provisions		

- SENTENCED TO TIME SERVED - LENGTH UNSPECIFIED.

163 | P a g e

Showing 1 to 3 of 3 entries

Previous 1 Next

↩ Return to Search Results (/html/case/searchResults.html)

IN THE CIRCUIT COURT IN AND FOR HILLSBOROUGH COUNTY, STATE OF FLORIDA

CASE NO. 17-CF-013214-B

STATE OF FLORIDA

VS

Division   C

Offense Date: 9/1/2017

Defense   Case Number: 17-CF-013214-B
Address: VASIGH, MAJID
101 N 12TH ST UNIT 104
TAMPA, FL 33602

JUDGMENT AND SENTENCE

The above named Defendant is now before the Court:

State: BROWN, CHRISTINE SHIVER

Cnt	Charge Description	Lev Deg	Plea	Disp Date	Disposition
2	787021 ARMED FALSE IMPRISONMENT	F2	GUILTY	07/16/18	NT - ADJUDGED GUILTY
3	7840211A AGGRAVATED ASSAULT WITH DEADLY WEAPON	F3	GUILTY	07/16/18	NT - ADJUDGED GUILTY
4	784031 BATTERY DOMESTIC VIOLENCE	M1	GUILTY	07/16/18	NT - ADJUDGED GUILTY

Ct.2,3 SENTENCE: CRIMINAL

Community Service (Hours: 50, Comment: @ 5/MO)
State Probation (24 Months)
Provisions

- MAY TRAVEL OUTSIDE COUNTY(INTERNATIONAL FLIGHT
- ABIDE ALL CONDITIONS OF INJUNCTION
- COMPLETION OF ANGER MANAGEMENT
- COMPLETION DOMESTIC VIOLENCE COURSE
- NO CONTACT WITH VICTIM
- COURT PERMITS RETURN PASSPORT CURRENTLY WITH HCSO
- COURT COSTS
- AUTOMATIC TERMINATION OF PROBATION ONCE PROOF OF RESIDENCY OF INDIA TO COURTS

Sentence Status (EACH COUNT CONCURRENT)

Ct.4 SENTENCE: CRIMINAL

Provisions

- SENTENCED TO TIME SERVED - LENGTH UNSPECIFIED

Fees :

- $411.88   CR-8884 INVESTIGATION COST - HCSO 938.27   FS AUTH: 938.27
- $100.00   CR-2399 INVESTIGATIVE COSTS SAO REVENUE FS 938.27(8)   FS AUTH: 938.27(8)
- $100.00   CR-8366 CFF CRIMES AGAINST MINORS -DOR-DCF GRANTS CHILD ADV   FS AUTH: 938.10(2)
- $50.00   CR-8450 DOR-DCF GRNT & DON -GRDN ADLITEM 938.10   FS AUTH: 938.10(2)
- $1.00   CR-R235 CRIMES AGAINST MINORS   FS AUTH: 938.10
- $50.00   CR-8081 CRIME PREVENTION   FS AUTH: 775.083(2)
- $65.00   CR-8097 ADDITIONAL COSTS (BOCC) - PROGRAMS   FS AUTH: 939.185(1)(a
- $49.00   CR-8311 FCCA CRIMES COMPENSATION TRUST FUND   FS AUTH: 938.03

- 17-CF-013214-B   Page 1 of 3   henry

07/25/2018 06:03:50 PM Electronically Filed: Hillsborough County/13th Judicial Circuit.   Page 1

165 | P a g e

- $17.00   CR-A362 CRIME STOPPERS TRUST FUND   **FS AUTH:** 938.06
- $200.00   CR-R252 ADDITIONAL COURT COST - CLERK - CIR CRIM   **FS AUTH:** 938.05(1)(a)
- $25.00   **FS AUTH:** 938.05(1)(a)
- $1.00   CR-R617 CRIMES COMPENSATION FEE 938.03   **FS AUTH:** 938.03
- $3.00   CR-RA20 CRIME STOPPERS TRUST FUND FEE   **FS AUTH:** 938.06
- $3.00   CR-2616 STATE ASSESSMENT (ADDL CRT COST CLEAR) 938.01   **FS AUTH:** 938.01
- $2.00   CR-2629 HILLSBOROUGH COUNTY LOCAL ASSESSMENT   **FS AUTH:** 938.15 318.18(11)(d)
- $6.00   CR-R229 FELONY PREP FEE FOR CRIMINAL JUDGMENT - 28.24(8)   **FS AUTH:** FS 28.24(8)
- $1.00   CR-R229D FELONY PREP FEE FOR CRIMINAL JUDGMENT - 28.24(8)   **FS AUTH:** FS 28.24(8)
- $6.00   CR-R228 FELONY PREP FEE FOR CRIM SATISFACTION - 28.24(8)   **FS AUTH:** FS 28.24(8)
- $1.00   CR-R228D FELONY PREP FEE FOR CRIM SATISFACTION - 28.24(8)   **FS AUTH:** FS 28.24(8)
- $9.00   CR-1100J RECORDING FEE FOR CRIMINAL JUDGMENT 28.24(12)(a)(b)   **FS AUTH:** FS 28.24(12)(a)(b)
- $10.00   CR-1100S RECORDING FEE FOR CRIM SATISFACTION 28.24(12)(a)(b)   **FS AUTH:** FS 28.24(12)(a)(b)

Fee Total : $1110.88

FEE TOTALS INCLUDE ALL OUTSTANDING FEES OWED ON THE CASE AT THE TIME OF THIS JUDGMENT, EXCEPT FOR COST OF SUPERVISION AND THE PROBATION SERVICE FEE. SEE ORDER OF PROBATION FOR DETAILS. THE ABOVE FEES INCLUDE THE ASSESSMENT OF JUDGMENT AND SATISFACTION FEES, AS APPLICABLE.

If you are a "qualifying offender" under section 943.325, Florida Statutes, you are required to submit a DNA sample in a manner consistent with Florida law.

The defendant SHALL pay all mandatory and discretionary costs, fines, fees, penalties, & surcharges applicable to this matter, per Florida Statutes and Hillsborough County Ordinances; as stated above.

Probation: If probation is ordered, the conditions of Probation will be provided to you on a separate written order prepared by the HCSO Probation Services or Florida Department of Corrections.

Jail: At the time of sentencing, if jail is ordered, the defendant may be taken into custody by the Sheriff of Hillsborough County, Florida or given a date to report for incarceration in the County Jail under supervision of the Board of Criminal Justice of Hillsborough County.

Judgment For Money Ordered To Be Paid: It is the order of the Court that a judgment is entered, on behalf of the Hillsborough County Clerk of Circuit and County Courts, on behalf of Hillsborough County, and on behalf of the State of Florida, on the money that is ordered to be paid as a result of the JUDGMENT AND SENTENCE to the charge(s) in this matter, **FOR WHICH LET EXECUTION ISSUE.**

Current Address of Lien Holder(s): State of Florida – Payable to the: Clerk of the Circuit Court, PO Box 3360 – Tampa, FL 33601

DONE AND ORDERED in open court in Tampa, Hillsborough County, Florida on, 7/16/2018.

17-CF-013214-B 7/25/2018 6:03:46 PM

17-CF-013214-B 7/25/2018 6:03:46 PM

Christopher C. Nash, PRESIDING JUDGE

Florida Statute 28.246(6), authorizes unpaid balances to be referred to a collection agent. This will add additional penalties of up to 40% of the amount owed. Pursuant to Florida Statute 322.245(5)(a), the Clerk of Court may notify the Department of Highway Safety Motor Vehicles (DHSMV) of your failure to pay financial obligations related to criminal offenses which will result in the suspension of your driver's license. To avoid additional costs, please remit payment in full immediately.

███████ - 17-CF-013214-B   Page 2 of 3   henry

CERTIFICATE OF SERVICE

I, PAT FRANK, Clerk of the Circuit and County Court of the County of Hillsborough, State of Florida, having by law the custody of the seal and all records, books, documents and papers of or appertaining to the County Court, do hereby certify that a true and correct copy of this document has been hand delivered, mailed or served electronically to the Office of the State Attorney, the Defense Attorney, and/or Defendant, if appearing Pro Se.

IN WITNESS WHEREOF, I have hereunto set my hand and seal of said County Court, this 30th day of July _____, 2018

PAT FRANK

As Clerk of the Circuit and County Court

As Deputy Clerk
Paulette Wong

- 17-CF-013214-B   Page 3 of 3   henry

07/25/2018 06:03:50 PM Electronically Filed: Hillsborough County/13th Judicial Circuit.   Page 3

167 | P a g e

STATE OF FLORIDA

VS.

FILED

CASE NUMBER: 17-CF- 013214-B

DEFENDANT

JUL 16 2018

CLERK OF CIRCUIT COURT

FINGERPRINTS OF DEFENDANT

1. Right Thumb	2. Right Index	3. Right Middle	4. Right Ring	5. Right Little
6. Left Thumb	7. Left Index	8. Left Middle	9. Left Ring	10. Left Little

Fingerprints taken by: DEP. R.VADASZ 235199   BAILIFF

NAME   TITLE

I HEREBY CERTIFY that the above and foregoing are the fingerprints of the defendant,

████████████████████, and that they were placed thereon by the defendant in my

presence in open court this date.

DONE AND ORDERED in open court in Hillsborough County, Florida, this 16TH day of

JULY , 20 18 .

JUDGE

07/25/2018 06:03:50 PM Electronically Filed: Hillsborough County/13th Judicial Circuit.   Page 4

168 | P a g e

STATE OF FLORIDA

IN THE THIRTEENTH JUDICIAL
CIRCUIT COURT, IN AND FOR
HILLSBOROUGH COUNTY

-VS-

████████████████████

Defendant

CASE NUMBER 17-CF-013214-B
DIVISION C
DC NUMBER C20014

ORDER OF PROBATION

This cause coming before the Court to be heard, and you, the defendant, being now present before the court, and you having

☒ entered a plea of guilty to

Count 2   ARMED FALSE IMPRISONMENT

Count 3   AGGRAVATED ASSAULT WITH DEADLY WEAPON

SECTION 1: JUDGMENT OF GUILT

☒ The court hereby adjudges you to be guilty of the above offense(s).

Now, therefore, it is ordered and adjudged that the imposition of sentence is hereby withheld and that you be placed on Probation for a period of 24 months, each count, each count to run concurrent under the supervision of the Department of Corrections, subject to Florida law.

IT IS FURTHER ORDERED that you shall comply with the following standard conditions of supervision as provided by Florida law:

(1) You will report to the probation officer as directed.

(2) You will pay the State of Florida the amount of $40.00 per month, as well as 4% surcharge, toward the cost of your supervision in accordance with s. 948.09, F.S., unless otherwise exempted in compliance with Florida Statutes.

(3) You will remain in a specified place. You will not change your residence or employment or leave the county of your residence without first procuring the consent of your officer.

(4) You will not possess, carry or own any firearm. You will not possess, carry, or own any weapon without first procuring the consent of your officer.

(5) You will live without violating any law. A conviction in a court of law is not necessary for such a violation of law to constitute a violation of your probation, community control, or any other form of court ordered supervision.

(6) You will not associate with any person engaged in any criminal activity.

(7) You will not use intoxicants to excess or possess any drugs or narcotics unless prescribed by a physician. Nor will you visit places where intoxicants, drugs or other dangerous substances are unlawfully sold, dispensed or used.

(8) You will work diligently at a lawful occupation, advise your employer of your probation status, and support any dependents to the best of your ability, as directed by your officer.

(9) You will promptly and truthfully answer all inquiries directed to you by the court or the officer, and allow your officer to visit in your home, at your employment site or elsewhere, and you will comply with all instructions your officer may give you.

(10) You will pay restitution, court costs, and/or fees in accordance with special conditions imposed or in accordance with the attached orders.

07/25/2018 06:10:15 PM Electronically Filed: Hillsborough County/13th Judicial Circuit.   Page 1

169 | Page

(11) You will submit to random testing as directed by your officer or the professional staff of the treatment center where you are receiving treatment to determine the presence or use of alcohol or controlled substances.

(12) You will submit a DNA sample, as directed by your officer, for DNA analysis as prescribed in ss. 943.325 and 948.014, F.S.

(13) You will submit to the taking of a digitized photograph by the department. This photograph may be displayed on the department's website while you are on supervision, unless exempt from disclosure due to requirements of s. 119.07, F.S.

(14) You will report in person within 72 hours of your release from incarceration to the probation office in Hillsborough County, Florida, unless otherwise instructed by the court or department. (This condition applies only if section 3 on the previous page is checked.) Otherwise, you must report immediately to the probation office located at 1313 N Tampa St Suite 124 Tampa, FL 33602.

SPECIAL CONDITIONS

☒ 1. You will successfully complete 50 hours of community service at a rate of 5 hours per month, at a work site approved by your officer.
Additional instructions ordered: _____

☒ 2. You will have no contact (direct or indirect) with the victim or the victim's family during the period of supervision.

☒ 3. You must successfully complete Anger Management / Batterer's Intervention Program, and be responsible for the payment of any costs incurred while receiving said treatment, unless waived. If convicted of a Domestic Violence offense, as defined in s. 741.28, F.S., you must attend and successfully complete a batterer's intervention program, unless otherwise directed by the court.
Additional instructions ordered: _____

☒ 4. The defendant can work off court costs by doing additional community service hours at the rate of $10.00 per hour.

☒ 5. The defendant may travel out of the county for purposes of international flight.

☒ 6. The defendant may automatically terminate probation once proof of residency in India is provided to the courts.

☒ 7. The defendant is required to abide by all terms of the injunction.

Effective for offenders whose crime was committed on or after September 1, 2005, there is hereby imposed, in additional to any other provision in this section, mandatory electronic monitoring as a condition of supervision for those who:
- Are placed on supervision for a violation of chapter 794, s. 800.04(4), (5), or (6), s. 827.071, or s. 847.0145 and the unlawful sexual activity involved a victim 15 years of age or younger and the offender is 18 years of age or older; or
- Are designated as a sexual predator pursuant to s. 775.21; or
- Has previously been convicted of a violation of chapter 794, s. 800.04(4), (5), or (6), s. 827.071, or s. 847.0145 and the unlawful sexual activity involved a victim 15 years of age or younger and the offender is 18 years of age or older.

You are hereby placed on notice that should you violate your probation or community control, and the conditions set forth in s. 948.063(1) or (2) are satisfied, whether your probation or community control is revoked or not revoked, you shall be placed on electronic monitoring in accordance with F.S. 948.063.

Effective for offenders who are subject to supervision for a crime that was committed on or after May 26, 2010, and who has been convicted at any time of committing, or attempting, soliciting, or conspiring to commit, any of the criminal offenses listed in s. 943.0435(1)(h)1.a.(I), or a similar offense in another jurisdiction, against a victim who was under the age of 18 at the time of the offense; the following conditions are imposed in addition to all other conditions:
(a) A prohibition on visiting schools, child care facilities, parks, and playgrounds, without prior approval from the offender's supervising officer. The court may also designate additional locations to protect a victim. The prohibition ordered under this paragraph does not prohibit the offender from visiting a school, child care facility, park, or playground for the sole purpose of attending a religious service as defined in s. 775.0861 or picking up or dropping off the offender's children or grandchildren at a child care facility or school.

Page 2 of 3   Revised 07-01-2017

07/25/2018 06:10:15 PM Electronically Filed: Hillsborough County/13th Judicial Circuit.   Page 2

170 | Page

(b) A prohibition on distributing candy or other items to children on Halloween; wearing a Santa Claus costume, or other costume to appeal to children, on or preceding Christmas; wearing an Easter Bunny costume, or other costume to appeal to children, on or preceding Easter; entertaining at children's parties; or wearing a clown costume; without prior approval from the court.

Effective for offenders whose crime was committed on or after October 1, 2014, and who is placed on probation or community control for a violation of chapter 794, s. 800.04, s. 827.071, s. 847.0135(5), or s. 847.0145, in addition to all other conditions imposed, is prohibited from viewing, accessing, owning, or possessing any obscene, pornographic, or sexually stimulating visual or auditory material unless otherwise indicated in the treatment plan provided by a qualified practitioner in the sexual offender treatment program. Visual or auditory material includes, but is not limited to, telephone, electronic media, computer programs, and computer services.

YOU ARE HEREBY PLACED ON NOTICE that the court may at any time rescind or modify any of the conditions of your probation, or may extend the period of probation as authorized by law, or may discharge you from further supervision. If you violate any of the conditions of your probation, you may be arrested and the court may revoke your probation, adjudicate you guilty if adjudication of guilt was withheld, and impose any sentence that it might have imposed before placing you on probation or require you to serve the balance of the sentence.

IT IS FURTHER ORDERED that when you have been instructed as to the conditions of probation, you shall be released from custody if you are in custody, and if you are at liberty on bond, the sureties thereon shall stand discharged from liability. (This paragraph applies only if section 1 or section 2 is checked.)

IT IS FURTHER ORDERED that you pay:
Court Costs, Fees, and Fines, as imposed at sentencing, in the total amount of: $1122.88

Payments processed through the Department of Corrections will be assessed a 4% surcharge pursuant to s. 945.31, F.S.
Pursuant to s. 948.09, F.S., you will be assessed an amount of $2.00 per month for each month of supervision for the Training Trust Fund Surcharge.

☐ Court Costs/Fines Waived
☐ Court Costs/Fines in the amount of _____ converted to _____ community service hours
☐ Court Costs/Fines in the amount of _____ reduced to civil judgment.

SPECIFIC INSTRUCTIONS FOR PAYMENT: _____

IT IS FURTHER ORDERED that the clerk of this court file this order in the clerk's office and provide certified copies of same to the officer for use in compliance with the requirements of law.

     DONE AND ORDERED, on July 16, 2018

17-CF-013214-B 7/25/2018 6:10:13 PM
_____
Christopher C. Nash, Circuit Judge

I acknowledge receipt of a copy of this order and that the conditions have been explained to me and I agree to abide by them.

Date: _____

                                          _____
                                          Defendant

Instructed by: _____
                Supervising Officer

Page 3 of 3   Revised 07-01-2017

07/25/2018 06:10:15 PM Electronically Filed: Hillsborough County/13th Judicial Circuit.   Page 3

171 | P a g e

IN THE CIRCUIT COURT OF THE THIRTEENTH JUDICIAL CIRCUIT
EN LA CORTE DEL CIRCUITO DEL DECIMOTERCER CIRCUITO JUDICIAL
HILLSBOROUGH COUNTY, FLORIDA
ESTADO DE FLORIDA, EN Y PARA EL CONDADO DE HILLSBOROUGH
CIRCUIT CRIMINAL DIVISION
DIVISIÓN CRIMINAL DE LA CORTE DEL CIRCUITO

STATE OF FLORIDA
ESTADO DE FLORIDA

CASE NO: 17-CF - 13214
NO. DE CASO:

v.

█████████████████

DIVISION: C
DIVISIÓN:

FILED

JUL 1 0 2019

DEFENDANT'S DATE OF BIRTH _____

CIRCUIT COURT

UNIFORM PLEA, ACKNOWLEDGMENT AND WAIVER OF RIGHTS FORM
FORMULARIO UNIFORME DE DECLARACIÓN, RECONOCIMIENTO Y RENUNCIA DE DERECHOS

CHARGE(S) *CARGO(S)*	MANDATORY MINIMUM *PENA MÍNIMA OBLIGATORIA*	MAXIMUM PENALTY *PENA MÁXIMA*
Armed False Imprisonment	Ø	30 yrs
Agg Assualt w/ Deadly Weapon	Ø	15 yr
Domestic battery	Ø	364 days

For sections 1 and 2, check either "a" or "b." *Para la sección 1 y 2, marque "a" o "b."*

☑ 1(a)   I am pleading guilty, and acknowledge (my guilt)(I feel it is in my best interest to do so).
Me declaro culpable y reconozco (mi culpabilidad) (pienso que es lo que más me conviene hacer).

OR / *O*

☐ 1(b)   I am pleading nolo contendere, and acknowledge I feel it is in my best interest to do so.
Me declaro no me opongo, y reconozco que es lo que más me conviene hacer.

☐ 2(a)   I am pleading open to the Court and understand there is no agreement as to what sentence I will receive, and the Court can sentence me within its discretion.
Me declaro abiertamente ante el juez y entiendo que no existe ningún acuerdo relacionado con la sentencia que voy a recibir y que el juez puede sentenciarme a su discreción.

OR / *O*

☑ 2(b)   I am pleading pursuant to a plea agreement and the terms of that agreement are as follows:
Me declaro conforme a un acuerdo de declaración y los términos son los siguientes:

FSP _____Ø_____   Psychological evaluation and treatment if necessary _____Ø_____
Prisión Estatal de Florida   *Evaluación psicológica y tratamiento (de ser necesario)*

County Jail _____Ø_____   Probation _24 months_   Specified Residency _____Ø_____
Cárcel del Condado   *Probatoria*   *Residencia Especificada*

Community Control _____Ø_____
Reclusión Domiciliaria

Page 1 of 4 – *Pagina 1 de 4*

Community Control II _____ ∅
Reclusión domiciliaria II

Restitution to: ____ ∅ ____ in the amount of: ∅ to be paid monthly @ ∅
Restitución a: por la cantidad de: para pagarse mensualmente a

Drug/Alcohol Evaluation (within 30 days) and treatment if necessary (counseling/urine screens) ∅
Evaluación de Alcohol/ Drogas (dentro de 30 días) y tratamiento de ser necesario (con un consejero/ exámenes de orina)

Community Service ____ 50 ____   Driver's License Revocation ∅
Servicio Comunitario   Revocación de Licencia de Conducir
at ____ 5 ____ hours per month   GED ∅   IC = $411.88
a   horas por mes   GED

Other _Abide by all terms of Injunction proceedings; No contact w/_
Otros _V, Anger Mngmnt DV Classes" No objection to Early Termination_

3. I understand if probation or community control is part of the plea agreement the Court may impose any [handwritten: D. show proof] special conditions it believes it should, but such special conditions will be orally pronounced by the Court at the time of sentencing. I understand the Court may require me to pay up to $1 per month to "First Step of Hillsborough, Inc." [handwritten: of residing in] as a special condition of probation or community control pursuant to section 948.039, Florida Statutes. [handwritten: Tudor] *Entiendo que si la probatoria a la reclusión domiciliaria forman parte del acuerdo declaratorio, la corte podría imponer cualesquiera condiciones especiales que crea deba imponer, pero dichas condiciones especiales se pronunciarán oralmente por el juez en el momento de la sentencia. Entiendo que la corte me requerirá pagar hasta $ 1 por mes para "First Step of Hillsborough, Inc." como una condición especial de probatoria o reclusión domiciliaria de acuerdo a la sección 948.039, Estatutos de la Florida.* [handwritten: & return passport currently in custody of HCSO back to defendant]

4. I understand I have a right to plead not guilty and the right to be tried by a jury to determine whether I am guilty or not guilty. I understand I have the right to be represented by an attorney at the trial and if I cannot afford one, the Court will appoint an attorney to represent me. I understand I have the right to compel the attendance of witnesses on my behalf, the right to confront and cross examine all witnesses testifying against me, and the right not to testify or be compelled to incriminate myself. I understand that if I plead guilty or nolo contendere, there will be no trial and I waive all the rights that go along with a trial. [handwritten: Free to travel out of county for purpose of internet flights] *Entiendo que tengo el derecho de declararme no culpable y el derecho de ser juzgado por un jurado que decidiría si soy culpable o no. Entiendo que tengo el derecho de ser representado por un abogado para el juicio y que si no tengo los medios para contratar a uno, la corte nombrará un abogado para que me represente. Entiendo que tengo el derecho de obligar la comparecencia de testigos para que declaren a mi favor, el derecho de repreguntar a todos los testigos de cargo y el derecho de no testificar o de ser obligado a incriminarme. Entiendo que si me declaro culpable o no me opongo, no habrá juicio y renuncio a todos los derechos propios de un juicio.*

5. I understand if I plead guilty or nolo contendere without reserving the right to appeal, I am waiving my rights to appeal all matters relating to the judgment including the issue of my guilt or innocence, but not impairing my right to review by appropriate collateral attack. I understand if I wish to take an appeal and cannot afford an attorney to help me in my appeal, the Court will appoint an attorney to represent me for that purpose. *Entiendo que si me declaro culpable o no me opongo sin reservarme el derecho a apelar, estoy renunciando a mis derechos de apelación sobre todos los elementos relacionados con la sentencia incluyendo el asunto de mi culpabilidad o inocencia, pero sin perjudicar mi derecho a reexaminar por medio de una refutación indirecta apropiada. Entiendo que si deseo apelar y no puedo contratar un abogado para ayudarme con mi apelación, la Corte asignará un abogado para representarme para ese propósito.*

6. I understand there are facts the State could use to prove the charge(s) against me. *Entiendo que existen hechos que el Estado podría usar para probar el o los cargos en mi contra.*

7. I understand if I plead guilty or nolo contendere the judge may ask me questions about the charge(s) to which I have just pled and if I am untruthful, my answer(s) may later be used against me in a prosecution for perjury. *Entiendo que si me declaro culpable o no me opongo, el juez podría hacerme preguntas respecto al cargo al cual me acabo de declarar y que si falto a la verdad, mis respuestas podrían ser usadas en mi contra en un proceso por perjurio.*

8. I understand that if I am not a citizen of the United States and I plead guilty or nolo contendere and the Court accepts my plea, regardless of whether adjudication of guilt is withheld, my plea and the Court's acceptance of my plea may have the additional consequence of changing my immigration status, including DEPORTATION or REMOVAL from the United States. I understand that I should consult with my attorney if I need additional information concerning potential immigration consequences of my plea. I understand that if I have not discussed the potential immigration

Page 2 of 4 – Pagina 2 de 4

consequences with my attorney, the Court will, upon my request, allow a reasonable amount of time for me to consider the appropriateness of my plea in light of the advisement in this section.

Entiendo que si no soy un ciudadano de los Estados Unidos y me he declarado culpable o no me opongo y la corte acepta mi declaración, ya sea que se haya retenido o nó la adjudicación de culpabilidad, mi declaración y la aceptación por la corte puede tener la consecuencia adicional de cambiar mi situación de inmigración, incluyendo DEPORTACIÓN o remoción de los Estados Unidos, exclusión de la readmisión a los Estados Unidos, detención, negación de la naturalización, o inelegibilidad para la ciudadanía de acuerdo con las leyes de los Estados Unidos. Entiendo que debo consultar con mi abogado si necesito información adicional concerniente a las posibles consecuencias sobre inmigración de mi declaración. Entiendo que si no he discutido con mi abogado sobre las posibles consecuencias sobre inmigración, la corte concederá, a mi pedido, un período de tiempo razonable para considerar apropiadamente mi declaración teniendo en cuenta la información contenida en esta sección.

9. I understand this plea could result in my driver's license being suspended or revoked if the charge(s) to which I am pleading is one where automatic, mandatory suspension or revocation is required by law.
    Entiendo que esta declaración podría resultar en la suspensión o revocación de mi licencia de conducir si el cargo al cual me estoy declarando es un delito donde se requiere la suspensión o revocación automática obligatoria por la ley.

10. I understand if I plead guilty or nolo contendere to a sexually violent offense or a sexually motivated offense, or if I have been previously convicted of such an offense, the plea may subject me to involuntary civil commitment as a sexually violent predator upon completion of any prison sentence or jail sentence on this or any other case.
    Entiendo que si me declaro culpable o no me opongo a un delito sexual con violencia, o a un delito motivado sexualmente, o si previamente he sido condenado por dicho delito, esta declaración me sujetaria a un confinamiento involuntario civil como un depredador sexual violento una vez que haya concluido cualquier sentencia de prisión o cárcel en este o cualquier otro caso.

11. I understand if I plead guilty or nolo contendere to a qualifying sexual offense, or if I have been previously convicted of such an offense or if I have been designated a sexual predator, I will be subject to mandatory electronic monitoring pursuant to section 948.30(3), Florida Statutes.
    Entiendo que si me declaro culpable o no me opongo a un delito de categoría sexual, o si he sido condenado previamente por dicho delito, o se me ha catalogado como depredador sexual, estaré sujeto a un control electrónico obligatorio conforme a la sección 948.30 (3), de los Estatutos de la Florida.

12. I understand my pleading guilty or nolo contendere will result in the Court imposing MANDATORY statutory costs. I also understand my plea may result in the Court imposing certain other costs and attorney's fees and I do not object to the imposition or amount of such costs and fees and I waive my right to a hearing on the imposition and amount of such costs and fees. I have had an opportunity to review with my attorney the mandatory costs (including fines and surcharges) that MUST be assessed against me and discretionary costs (including fines and surcharges) that MAY be assessed against me. I understand if I fail to pay the imposed costs and fees my driver's license may be suspended.
    Entiendo que si me declaro culpable o no me opongo traerá como resultado que el juez imponga las costas OBLIGATORIAS de ley. Asimismo, entiendo que mi declaración podría hacer que el juez imponga ciertos costos y honorarios del abogado. No me opongo a la imposición o la cantidad de costos y honorarios y renuncio a mi derecho a una audiencia respecto a la imposición y la cantidad de costos y honorarios. He tenido la oportunidad de revisar con mi abogado la lista adjunta de costas obligatorias (multas y recargos) que me TIENEN que ser impuestos y costas opcionales (incluyendo multas y recargos) que me puedan imponer. Entiendo que si no pago los costos y honorarios impuestos, mi licencia de conducir podría ser suspendida.

13. I understand a conviction for an offense to which I am pleading guilty or nolo contendere may serve to enhance the sentence for any offense for which I may be convicted of in the future.
    Entiendo que una condena por un delito al cual me estoy declarando culpable o no me opongo podría servir para aumentar la sentencia por cualquier delito por el cual se me podría condenar en el futuro.

14. I am not under the influence of drugs, an alcoholic beverage or medication, but I am taking this medication:

    _____

    No me encuentro bajo los efectos de drogas ni bebidas alcohólicas, aunque estoy tomando este medicamento:

15. I do not have any mental illness that would keep me from understanding this plea and its consequences.
    No padezco de ninguna enfermedad mental que podría impedirme entender esta declaración y sus consecuencias.

16. I certify that no one has threatened or coerced me in any way in order to get me to enter this plea, and I am pleading freely and voluntarily. Other than the terms of the plea negotiation as set forth above (if applicable), no one has promised me anything upon which I have relied in order to influence me to enter this plea.
    Certifico que nadie me ha amenazado ni coaccionado de ninguna manera para que yo asiente esta declaración y me declaro libre y voluntariamente. Aparte del acuerdo declaratorio, como se estipula en el párrafo antes mencionado (si es aplicable), nadie me ha prometido nada en lo cual yo me he basado con el motivo de influenciarme para que yo asiente esta declaración.

17. I certify that I have discussed the charges with my attorney including the maximum possible and mandatory minimum (if any) penalties and possible defenses and am fully satisfied with the representation of my attorney. I understand by entering this plea there is no guarantee what gain time, if any, the Department of Corrections or any county jail may award me.

Certifico que he revisado los cargos con mi abogado, incluso las penas máximas posibles y mínimas obligatorias (si las hubiera) y defensas posibles y estoy completamente satisfecho con la representación de mi abogado. Entiendo que al asentar esta declaración no hay garantía del tiempo ganado, de haberlo, que el Departamento de Corrección o cualquier cárcel del condado podrán conceder me.

18. I have reviewed my criminal punishment code scoresheet and it is correct.

He revisado mi hoja de puntuación y está correcta.

19. I have reviewed the standard terms of supervision and I understand I must follow them as well as any special conditions the Court thinks are appropriate.

He revisado las condiciones generales de supervisión y entiendo que debo cumplirlas, así como cualesquiera otras condiciones que la corte considere apropiadas.

20. I understand no one, including my attorney, can accurately predict the actual time I will serve on a sentence and I may be required to serve the entire sentence.

Entiendo que nadie, incluyendo mi abogado, puede predecir con certeza el tiempo real que cumpliré por una sentencia y que podría requerirse que cumpla la sentencia completa.

21. I certify that there are not any other witnesses I want my attorney to investigate or call, nor is there any other type of discovery or investigation I want my attorney to do, or any other motions I want my attorney to file and set for hearing prior to entering this plea.

Certifico que no hay otros testigos que quiero que mi abogado investigue o llame, ni tampoco existe otro tipo de prueba o investigación que quiero que mi abogado haga, o algunas otras peticiones que quiero que mi abogado presente y fije para una audiencia antes de asentar esta declaración.

22. I certify that no one, including my attorney, has made any promises concerning the jail credit or prison credit I am to receive other than the fact that I am going to receive credit for every day I actually spent incarcerated on this case, which is _____ days.

Certifico que nadie, incluyendo mi abogado (a) me ha hecho ninguna promesa respecto al tiempo que será acreditado de la cárcel o prisión además del hecho que voy a recibir crédito por cada día que realmente pasé encarcelado en este caso, cual son _____ días.

_____	7/16/2018
Defendant / *Acusado*	Date / *Fecha*

STATEMENT OF ATTORNEY
DECLARACIÓN DEL LICENCIADO

I have reviewed this plea form and the mandatory costs with my client, the Defendant in this case, and it is my belief the Defendant fully understands its contents.

Yo he revisado este convenio declaratorio y los costos obligatorios con mi cliente, el Acusado en este caso, y en mi opinión el Acusado entiende completamente el contenido del convenio.

_____	7/16/2018
Defense Attorney's Signature / *Licenciado*	Date / *Fecha*

MAS VASIGH
Defense Attorney's Name - Printed / *Licenciado*

(Revised 11/2/15)

Case Information

Uniform Case Number: 292017CF013214000CHC
STATE OF FLORIDA VS KALSI, BHUPINDER

Icon Keys Summary Parties Events\Documents Charges Hearings Financial Bonds Disposition
File Location

Case Information

Case Number \ Citation

Case Number: 17-CF-013214-C

Citation Number:

Booking Numbers

Booking Numbers
2017-32346
17032346

Case Information

Case Category Description: Criminal

Case Type Description: FELONY

Case Sub Type Description:

Case Status: CLOSED

Case Filed On: 2017-09-22

Financial Information

Balance Due: $1,118.63

Due Date: 07/23/2020

Judge Assignment

Judge: Nash, C., Christopher

Division: Division C

Judge Assignment History ▾

Return to Search Results (/html/case/searchResults.html)

Case Information

Uniform Case Number: 292017CF013214000CHC

STATE OF FLORIDA VS ███████████

Icon Keys   Summary   Parties   Events/Documents   Charges   Hearings   Financial   Bonds   Disposition

File Location

Parties on the Case

Show 25 entries   Column visibility   Excel   CSV   Search:

Party Type	Name	Party Demographics	Attorney Name	Attorney Contact
Plaintiff	STATE OF FLORIDA 11 TAMPA, FL 33602		BROWN , CHRISTINE SHIVER	Telephone: 813-272-5400 419 N PIERCE ST TAMPA, FL 33602
Defendant	███████████	Date of Birth: 11/02/1955 Height (inches): 63 Weight: 135 Race: White Gender: Female	VASIGH , MAJID	Telephone: 813-800-1111 101 N 12TH ST UNIT 104 TAMPA, FL 33602

Showing 1 to 2 of 2 entries   Previous 1 Next

Return to Search Results (/html/case/searchResults.html)

Case Information

Icon Keys   Summary   Parties   Events/Documents   Charges   Hearings   Financial   Bonds   Disposition

File Location

Charges

Show [25] entries   Column visibility Excel CSV   Search: [   ]

Select	Charge Number	Offense Description	Offense Date	Degree Description	Disposition
	4	784031-BATT1102 (MF) BATTERY DOMESTIC VIOLENCE	09/01/2017	FIRST DEGREE MISDEMEANOR	NT - ADJUDICATION WITHHELD

Arrest Information

Arrest Date: 09/02/2017

Plea Information

| Date: 07/16/2018 | Plea: GUILTY |
| Date: 09/19/2017 | Plea: WRITTEN PLEA OF NOT GUILTY |

Prosecutor Information

| Date: 09/22/2017 | Description: FILED |

CriminalDispo Information

| Date: 07/16/2018 | Description: NT - ADJUDICATION WITHHELD | Judge: Nash, Christopher C. |

Sentence Information

| Date: 07/16/2018 | Description: NT - ADJUDICATION WITHHELD | Code: NTAW |

Select	Charge Number	Offense Description	Offense Date	Degree Description	Disposition
	2	392052-CHAB2054 (FT) FAILURE TO REPORT CHILD ABUSE	09/01/2017	THIRD DEGREE FELONY	NT - NO INFORMATION FILED

Arrest Information

Arrest Date: 09/02/2017

Prosecutor Information

| Date: 09/22/2017 | Description: NO INFORMATION FILED |

CriminalDispo Information

| Date: 09/22/2017 | Description: NT - NO INFORMATION FILED | Judge: Nash, Christopher C. |

Select	Charge Number	Offense Description	Offense Date	Degree Description	Disposition
	1	787021-KIDN5003 (FT) FALSE IMPRISONMENT	09/01/2017	THIRD DEGREE FELONY	NT - ADJUDICATION WITHHELD

Plea Information

| Date: 07/16/2018 | Plea: GUILTY |
| Date: 09/19/2017 | Plea: WRITTEN PLEA OF NOT GUILTY |

Prosecutor Information

| Date: 09/22/2017 | Description: FILED |

CriminalDispo Information

| Date: 07/16/2018 | Description: NT - ADJUDICATION WITHHELD | Judge: Nash, Christopher C. |

Sentence Information

| Date: 07/16/2018 | Description: NT - ADJUDICATION WITHHELD | Code: NTAW |

Showing 1 to 3 of 3 entries   Previous 1 Next

⇖ Return to Search Results (/html/case/searchResults.html)

Case Information

Uniform Case Number: 292017CF013214000CHC

STATE OF FLORIDA VS █████████

Icon Keys   Summary   Parties   Events\Documents   Charges   Hearings   Financial   Bonds   Disposition

File Location

Disposition (Charge Sentence Information)

Show [25] entries   Column visibility   Excel   CSV   Search: [   ]

Document Index	Charge Number	Offense Date	Charge Offense Description	Degree Description	Citation Number
	1	09/01/2017	787021-KIDN5003 (FT) FALSE IMPRISONMENT	THIRD DEGREE FELONY	

Sentence Information

Plea	07/16/2018	GUILTY		
Disposition	07/16/2018	NT - ADJUDICATION WITHHELD		
Sentence	07/16/2018	CRIMINAL		
		Community Service (Hours: 50. Comment: @ 5 MNTH)		
		State Probation (24 Mo)		
		Provisions		

  - ATTEND AND COMPLETE ANGER MANAGEMENT,
  - NO CONTACT WITH VICTIM OR PROPERTY,
  - OTHER COURT RESTRICTIONS,

  Comment: MAY TRAVEL OUT OF COUNTY (INTE

Prosecutor: BROWN CHRISTINE SHIVER
Defense: VASIGH MAJID

| | 4 | 09/01/2017 | 784031-BATT1102 (MF) BATTERY DOMESTIC VIOLENCE | FIRST DEGREE MISDEMEANOR | |

Sentence Information

Plea	07/16/2018	GUILTY		
Disposition	07/16/2018	NT - ADJUDICATION WITHHELD		
Sentence	07/16/2018	CRIMINAL		
		Provisions		

  - SENTENCED TO TIME SERVED - LENGTH UNSPECIFIED.

Showing 1 to 2 of 2 entries   Previous   1   Next

Return to Search Results (/html/case/searchResults.html)

IN THE CIRCUIT COURT IN AND FOR HILLSBOROUGH COUNTY, STATE OF FLORIDA

CASE NO. 17-CF-013214-C

STATE OF FLORIDA

VS

Division   C

Offense Date: 9/1/2017

Defense Case Number: 17-CF-013214-C
Address: VASIGH , MAJID
101 N 12TH ST UNIT 104
TAMPA, FL 33602

JUDGMENT AND SENTENCE

The above named Defendant is now before the Court:

State: BROWN , CHRISTINE SHIVER

Cnt	Charge Description	Lev Deg	Plea	Disp Date	Disposition
1	787021 FALSE IMPRISONMENT	F3	GUILTY	07/16/18	NT - ADJUDICATION WITHHELD
4	784031 BATTERY DOMESTIC VIOLENCE	M1	GUILTY	07/16/18	NT - ADJUDICATION WITHHELD

Ct.1 SENTENCE: CRIMINAL

Community Service (Hours: 50, Comment: AT 5/ MONTH)
State Probation (24 Months)
Provisions
- MAY TRAVEL OUT OF COUNTRY (INTERNATIONAL FLIGHT)
- AUTOMATIC TERMINATION ONCE PROOF OF RESIDENCY OF INDIA TO COURTS
- NO CONTACT WITH VICTIM
- ABIDE BY ALL TERMS OF INJUNCTIONS
- ATTEND AND COMPLETE ANGER MANAGEMENT
- COMPLETE DOMESTIC VIOLENCE COURSE

Ct.4 SENTENCE: CRIMINAL

Provisions
- SENTENCED TO TIME SERVED - LENGTH UNSPECIFIED

Fees :
- $362.63 CR-8884 INVESTIGATION COST - HCSO 938.27 FS AUTH: 938.27
- $100.00 CR-2399 INVESTIGATIVE COSTS SAO REVENUE FS 938.27(8) FS AUTH: 938.27(8)
- $100.00 CR-8366 CFF CRIMES AGAINST MINORS -DOR-DCF GRANTS CHILD ADV FS AUTH: 938.10(2)
- $50.00 CR-8450 DOR-DCF GRNT & DON -GRDN ADLITEM 938.10 FS AUTH: 938.10(2)
- $1.00 CR-R235 CRIMES AGAINST MINORS FS AUTH: 938.10
- $50.00 CR-8081 CRIME PREVENTION FS AUTH: 775.083(2)
- $65.00 CR-8097 ADDITIONAL COSTS (BOCC) - PROGRAMS FS AUTH: 939.185(1)(a
- $49.00 CR-8311 FCCA CRIMES COMPENSATION TRUST FUND FS AUTH: 938.03
- $17.00 CR-A362 CRIME STOPPERS TRUST FUND FS AUTH: 938.06

KALSI, BHUPINDER - 17-CF-013214-C   Page 1 of 3   whitney.scott

07/25/2018 04:48:37 PM Electronically Filed: Hillsborough County/13th Judicial Circuit.   Page 1

181 | P a g e

- **$200.00** CR-R252 ADDITIONAL COURT COST - CLERK - CIR CRIM **FS AUTH:** 938.05(1)(a)
- **$25.00** **FS AUTH:** 938.05(1)(a)
- **$1.00** CR-R617 CRIMES COMPENSATION FEE 938.03 **FS AUTH:** 938.03
- **$3.00** CR-RA20 CRIME STOPPERS TRUST FUND FEE **FS AUTH:** 938.06
- **$49.00** CR-2780 PD APP FEE - INDIGENT CRIMINAL TRUST FUND **FS AUTH:** 27.52(1)(b)
- **$0.80** CR-3991 PD APP FEE- INDIGENT CRIM TR FEE 2%- CLERKS OF CT TF **FS AUTH:** 27.52(1)(b)
- **$0.20** CR-4005 PD APP ADDL FEE - CLERK OF COURT T.F./DOR/GEN FUND **FS AUTH:** 27.52(1)(b)
- **$6.00** CR-R229 FELONY PREP FEE FOR CRIMINAL JUDGMENT - 28.24(8) **FS AUTH:** FS 28.24(8)
- **$1.00** CR-R229D FELONY PREP FEE FOR CRIMINAL JUDGMENT - 28.24(8) **FS AUTH:** FS 28.24(8)
- **$6.00** CR-R228 FELONY PREP FEE FOR CRIM SATISFACTION - 28.24(8) **FS AUTH:** FS 28.24(8)
- **$1.00** CR-R228D FELONY PREP FEE FOR CRIM SATISFACTION - 28.24(8) **FS AUTH:** FS 28.24(8)
- **$9.00** CR-1100J RECORDING FEE FOR CRIMINAL JUDGMENT 28.24(12)(a)(b) **FS AUTH:** FS 28.24(12)(a)(b)
- **$10.00** CR-1100S RECORDING FEE FOR CRIM SATISFACTION 28.24(12)(a)(b) **FS AUTH:** FS 28.24(12)(a)(b)

Fee Total : $1106.63

**FEE TOTALS INCLUDE ALL OUTSTANDING FEES OWED ON THE CASE AT THE TIME OF THIS JUDGMENT, EXCEPT FOR COST OF SUPERVISION AND THE PROBATION SERVICE FEE. SEE ORDER OF PROBATION FOR DETAILS. THE ABOVE FEES INCLUDE THE ASSESSMENT OF JUDGMENT AND SATISFACTION FEES, AS APPLICABLE.

If you are a "qualifying offender" under section 943.325, Florida Statutes, you are required to submit a DNA sample in a manner consistent with Florida law.

The defendant SHALL pay all mandatory and discretionary costs, fines, fees, penalties, & surcharges applicable to this matter, per Florida Statutes and Hillsborough County Ordinances; as stated above.

Probation: If probation is ordered, the conditions of Probation will be provided to you on a separate written order prepared by the HCSO Probation Services or Florida Department of Corrections.

Jail: At the time of sentencing, if jail is ordered, the defendant may be taken into custody by the Sheriff of Hillsborough County, Florida or given a date to report for incarceration in the County Jail under supervision of the Board of Criminal Justice of Hillsborough County.

Judgment For Money Ordered To Be Paid: It is the order of the Court that a judgment is entered, on behalf of the Hillsborough County Clerk of Circuit and County Courts, on behalf of Hillsborough County, and on behalf of the State of Florida, on the money that is ordered to be paid as a result of the JUDGMENT AND SENTENCE to the charge(s) in this matter, **FOR WHICH LET EXECUTION ISSUE.**

KALSI, BHUPINDER - 17-CF-013214-C   Page 2 of 3   whitney.scott

07/25/2018 04:48:37 PM Electronically Filed: Hillsborough County/13th Judicial Circuit.   Page 2

182 | P a g e

Current Address of Lien Holder(s): State of Florida – Payable to the: Clerk of the Circuit Court, PO Box 3360 – Tampa, FL 33601

DONE AND ORDERED in open court in Tampa, Hillsborough County, Florida on, 7/16/2018.

17-CF-013214-C 7/25/2018 4:48:31 P

17-CF-013214-C 7/25/2018 4:48:31 PM

Christopher C. Nash, PRESIDING JUDGE

Florida Statute 28.246(6), authorizes unpaid balances to be referred to a collection agent. This will add additional penalties of up to 40% of the amount owed. Pursuant to Florida Statute 322.245(5)(a), the Clerk of Court may notify the Department of Highway Safety Motor Vehicles (DHSMV) of your failure to pay financial obligations related to criminal offenses which will result in the suspension of your driver's license. To avoid additional costs, please remit payment in full immediately.

<u>CERTIFICATE OF SERVICE</u>

I, PAT FRANK, Clerk of the Circuit and County Court of the County of Hillsborough, State of Florida, having by law the custody of the seal and all records, books, documents and papers of or appertaining to the County Court, do hereby certify that a true and correct copy of this document has been hand delivered, mailed or served electronically to the Office of the State Attorney, the Defense Attorney, and/or Defendant, if appearing Pro Se.

IN WITNESS WHEREOF, I have hereunto set my hand and seal of said County Court, this 30th day of
July , 2018

PAT FRANK

As Clerk of the Circuit and County Court

As Deputy Clerk
Paulette Wong

KALSI, BHUPINDER - 17-CF-013214-C   Page 3 of 3   whitney.scott

07/25/2018 04:48:37 PM Electronically Filed: Hillsborough County/13th Judicial Circuit.   Page 3

183 | P a g e

STATE OF FLORIDA

VS.

CASE NUMBER: 17-CF-013214-C

█████████████████████

DEFENDANT

FILED

JUL 16 2018

CLERK OF CIRCUIT COURT

FINGERPRINTS OF DEFENDANT

1. Right Thumb	2. Right Index	3. Right Middle	4. Right Ring	5. Right Little

6. Left Thumb	7. Left Index	8. Left Middle	9. Left Ring	10. Left Little

Fingerprints taken by: DEP. R. VADASZ 235199   BAILIFF

NAME   TITLE

I HEREBY CERTIFY that the above and foregoing are the fingerprints of the defendant, █████████████████████ , and that they were placed thereon by the defendant in my presence in open court this date.

DONE AND ORDERED in open court in Hillsborough County, Florida, this 16TH day of JULY , 20 18 .

_____
JUDGE

07/25/2018 04:48:37 PM Electronically Filed: Hillsborough County/13th Judicial Circuit.   Page 4

184 | P a g e

STATE OF FLORIDA

-VS-

████████████████

Defendant

IN THE THIRTEENTH JUDICIAL
CIRCUIT COURT, IN AND FOR
HILLSBOROUGH COUNTY

CASE NUMBER   17-CF-013214-C
DIVISION C
DC NUMBER   A00014

ORDER OF PROBATION

This cause coming before the Court to be heard, and you, the defendant, being now present before the court, and you having

☒   entered a plea of guilty to

Count 1   FALSE IMPRISONMENT

SECTION 2: ORDER WITHHOLDING ADJUDICATION

☒   Now, therefore, it is ordered and adjudged that the adjudication of guilt is hereby withheld and that you be placed on Probation for a period of 24 months under the supervision of the Department of Corrections, subject to Florida law.

IT IS FURTHER ORDERED that you shall comply with the following standard conditions of supervision as provided by Florida law:

(1) You will report to the probation officer as directed.

(2) You will pay the State of Florida the amount of $40.00 per month, as well as 4% surcharge, toward the cost of your supervision in accordance with s. 948.09, F.S., unless otherwise exempted in compliance with Florida Statutes.

(3) You will remain in a specified place. You will not change your residence or employment or leave the county of your residence without first procuring the consent of your officer.

(4) You will not possess, carry or own any firearm. You will not possess, carry, or own any weapon without first procuring the consent of your officer.

(5) You will live without violating any law. A conviction in a court of law is not necessary for such a violation of law to constitute a violation of your probation, community control, or any other form of court ordered supervision.

(6) You will not associate with any person engaged in any criminal activity.

(7) You will not use intoxicants to excess or possess any drugs or narcotics unless prescribed by a physician. Nor will you visit places where intoxicants, drugs or other dangerous substances are unlawfully sold, dispensed or used.

(8) You will work diligently at a lawful occupation, advise your employer of your probation status, and support any dependents to the best of your ability, as directed by your officer.

(9) You will promptly and truthfully answer all inquiries directed to you by the court or the officer, and allow your officer to visit in your home, at your employment site or elsewhere, and you will comply with all instructions your officer may give you.

(10) You will pay restitution, court costs, and/or fees in accordance with special conditions imposed or in accordance with the attached orders.

(11) You will submit to random testing as directed by your officer or the professional staff of the treatment center where you are receiving treatment to determine the presence or use of alcohol or controlled substances.

07/25/2018 06:11:54 PM Electronically Filed: Hillsborough County/13th Judicial Circuit.   Page 1

185 | Page

(12) You will submit a DNA sample, as directed by your officer, for DNA analysis as prescribed in ss. 943.325 and 948.014, F.S.

(13) You will submit to the taking of a digitized photograph by the department. This photograph may be displayed on the department's website while you are on supervision, unless exempt from disclosure due to requirements of s. 119.07, F.S.

(14) You will report in person within 72 hours of your release from incarceration to the probation office in Hillsborough County, Florida, unless otherwise instructed by the court or department. (This condition applies only if section 3 on the previous page is checked.) Otherwise, you must report immediately to the probation office located at 1313 N Tampa St Suite 124 Tampa, FL 33602.

SPECIAL CONDITIONS

☒   1. You will successfully complete 50 hours of community service at a rate of 5 hours per month, at a work site approved by your officer.
Additional instructions ordered: _____

☒   2. You will have no contact (direct or indirect) with the victim or the victim's family during the period of supervision.

☒   3. You must successfully complete Anger Management / Batterer's Intervention Program, and be responsible for the payment of any costs incurred while receiving said treatment, unless waived. If convicted of a Domestic Violence offense, as defined in s. 741.28, F.S., you must attend and successfully complete a batterer's intervention program, unless otherwise directed by the court.
Additional instructions ordered: _____

☒   4. The defendant can work off court costs by doing additional community service hours at the rate of $10.00 per hour.

☒   5. The defendant may travel out of the county for purposes of international flight.

☒   6. The defendant may automatically terminate probation once proof of residency in India is provided to the courts.

☒   7. The defendant is required to abide by all terms of the injunction.

Effective for offenders whose crime was committed on or after September 1, 2005, there is hereby imposed, in additional to any other provision in this section, mandatory electronic monitoring as a condition of supervision for those who:
  • Are placed on supervision for a violation of chapter 794, s. 800.04(4), (5), or (6), s. 827.071, or s. 847.0145 and the unlawful sexual activity involved a victim 15 years of age or younger and the offender is 18 years of age or older; or
  • Are designated as a sexual predator pursuant to s. 775.21; or
  • Has previously been convicted of a violation of chapter 794, s. 800.04(4), (5), or (6), s. 827.071, or s. 847.0145 and the unlawful sexual activity involved a victim 15 years of age or younger and the offender is 18 years of age or older.

You are hereby placed on notice that should you violate your probation or community control, and the conditions set forth in s. 948.063(1) or (2) are satisfied, whether your probation or community control is revoked or not revoked, you shall be placed on electronic monitoring in accordance with F.S. 948.063.

Effective for offenders who are subject to supervision for a crime that was committed on or after May 26, 2010, and who has been convicted at any time of committing, or attempting, soliciting, or conspiring to commit, any of the criminal offenses listed in s. 943.0435(1)(h)1.a.(I), or a similar offense in another jurisdiction, against a victim who was under the age of 18 at the time of the offense; the following conditions are imposed in addition to all other conditions:

(a) A prohibition on visiting schools, child care facilities, parks, and playgrounds, without prior approval from the offender's supervising officer. The court may also designate additional locations to protect a victim. The prohibition ordered under this paragraph does not prohibit the offender from visiting a school, child care facility, park, or playground for the sole purpose of attending a religious service as defined in s. 775.0861 or picking up or dropping off the offender's children or grandchildren at a child care facility or school.

(b) A prohibition on distributing candy or other items to children on Halloween; wearing a Santa Claus costume, or other costume to appeal to children, on or preceding Christmas; wearing an Easter Bunny costume, or other costume to appeal to children, on or preceding Easter; entertaining at children's parties; or wearing a clown costume; without prior approval from the court.

Page 2 of 3   Revised 07-01-2017

07/25/2018 06:11:54 PM Electronically Filed: Hillsborough County/13th Judicial Circuit.   Page 2

186 | P a g e

Effective for offenders whose crime was committed on or after October 1, 2014, and who is placed on probation or community control for a violation of chapter 794, s. 800.04, s. 827.071, s. 847.0135(5), or s. 847.0145, in addition to all other conditions imposed, is prohibited from viewing, accessing, owning, or possessing any obscene, pornographic, or sexually stimulating visual or auditory material unless otherwise indicated in the treatment plan provided by a qualified practitioner in the sexual offender treatment program. Visual or auditory material includes, but is not limited to, telephone, electronic media, computer programs, and computer services.

YOU ARE HEREBY PLACED ON NOTICE that the court may at any time rescind or modify any of the conditions of your probation, or may extend the period of probation as authorized by law, or may discharge you from further supervision. If you violate any of the conditions of your probation, you may be arrested and the court may revoke your probation, adjudicate you guilty if adjudication of guilt was withheld, and impose any sentence that it might have imposed before placing you on probation or require you to serve the balance of the sentence.

IT IS FURTHER ORDERED that when you have been instructed as to the conditions of probation, you shall be released from custody if you are in custody, and if you are at liberty on bond, the sureties thereon shall stand discharged from liability. (This paragraph applies only if section 1 or section 2 is checked.)

IT IS FURTHER ORDERED that you pay:
Court Costs, Fees, and Fines, as imposed at sentencing, in the total amount of: $1118.63

Payments processed through the Department of Corrections will be assessed a 4% surcharge pursuant to s. 945.31, F.S.
Pursuant to s. 948.09, F.S., you will be assessed an amount of $2.00 per month for each month of supervision for the Training Trust Fund Surcharge.

☐ Court Costs/Fines Waived
☐ Court Costs/Fines in the amount of _____ converted to _____ community service hours
☐ Court Costs/Fines in the amount of _____ reduced to civil judgment.

SPECIFIC INSTRUCTIONS FOR PAYMENT: _____

IT IS FURTHER ORDERED that the clerk of this court file this order in the clerk's office and provide certified copies of same to the officer for use in compliance with the requirements of law.

    DONE AND ORDERED, on July 16, 2018

17-CF-013214-C 7/25/2018 6:11:51 P
17-CF-013214-C 7/25/2018 6:11:51 PM

Christopher C. Nash, Circuit Judge

    I acknowledge receipt of a copy of this order and that the conditions have been explained to me and I agree to abide by them.

Date: _____

Instructed by: _____
      Supervising Officer

Defendant _____

IN THE CIRCUIT COURT OF THE THIRTEENTH JUDICIAL CIRCUIT
EN LA CORTE DEL CIRCUITO DEL DECIMOTERCER CIRCUITO JUDICIAL
HILLSBOROUGH COUNTY, FLORIDA
ESTADO DE FLORIDA, EN Y PARA EL CONDADO DE HILLSBOROUGH
CIRCUIT CRIMINAL DIVISION
DIVISIÓN CRIMINAL DE LA CORTE DEL CIRCUITO

STATE OF FLORIDA
ESTADO DE FLORIDA

CASE NO: Π-CF-13214
NO. DE CASO:

v.

DIVISION: C
DIVISIÓN:

FILED

JUL 16 2018

DEFENDANT'S DATE OF BIRTH_____

CLERK OF CIRCUIT COURT

UNIFORM PLEA, ACKNOWLEDGMENT AND WAIVER OF RIGHTS FORM
FORMULARIO UNIFORME DE DECLARACIÓN, RECONOCIMIENTO Y RENUNCIA DE DERECHOS

CHARGE(S) *CARGO(S)*	MANDATORY MINIMUM *PENA MÍNIMA OBLIGATORIA*	MAXIMUM PENALTY *PENA MÁXIMA*
~~Count 2~~ MW ~~Armed~~ False Imprisonment	0	~~5~~ 5 years
~~Aggg Assault~~ w/ ~~Deadly Weapon~~		~~5~~
Count 4 Domestic Battery	0	364 days

For sections 1 and 2, check either "a" or "b." *Para la sección 1 y 2, marque "a" o "b."*

☑ 1(a) I am pleading guilty, and acknowledge (my guilt)(I feel it is in my best interest to do so).
Me declaro culpable y reconozco (mi culpabilidad) (pienso que es lo que más me conviene hacer).

OR / *O*

☐ 1(b) I am pleading nolo contendere, and acknowledge I feel it is in my best interest to do so.
Me declaro no me opongo, y reconozco que es lo que más me conviene hacer.

☐ 2(a) I am pleading open to the Court and understand there is no agreement as to what sentence I will receive, and the Court can sentence me within its discretion.
Me declaro abiertamente ante el juez y entiendo que no existe ningún acuerdo relacionado con la sentencia que voy a recibir y que el juez puede sentenciarme a su discreción.

OR / *O*

☑ 2(b) I am pleading pursuant to a plea agreement and the terms of that agreement are as follows:
Me declaro conforme a un acuerdo de declaración y los términos son los siguientes:

FSP ___0___   Psychological evaluation and treatment if necessary ___0___
Prisión Estatal de Florida   *Evaluación psicológica y tratamiento (de ser necesario)*

County Jail ___0___   Probation 24 month Specified Residency ___0___
Cárcel del Condado   *Probatoria*   *Residencia Especificada*

Community Control ___0___
Reclusión Domiciliaria

Page 1 of 4 — *Página 1 de 4*

Community Control II _____ Ø
Reclusión domiciliaria II

Restitution to: _____ Ø _____ in the amount of: ___ Ø ___ to be paid monthly @ ___ Ø ___
Restitución a: *por la cantidad de:*   *para pagarse mensualmente a*

Drug/Alcohol Evaluation (within 30 days) and treatment if necessary (counseling/urine screens) Ø
Evaluación de Alcohol/ Drogas (dentro de 30 días) y tratamiento de ser necesario (con un consejero/ exámenes de orina)

Community Service ___ 50 ___   Driver's License Revocation Ø
Servicio Comunitario   *Revocación de Licencia de Conducir*
at __ 5 __ hours per month   GED Ø   *IC = $362.63*
a   *horas por mes*   GED

Other *Abide by all terms of Injunction proceedings" No. contact w/*
Otros
Angeso Margaret DU Classel, No objection to Early Termination once

3.   I understand if probation or community control is part of the plea agreement the Court may impose any *show proof*
special conditions it believes it should, but such special conditions will be orally pronounced by the Court at the time *of*
of sentencing. I understand the Court may require me to pay up to $1 per month to "First Step of Hillsborough, Inc." *residing in India*
as a special condition of probation or community control pursuant to section 948.039, Florida Statutes. *& return*
Entiendo que si la probatoria o la reclusión domiciliaria forman parte del acuerdo declaratorio, la corte podría imponer *passport*
cualesquiera condiciones especiales que crea deba imponer, pero dichas condiciones especiales se pronunciarán oralmente por el *currently*
juez en el momento de la sentencia. Entiendo que la corte me requerirá pagar hasta $1 por mes para "First Step of Hillsborough, *in control*
Inc." como una condición especial de probatoria o reclusión domiciliaria de acuerdo a la sección 948.039, Estatutos de la *of HCSO*
Florida. *to defendt*

4.   I understand I have a right to plead not guilty and the right to be tried by a jury to determine whether I am
guilty or not guilty. I understand I have the right to be represented by an attorney at the trial and if I cannot afford *Free to Travel*
one, the Court will appoint an attorney to represent me. I understand I have the right to compel the attendance of *out of*
witnesses on my behalf, the right to confront and cross examine all witnesses testifying against me, and the right not *Court*
to testify or be compelled to incriminate myself. I understand if I plead guilty or nolo contendere, there will be no *for purpose*
trial and I waive all the rights that go along with a trial. *of Interpreted*
Entiendo que tengo el derecho de declararme no culpable y el derecho de ser juzgado por un jurado que decidiría si soy culpable o *flight*
no. Entiendo que tengo el derecho de ser representado por un abogado para el juicio y que si no tengo los medios para contratar a
uno, la corte nombrará un abogado para que me represente. Entiendo que tengo el derecho de obligar la comparecencia de
testigos para que declaren a mi favor, el derecho de repreguntar a todos los testigos de cargo y el derecho de no testificar o de ser
obligado a incriminarme. Entiendo que si me declaro culpable o no me opongo, no habrá juicio y renuncio a todos los derechos
propios de un juicio.

5.   I understand if I plead guilty or nolo contendere without reserving the right to appeal, I am waiving my rights to
appeal all matters relating to the judgment including the issue of my guilt or innocence, but not impairing my right to
review by appropriate collateral attack. I understand if I wish to take an appeal and cannot afford an attorney to help
me in my appeal, the Court will appoint an attorney to represent me for that purpose.
Entiendo que si me declaro culpable o no me opongo sin reservarme el derecho a apelar, estoy renunciando a mis derechos de
apelación sobre todos los elementos relacionados con la sentencia incluyendo el asunto de mi culpabilidad o inocencia, pero sin
perjudicar mi derecho a reexaminar por medio de una refutación indirecta apropiada. Entiendo que si deseo apelar y no puedo
contratar un abogado para ayudarme con mi apelación, la Corte asignará un abogado para representarme para ese propósito.

6.   I understand there are facts the State could use to prove the charge(s) against me.
Entiendo que existen hechos que el Estado podría usar para probar el o los cargos en mi contra.

7.   I understand if I plead guilty or nolo contendere the judge may ask me questions about the charge(s) to which I have
just pled and if I am untruthful, my answer(s) may later be used against me in a prosecution for perjury.
Entiendo que si me declaro culpable o no me opongo, el juez podría hacerme preguntas respecto al cargo al cual me acabo de
declarar y que si falto a la verdad, mis respuestas podrían ser usadas en mi contra en un proceso por perjurio.

8.   I understand that if I am not a citizen of the United States and I plead guilty or nolo contendere and the Court accepts
my plea, regardless of whether adjudication of guilt is withheld, my plea and the Court's acceptance of my plea may
have the additional consequence of changing my immigration status, including DEPORTATION or REMOVAL from
the United States. I understand that I should consult with my attorney if I need additional information concerning
potential immigration consequences of my plea. I understand that if I have not discussed the potential immigration

consequences with my attorney, the Court will, upon my request, allow a reasonable amount of time for me to consider the appropriateness of my plea in light of the advisement in this section.

Entiendo que si no soy un ciudadano de los Estados Unidos y me he declarado culpable o no me opongo y la corte acepta mi declaración, ya sea que se haya retenido o nó la adjudicación de culpabilidad, mi declaración y la aceptación por la corte puede tener la consecuencia adicional de cambiar mi situación de inmigración, incluyendo DEPORTACIÓN o remoción de los Estados Unidos, exclusión de la readmisión a los Estados Unidos, detención, negación de la naturalización, o inelegibilidad para la ciudadanía de acuerdo con las leyes de los Estados Unidos. Entiendo que debo consultar con mi abogado si necesito información adicional concerniente a las posibles consecuencias sobre inmigración de mi declaración. Entiendo que si no he discutido con mi abogado sobre las posibles consecuencias sobre inmigración, la corte concederá, a mi pedido, un período de tiempo razonable para considerar apropiadamente mi declaración teniendo en cuenta la información contenida en esta sección.

9. I understand this plea could result in my driver's license being suspended or revoked if the charge(s) to which I am pleading is one where automatic, mandatory suspension or revocation is required by law.
Entiendo que esta declaración podría resultar en la suspensión o revocación de mi licencia de conducir si el cargo al cual me estoy declarando es un delito donde se requiere la suspensión o revocación automática obligatoria por la ley.

10. I understand if I plead guilty or nolo contendere to a sexually violent offense or a sexually motivated offense, or if I have been previously convicted of such an offense, the plea may subject me to involuntary civil commitment as a sexually violent predator upon completion of any prison sentence or jail sentence on this or any other case.
Entiendo que si me declaro culpable o no me opongo a un delito sexual con violencia, o a un delito motivado sexualmente, o si previamente he sido condenado por dicho delito, esta declaración me sujetaría a un confinamiento involuntario civil como un depredador sexual violento una vez que haya concluido cualquier sentencia de prisión o cárcel en este o cualquier otro caso.

11. I understand if I plead guilty or nolo contendere to a qualifying sexual offense, or if I have been previously convicted of such an offense or if I have been designated a sexual predator, I will be subject to mandatory electronic monitoring pursuant to section 948.30(3), Florida Statutes.
Entiendo que si me declaro culpable o no me opongo a un delito de categoria sexual, o si he sido condenado previamente por dicho delito, o se me ha catalogado como depredador sexual, estaré sujeto a un control electrónico obligatorio conforme a la sección 948.30 (3), de los Estatutos de la Florida.

12. I understand my pleading guilty or nolo contendere will result in the Court imposing MANDATORY statutory costs. I also understand my plea may result in the Court imposing certain other costs and attorney's fees and I do not object to the imposition or amount of such costs and fees and I waive my right to a hearing on the imposition and amount of such costs and fees. I have had an opportunity to review with my attorney the mandatory costs (including fines and surcharges) that MUST be assessed against me and discretionary costs (including fines and surcharges) that MAY be assessed against me. I understand if I fail to pay the imposed costs and fees my driver's license may be suspended.
Entiendo que si me declaro culpable o no me opongo traerá como resultado que el juez imponga las costas OBLIGATORIAS de ley. Asimismo, entiendo que mi declaración podría hacer que el juez imponga ciertas costas y honorarios del abogado. No me opongo a la imposición o a la cantidad de costos y honorarios y renuncio a mi derecho a una audiencia respecto a la imposición y la cantidad de costos y honorarios. He tenido la oportunidad de revisar con mi abogado la lista adjunta de costas obligatorias (multas y recargos) que me TIENEN que ser impuestos y las costa opcionales (incluyendo multas y recargos) que me puedan imponer. Entiendo que si no pago los costos y honorarios impuestos, mi licencia de conducir podría ser suspendida.

13. I understand a conviction for an offense to which I am pleading guilty or nolo contendere may serve to enhance the sentence for any offense for which I may be convicted of in the future.
Entiendo que una condena por un delito al cual me estoy declarando culpable o no me opongo podría servir para aumentar la sentencia por cualquier delito por el cual se me podría condenar en el futuro.

14. I am not under the influence of drugs, an alcoholic beverage or medication, but I am taking this medication:

_____

No me encuentra bajo los efectos de drogas ni bebidas alcohólicas, aunque estoy tomando este medicamento:

15. I do not have any mental illness that would keep me from understanding this plea and its consequences.
No padezco de ninguna enfermedad mental que podría impedirme entender esta declaración y sus consecuencias.

16. I certify that no one has threatened or coerced me in any way in order to get me to enter this plea, and I am pleading freely and voluntarily. Other than the terms of the plea negotiation as set forth above (if applicable), no one has promised me anything upon which I have relied in order to influence me to enter this plea.
Certifico que nadie me ha amenazado ni coaccionado de ninguna manera para que yo asiente esta declaración y me declaro libre y voluntariamente. Aparte del acuerdo declaratorio, como se estipula en el párrafo antes mencionado (si es aplicable), nadie me ha prometido nada en lo cual yo me he basado con el motivo de influenciarme para que yo asiente esta declaración.

17.   I certify that I have discussed the charges with my attorney including the maximum possible and mandatory minimum (if any) penalties and possible defenses and am fully satisfied with the representation of my attorney. I understand by entering this plea there is no guarantee what gain time, if any, the Department of Corrections or any county jail may award me.

Certifico que he revisado los cargos con mi abogado, incluso las penas máximas posibles y mínimas obligatorias (si las hubiera) y defensas posibles y estoy completamente satisfecho con la representación de mi abogado. Entiendo que al asentar esta declaración no hay garantía del tiempo ganado, de haberlo, que el Departamento de Corrección o cualquier cárcel del condado podrán concederme.

18.   I have reviewed my criminal punishment code scoresheet and it is correct.
He revisado mi hoja de puntuación y está correcta.

19.   I have reviewed the standard terms of supervision and I understand I must follow them as well as any special conditions the Court thinks are appropriate.
He revisado las condiciones generales de supervisión y entiendo que debo cumplirlas, así como cualesquiera otras condiciones que la corte considere apropiadas.

20.   I understand no one, including my attorney, can accurately predict the actual time I will serve on a sentence and I may be required to serve the entire sentence.
Entiendo que nadie, incluyendo mi abogado, puede predecir con certeza el tiempo real que cumpliré por una sentencia y que podría requerirse que cumpla la sentencia completa.

21.   I certify that there are not any other witnesses I want my attorney to investigate or call, nor is there any other type of discovery or investigation I want my attorney to do, or any other motions I want my attorney to file and set for hearing prior to entering this plea.
Certifico que no hay otros testigos que quiero que mi abogado investigue o llame, ni tampoco existe otro tipo de prueba o investigación que quiero que mi abogado haga, o algunas otras peticiones que quiero que mi abogado presente y fije para una audiencia antes de asentar esta declaración.

22.   I certify that no one, including my attorney, has made any promises concerning the jail credit or prison credit I am to receive other than the fact that I am going to receive credit for every day I actually spent incarcerated on this case, which is _____ days.
Certifico que nadie, incluyendo mi abogado (a) me ha hecho ninguna promesa respecto al tiempo que será acreditado de la cárcel o prisión además del hecho que voy a recibir crédito por cada día que realmente pasé encarcelado en este caso, cual son _____ días.

_____	7/16/2018
Defendant / *Acusado*	Date / *Fecha*

STATEMENT OF ATTORNEY
DECLARACIÓN DEL LICENCIADO

I have reviewed this plea form and the mandatory costs with my client, the Defendant in this case, and it is my belief the Defendant fully understands its contents.

Yo he revisado este convenio declaratorio y los costos obligatorios con mi cliente, el Acusado en este caso, y en mi opinión el Acusado entiende completamente el contenido del convenio.

_____	7/16/2018
Defense Attorney's Signature / *Licenciado*	Date / *Fecha*

MAJ VASIGH
Defense Attorney's Name - Printed / *Licenciado*

(Revised 11/23/15)

EXHIBIT #11

APPLICANT'S INITIAL ASSESSMENT AND DIAGNOSTIC
IMPRESSION (PTSD)

Life Balance & Beauty

LIFE BALANCE AND BEAUTY
INITIAL ASSESSMENT AND DIAGNOSTIC
IMPRESSION

Client: ███████   Birth Date: 11/28/1983

Insurer(s):   Aetna

Intake Date: 01/03/2018   Staff Member(s):   Brigit Towey, LMHC (NPI: 1629335377)

Referral Source(s):   Devereux   Case #

Diagnostic Impressions:

309.81 (F43.10) Post Traumatic Stress Disorder

Client's initial explanation of the problem(s), duration and precipitant cause:

Patient is a 34 Indian American Female. She was referred for Individual and Child Parent Psychotherapy due to a history of trauma related to family violence and removal of her daughter. Client has also been referred to have a mental health and domestic violence evaluation completed as a part of her dependency case plan. Client was interested in therapy, despite the case plan requirements, as she has trauma symptoms such as sleep difficulties, hypervigilent with an exaggerated startle response, recurring memories, flashbacks and thoughts, fear, isolation, and depressive symptoms (crying).

Therapist's observations of Client's Presentation and Family Interactions:

Client and her one-year old daughter are very isolated. They do not venture into the community out of fear that she may encounter the father. Client does not have a strong support system. Her parents reside in India, however, they will be traveling to the United States soon to spend time with client and baby. Client indicated that she does not have any friends, as the friends that she had were common friends with her estranged husband. The mother also has an impending fear as she does not know where the father is, or if and when he could find them.

LIFE BALANCE AND BEAUTY
INITIAL ASSESSMENT AND DIAGNOSTIC IMPRESSION

Client: ▮▮▮▮▮▮   Birth Date: 11/28/1983

Insurer(s):   Aetna

Intake Date: 01/03/2018   Staff Member(s):   Brigit Towey, LMHC (NPI: 1629335377)

Referral Source(s):   n/a   Case #

Mental Status Exam

Appearance: Within Normal Limits, clean, well-dressed

Orientation: Within Normal Limits x 3

Behavior: nervous but cooperative

Speech: Within Normal Limits

Affect: flat, withdrawn

Mood: Within Normal Limits, anxious: moderate

Thought Process: Within Normal Limits, goal directed

Thought Content: Within Normal Limits, concrete thinking

Perception: Within Normal Limits

Judgement: Within Normal Limits, appropriate

Insight: Within Normal Limits, full, intellectual

Appetite: Within Normal Limits

Sleep: impaired

Suicidal: Not Present

Pertinent History: (including family, social, psychological, and medical) Any prior therapy:

There are multiple legal cases involved with this client;
Dependency/Child Welfare; Criminal-against husband and
in-laws; Injunction for protection to keep the father away
from client and child; Family-Divorce Proceedings;
Immigration-husband could be deported if found guilty.

The Client received some services for domestic violence to include psycho-social and educational groups and domestic violence classes

while at The Spring, a domestic violence shelter. Client found this information to be very helpful and assisted her in understanding the

cycle of violence, identifying red flags and protecting herself and her daughter in the future.

The Client has some medical issues (dermatology / plastic surgery) related to the domestic violence that she is being treated for. She

sustained a blow to the head that resulted in a cyst or growth. She has seen a specialist to have this assessed and treated.

Client denies a history of substance abuse.

LIFE BALANCE AND BEAUTY

INITIAL ASSESSMENT AND DIAGNOSTIC IMPRESSION

Client: ███████████   Birth Date: 11/28/1983

Insurer(s):   Aetna

Intake Date: 01/03/2018   Staff Member(s):   Brigit Towey, LMHC (NPI: 1629335377)

Referral Source(s):   n/a   Case #

Family/Psychosocial Assessment:

Patient resides with her one-year old daughter. The husband/father has no contact with the client and child due to a pending criminal, dependency and family court proceedings related to his arrest for false imprisonment and battery against the mother/client. The client was a victim of domestic violence throughout her four-year marriage to her husband.

The client reported that she came from a large, supportive, loving and nurturing family in India. She moved to the United States when she was 23 years old and obtained a Masters Degree in Finance. She stated that she met her husband while in the United States for College. They are both from India. The client stated that while dating, there was no violence, but in hindsight, after learning about the power and control dynamics and manipulations that many abusers have, that there were "red flags", however, she had never been in a violent relationship prior and did not know what to "look out for". The couple dated for five years. The client reported that the physical abuse began immediately after they were married.

The client reported that her husband, "always made me feel guilty, like he was unloved", and talked about the abuse he endured in his childhood. The client reported that her husband exhibited the typical "cycle of abuse" to include manipulation, control and psychological abuse. The husband had isolated the client from her family and friends. She indicated that she started to feel "ashamed, confused and stupid". However, she also felt unable to leave, due to conflicting cultural beliefs and values (a wife listens to/obeys her husband, a good wife will do as her husband says, etc.).

When the mother became pregnant, the violence continued, but was mostly emotional/psychological. The client also had family visiting during the pregnancy and her husband refrained from violence in presence of others. However, the husband did NOT allow the family to be present at the hospital at the time of the baby's birth in December 2016. After the birth of their child the physical violence continued, and the father threatened on several occasions to kill the client, the baby and himself "before the police would even arrive". The husband provided details on how he would kill the family, to include the length of time it would take for the police to arrive, opposed to the length of time is would take for him to murder them.

LIFE BALANCE AND BEAUTY
INITIAL ASSESSMENT AND DIAGNOSTIC IMPRESSION

Client: ███████   Birth Date: 11/28/1983

Insurer(s):   Aetna

Intake Date: 01/03/2018   Staff Member(s):   Brigit Towey, LMHC (NPI: 1629335377)

Referral Source(s):   n/a   Case #

The husband sent for his parents in India to travel to the family home and "discipline" the mother. The in-laws and the husband proceeded to assault the client, physically and mentally, and prevented her from calling the police or leaving the home. The client was able to contact her parents in India and her parents contacted Law Enforcement who responded to the home and rescued the client and baby and arrested the father and grandparents for battery and false imprisonment. After the police intervention the mother and child were required to reside in a domestic violence shelter for three months. The baby was removed from the mother/client and placed in foster care for three days. She was returned to the care of her mother and they were allowed to return to the family home, under the conditions that the father not be involved.

This case became a high profile media case in the local, national and international news. The client has done her own research and self/personal growth on domestic violence and trauma. She is resourceful and has secured supports through Margaret Petros - Mothers Against Murder (MAM), The Spring, and Early Steps.

Evidence of potential or actual risk(s):

The mother and child remain at risk of violence from the

father. There is not a current injunction for protection as the

case has been continued on numerous occasions.

Client made contract to cover risk(s): *Yes*

Security System in the home.

Develop a back-up/ safety plan for child in the event of an emergency(who will pick her up from daycare, care for her etc.)

Client/Family strengths (including support system(s)):

The client is employed. She has sufficient income and resources to support herself and the child.

The client is very resourceful. The mother is strong and has the will power to follow through with the various court

proceedings.

Client has a brother in Orlando.

Clients parents will be visiting from India for 6 months which will be a

great support.

LIFE BALANCE AND BEAUTY

INITIAL ASSESSMENT AND DIAGNOSTIC IMPRESSION

Client: ██████   Birth Date: 11/28/1983

Insurer(s):   Aetna

Intake Date: 01/03/2018   Staff Member(s):   Brigit Towey, LMHC (NPI: 1629335377)

Referral Source(s):   n/a   Case #

Tentative goals and plans:

Client is recommended to participate in individual therapy and Child Parent Psycho-Therapy. Client has received domestic violence treatment and services at The Spring. She has applied the skills and information learned through these services to proceed with the various legal proceedings, establish a safety plan for her and her daughter and be able to react/prevent future incidences or involvement with romantic partners who are violent or controlling. The client intends to fully pursue the legal charges against her estranged husband. She is hopeful that he will be prosecuted for the trauma and damage that he has caused to this client and their child. The goals for individual and Child Parents Psychotherapy are as follows: Psycho-Education on Trauma and the effects on Early Childhood Development; Identifying trauma triggers and developing coping skills, Relationship Building Activities, and creating a safe place.

Who will be involved in treatment?:

Client Child and the Life Balance and Beauty clinical team (Brigit Towey, LMHC and Karah Moody, LMHC, CPP)

Expected length of treatment: 6 months

Is client appropriate for agency services?: Yes

Special needs of client (e.g. need for interpreter, interpreter for the deaf, religious consultant, etc.): None

Cultural variables?:

Indian American

Language Barriers - minimal

Educational or vocational problems or needs: None

Clinician Signature: _Brigit Towey_ LMHC   Date: 01·03·2018

Brigit Towey, MS, LMHC
Florida Licensure #MH11514
Clinical Director / Owner/Operator
Life Balance and Beauty

EXHIBIT #12

APPLICANT'S MEDICAL RECORDS

Tampa General Medical Group [TGMG]

TGMG Family Care
Center Riverview
10647 Big Bend Road, Suite 212
Riverview FL 33579-7176
Phone: 813-844-4600
Fax: 813-844-1960

December 27, 2017

Patient: ████████
Date of Birth: 11/28/1983
Date of Visit: **12/27/2017**

To Whom it May Concern:

████████ was seen in my office on 12/27/2017. She may return to work on 12/28/2017. Last visit pt was referred to dermatologist for eval of lump to Left side of face. Lump could have developed after trauma. Dermatological eval recommended for further eval and possible removal.

If you have any questions or concerns, please don't hesitate to call.

Sincerely,

N Calderon-polanco ARNP

Calderon Polanco, Nancy, ARNP

↑ARRIOR
FACIAL PLASTIC SURGERY

FELLOW AMERICAN COLLEGE OF SURGEONS
AMERICAN ACADEMY OF FACIAL PLASTIC & RECONSTRUCTIVE SURGERY

AMERICAN BOARD OF OTOLARYNGOLOGY
AMERICAN BOARD OF FACIAL PLASTIC AND RECONSTRUCTIVE SURGERY

February 16, 2018

██████████

Dear ███,

It was a pleasure meeting you during your consultation.

The mass on your forehead is either a neuroma or a cyst caused by the trauma.

The best management is to have it removed. If it is not removed it will enlarge over time and could become more painful and destructive.

The surgery will not be extensive or complex and could be performed under local anesthesia.

Should you require any additional information, please do not hesitate to contact the office.

Respectfully,

Edward H Farrior, M.D., F.A.C.S.
Facial Plastic Surgery

EXHIBIT #13

PHOTOGRAPHS OF APPLICANT'S INJURIES

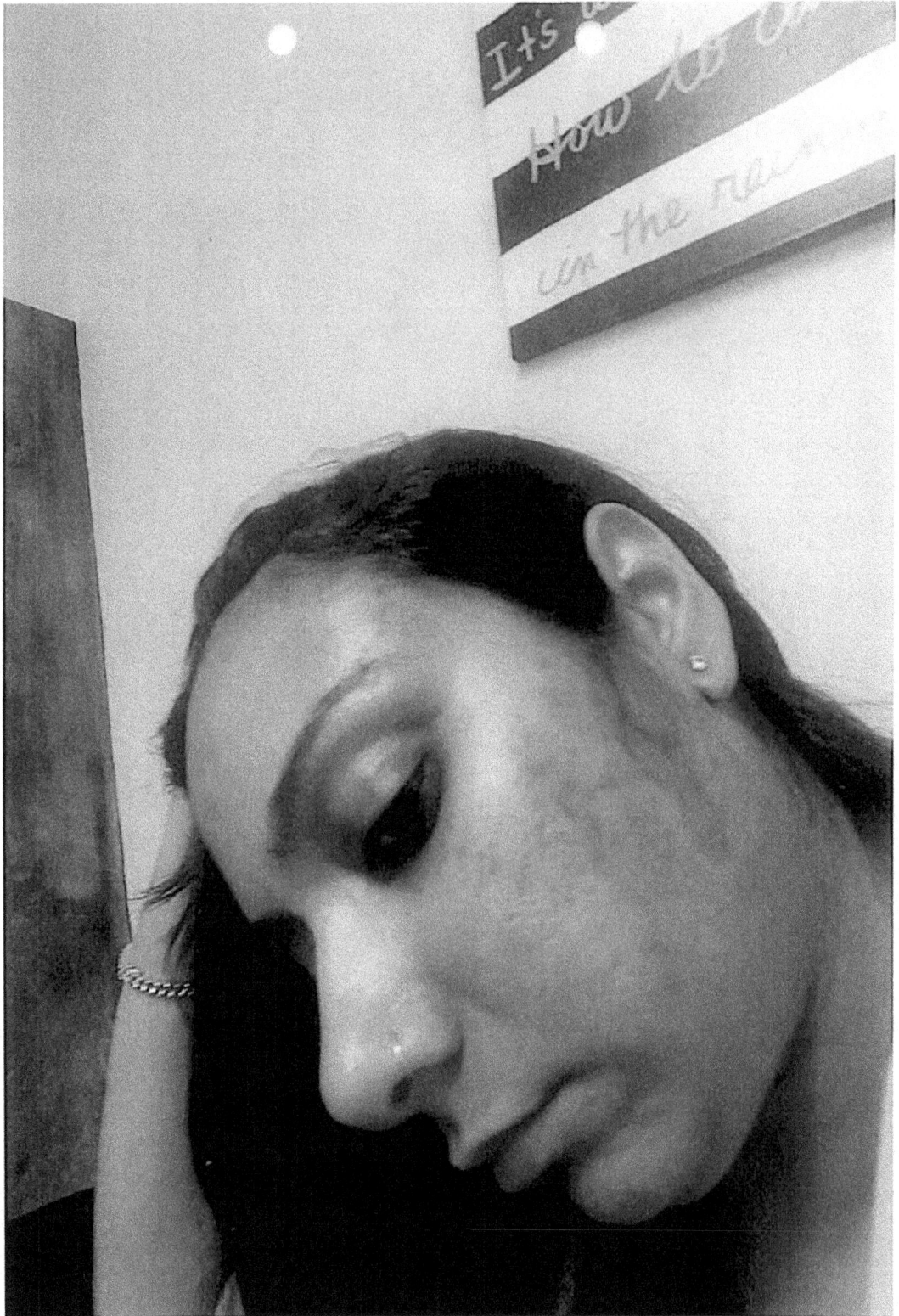

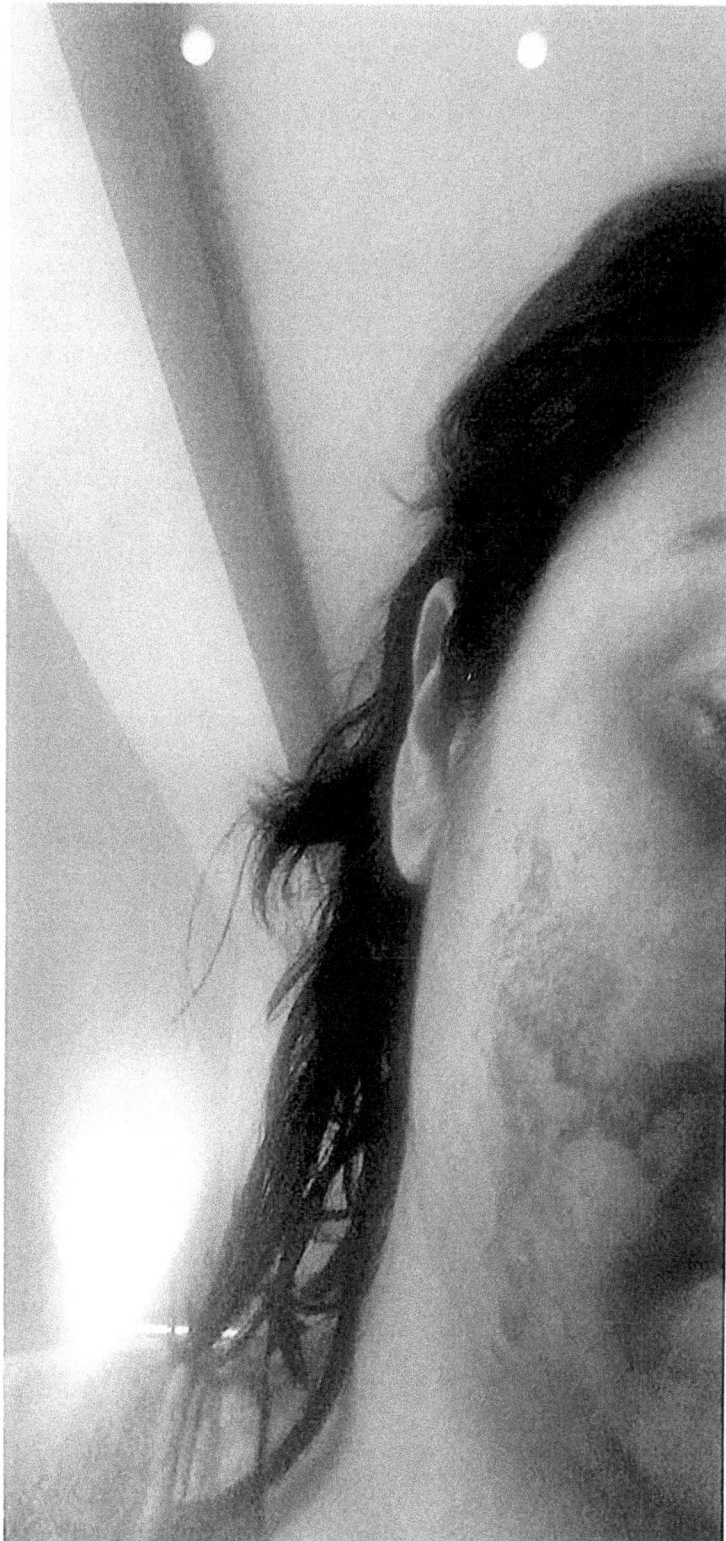

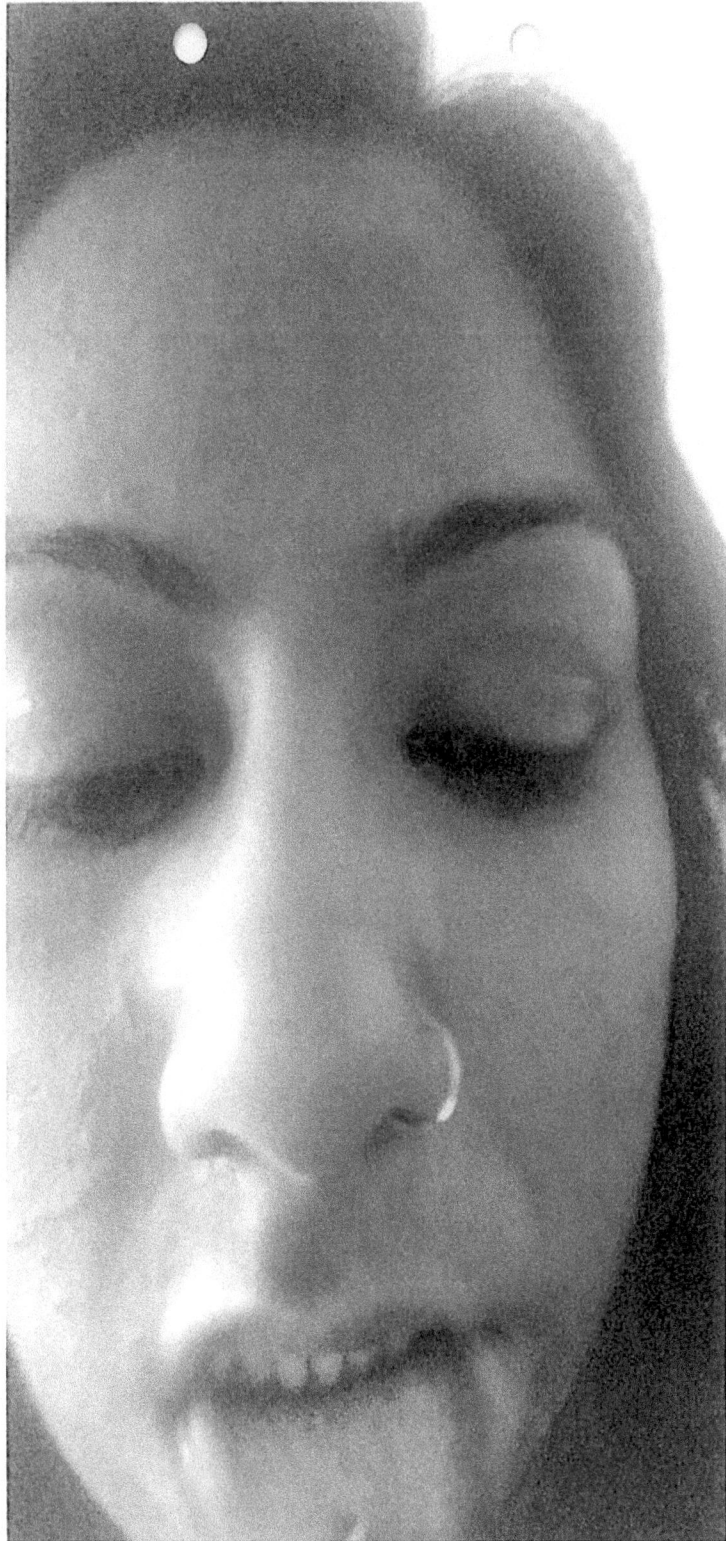

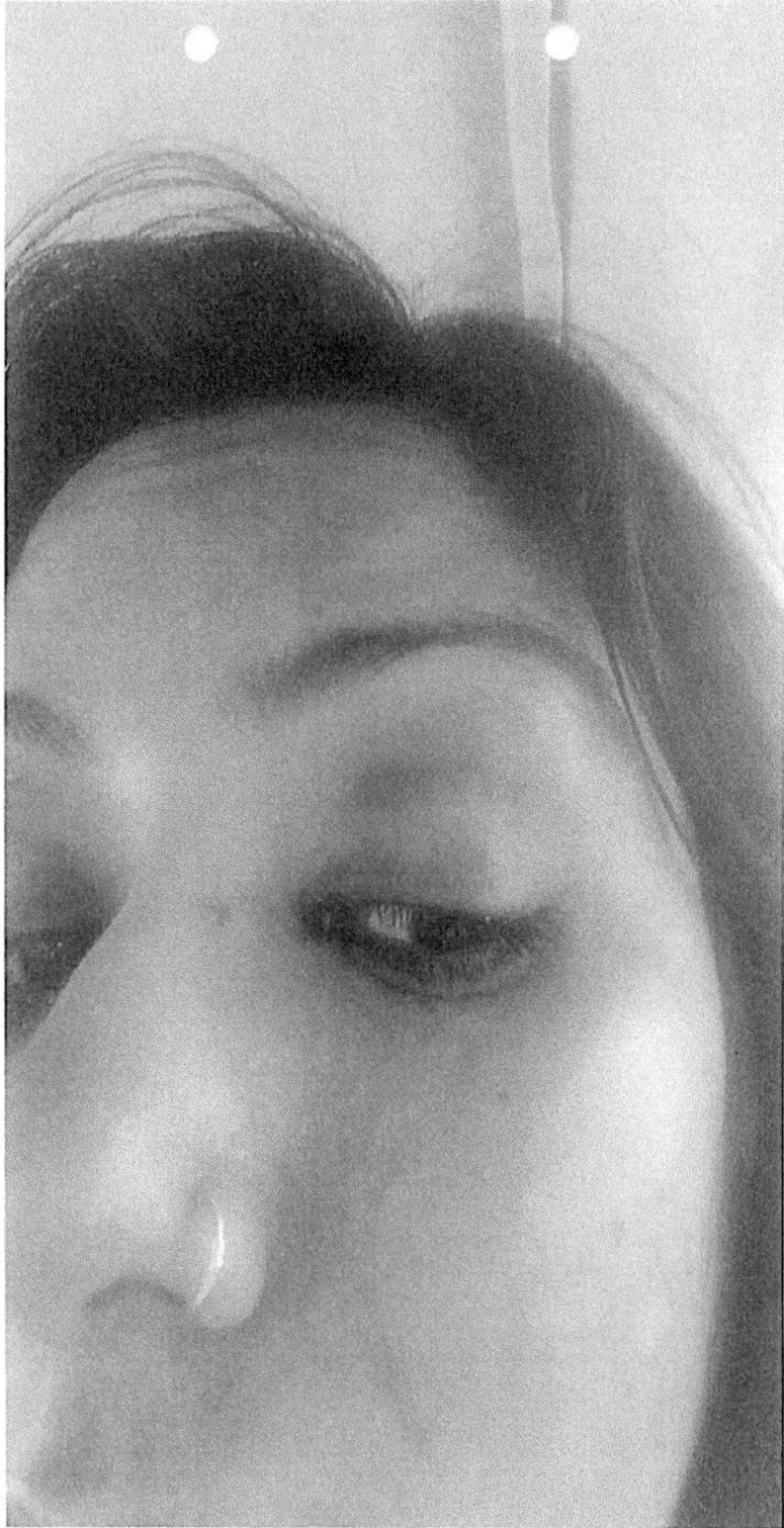

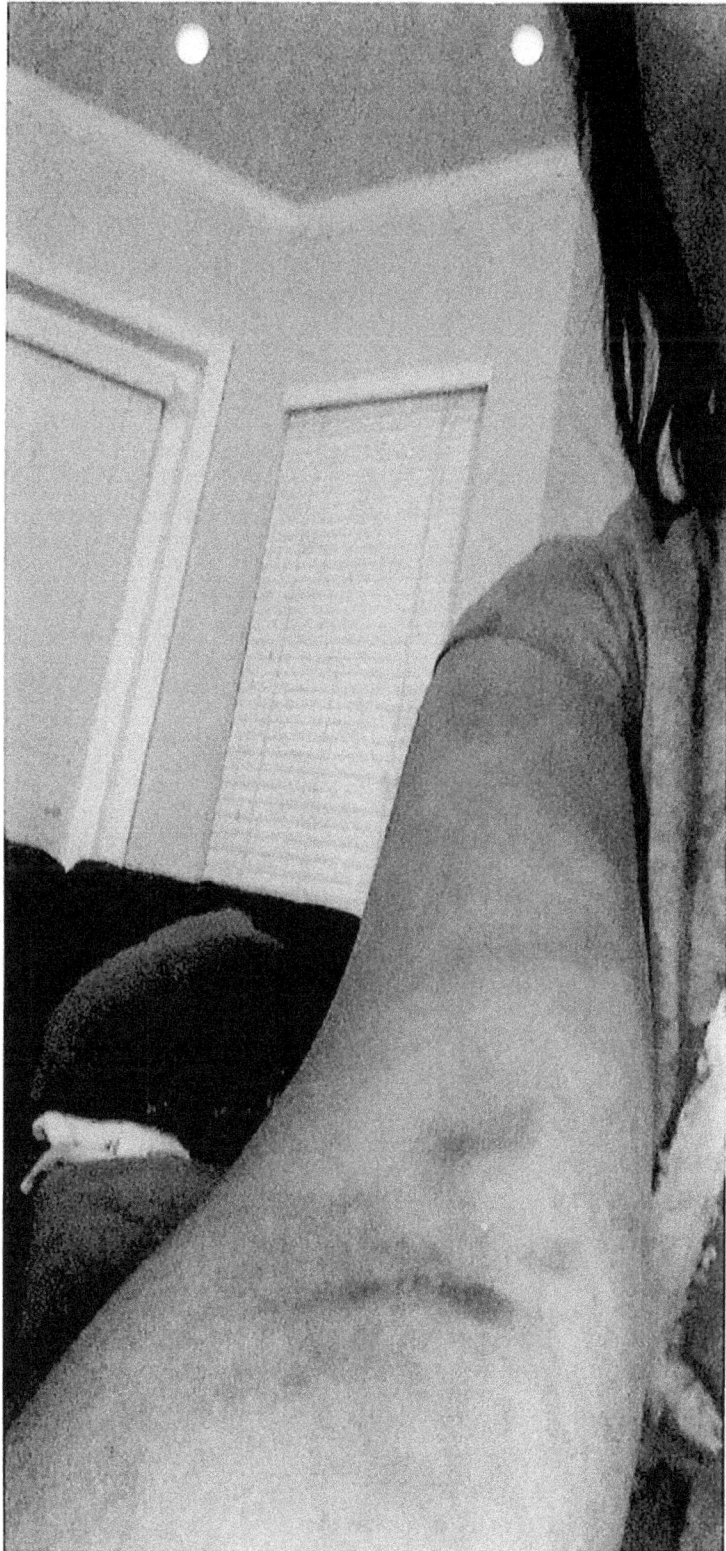

EXHIBIT #14

NEW ARTICLES REGARDING APPLICANT'S ABUSE AND SUFFERING

Morning Mix

A Florida man had his parents travel from India to help him beat his wife, police say

By Rachel Siegel
September 6, 2017

Looking to "counsel and discipline" his wife, ▮▮▮▮ asked his parents to travel from India to his home near Tampa and help imprison and beat his wife. Soon they came, police say.

On Saturday, desperate to save herself, ▮▮▮▮▮▮▮▮, called her parents in India so they could contact local authorities and help launch her rescue. And so they did.

It was that phone call that led to a knock on the door by deputies from the Hillsborough County Sheriff's Office at the home ▮▮▮▮ shared with their 1-year-old daughter. But at around 6:30 a.m. Saturday, the knocks at first went unanswered.

Sheriff's office officials told the Tampa Bay Times that Gaind, 33, eventually came to the door and "screamed for the deputy to save her and her child." Deputies forced the door open, only to find Devbir Kalsi, 33, straining to push the door closed. Officials found ▮▮▮▮▮▮ and ▮▮▮▮ in the home as well.

Investigators now say that ▮▮▮▮ had complained about his wife's disobedience to his parents, who left their home in Punjab to hold ▮▮ against her will at the home in Riverview, Fla. Meanwhile, the beatings continued, and deputies described ▮▮ as "badly beaten and bruised over her entire body" from abuse that had "been ongoing for an extended period of time," according to the Tampa Bay Times. Police did not indicate how long the elder Kalsis had been at the home.

An arrest report cited by the ne[??]paper said Devbir Kalsi and Gain[??] [??]ere arguing Friday night when he struck her "repeatedly and forcefully." ████ tried to defend herself, only to take more hits to her face, neck and torso from her in-laws. The report said ████████ threatened to stab her with a kitchen knife.

The same report referenced by the Tampa Bay Times said ████ was holding her young daughter during her fight with her husband, and that the child was hit in the face as a result. Deputies said Kalsi then took away his wife's phone, dragged her into another room and had his parents lock her inside.

Online arrest records from the sheriff's office said Devbir Kalsi, who is described as employee of electronics company Jabil Circuit, is in jail and faces charges of felony battery, false imprisonment, harassing a witness and child abuse.

His father is also in jail and has been charged with child abuse, aggravated assault with a deadly weapon, harassing a witness and false imprisonment. Kalsi's mother faces charges of domestic violence battery and failure to report child abuse.

All three were arrested and booked on Saturday, according to online records.

No lawyer for any of those charged could be located.

The case has also drawn coverage in the Indian press, with articles from the Times of India and the Hindustan Times. All parties involved are Indian nationals, officials said.

Wife-beating is a worldwide scourge. The notion of a man summoning his mother and father to discipline his wife may sound strange to American sensibilities. But it's a familiar issue in India.

A 2012 UNICEF report said 57 ⟨ cent of young Indian men said w᷄ beating was justified. Legal Service India, an online legal resource provider, said domestic violence there is largely propagated by the husband or his relatives.

"Indian mothers-in law are consistently legally implicated in violence against their daughters-in-law, particularly in dowry-related cases," said a 2013 study called "Violence Between Female In-laws in India."

It linked the problem to "patrilocality," by which "sons stay within their parents' home even after marriage, while married women join their husbands in their in-laws household," often giving mothers-in-law "a vested interest in perpetuating practices of control and power over their daughters-in-law."

According to the local news channel WFLA, the Florida Abuse Hotline and Immigration and Customs Enforcement were notified of the case. ▆▆▆ and her daughter have since been "provided a safe place for refuge."

WFLA quoted a neighbor, ▆▆▆▆▆▆▆▆ who said the incident left her "both sad and scared."

"I'm upset that this was all going on right across the street from me and I couldn't do anything about it and couldn't help her," Payne said.

Another neighbor, who asked not to be identified, was simply shocked.

"Who beats their wife up and has their mother and dad help him?" the neighbor said. "Who does that?"

More from Morning Mix:

Getting to Harvard, the Corey Lewandowski way

Utah hospital to police: Stay away from our nurses

Robert E. Lee 'descendant' — and denouncer — quits N.C. pastor post over 'hurtful' reaction to VMAs spee

Count on North Korea's 'pink lady' broadcaster for joyful news of bombs and missiles

Rachel Siegel
Rachel Siegel is a national business reporter. She previously contributed to the Post's Metro desk, The Marshall Project and The Dallas Morning News. Follow 🐦

FOX NEWS.com

Indian man's parents fly to Florida to beat son's wife for being 'disobedient,' police say

By .

Published September 19, 2017

Fox News

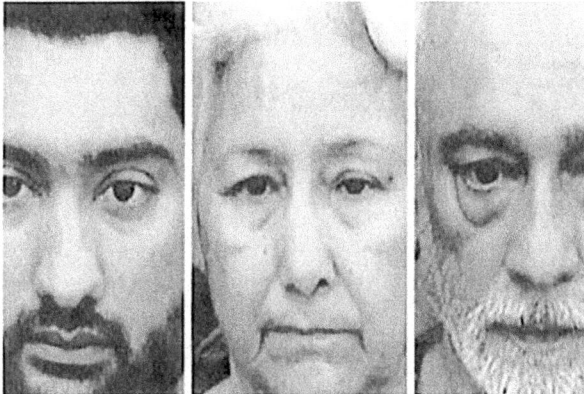

Devbir Kalsi, 33, and his parents Bhupinder Kalsi, 61, and Jasbir Kalsi, 67, were arrested for assaulting Devbir's wife, ███ 33, Saturday, in Riverview, Fla. (The Hillsborough County Sheriff's Office)

Florida police rescued an Indian woman Saturday who was beaten by her husband and his parents who traveled from India to help assist him with the assault.

The Hillsborough County Sheriff's ██████████████, called her parents in India to tell them of the abuse. They then called the authorities.

Police said ███ was being held in the Riverview home by her husband Devbir Kalsi, 33, and his parents Jasbir, 67, and Bhupinder Kalsi, 61, who traveled from India to help their son "counsel and discipline his wife for being disobedient" after he asked for their assistance, according to Fox 13.

3 FLORIDA TEENS CHARGED IN MMA FIGHTER'S SHOOTING DEATH

When a deputy arrived at the residence, no one responded to a repeated knock. Then Gaind attempted to open the door and screamed for him to help her and her 1-year-old daughter.

The deputy forced his way in despite Kalsi trying to keep the door closed. While the deputy started to handcuff Kalsi, his parents confronted the officer, according to the Tampa Bay Times.

Kalsi and Gaind argued Friday night where he battered her "repeatedly and forcefully," according to the arrest report. Kalsi's parents started striking her after Gaind attempted to defend herself. The infant was accidentally struck in the face while Gaind was holding her during the attack, the report stated.

Kalsi was threatened with a knife by Jasbir Kalsi. After the incident, Gaind was locked in a room and her cell phone was taken from her.

VIDEO SHOWS VEHICLE CRASHING INTO FLORIDA GAME STORE

"Awful, nobody should go through that," an unidentified neighbor told Fox 13. "It really is heartbreaking. There's a brand new baby But who beats their wife up and his mother and dad help him? Who does that?"

Devbir and Jasbir Kalsi may face "charges of f...e imprisonment, child abuse and denying access to 9...", according to the Tampa Bay Times. Devbir Kalsi also could face felon... ...ery charge, and Jasbir Kalsi was accused of "aggra... ...u battery with a deadly weapon," the paper reported. Bhupinder Kalsi could face "charges of battery domestic violence and failure to report child abuse."

They were all booked into Hillsborough County Jail and were being held without bond. Fox 13 reported that the three could face deportation back to India. Gaind and her infant were put in a safe place, the sheriff's office said.

The Associated Press contributed to this report.

Print   Close

URL
https://www.foxnews.com/us/indian-mans-parents-fly-to-florida-to-beat-sons-wife-for-being-disobedient-police-say

FEATURED

Florida Wife Allegedly Abused by Husband, In-Laws, Finally Allowed to Leave Shelter for Battered Women

SUNITA SOHRABJI, India-West Staff Reporter   Nov 24, 2017

Riverview, Florida resident Silky Gaind (right) who was allegedly repeatedly battered by her husband, Devbir (left), and her in-laws, was released last month from a shelter for victims of domestic violence. (Facebook photo)

An Indian American woman residing in Riverview, Florida, who allegedly suffered repeated battery at the hands of her husband and in-laws, was allowed to leave a court-mandated shelter for abused women last month, after supporters from the community rallied on her behalf.

According to police reports, ███████████ was allegedly repeatedly beaten by her husband Devbir Kalsi, also 33, who then called in his mother and father from Ludhiana, Jasbir and Bhupinder, to "help control" his wife. ███ d was falsely imprisoned by the Kalsis in her home, according to police, and her baby – who has not been named – also suffered abuse by the Kalsis. (see earlier India-West story here.)

The Kalsis were arrested Sept. 2, and charged with various offenses. According to the inmate locator for The Hillsboro County Sheriff's Office, Devbir Kalsi was charged with felony battery, false imprisonment, harassing a witness, and child abuse. He was held in custody in $32,000 bail, and ordered to turn in his passport and visa to the Hillsboro County Sheriff's office.

Jasbir Singh Khalsi, 67, was charged with child abuse, aggravated assault with a deadly weapon – a knife – false imprisonment, and harassing a witness. He was held on $27,000 bail.

Bhupinder Singh Khalsi, 62, was held on $9,500 bail, and charged with battery domestic violence, and failure to report child abuse. Bhupinder has also allegedly violated immigration laws, though her booking sheet did not give details of the latter charge.

Jasbir and Bhupinder were released from custody on Sept. 20. Devbir was released on Oct. 2.

After the arrests ███████ and her baby were immediately taken to a shelter for battered women. Magaret Petros, executive director of the Los Altos, Calif.-based Mothers Against Murder, told India-West in an e-mail that Gaind was ordered by the county's Child Protection Investigation service to remain at the shelter or have her child taken from her and moved to foster care.

"This is a cruel decision that a non-offending p███ ███, victim of domestic violence, should not have to face," wrote Petros in a petition, which was del████ ███d with 575 signatures to Devereux Advanced Behavioral Health Eckerd Kids in Tampa, Florida.

In her petition, Petros asked that ████ be allowed to return home as soon as possible, with a security alarm installed at her residence, and a pro bono attorney to represent her case.

Gaind was allowed to leave the shelter Oct. 13, after an ADT alarm was installed.

It is unclear whether ████ has a restricting order against her husband and in-laws to ban them from entering the property.

"The re-victimization that happened to ████ by the system that is in place to supposedly help happens to millions of other crime victims every year in the United States. Victims have rights that are often ignored. An aggressive approach to force those who work the system to honor victims' rights is necessary," wrote Petros.

What is your reaction? (2 votes)   Powered by Vuukle

happy	unmoved	amused	excited	angry	sad
50%	0%	0%	0%	0%	50%

ndian American, parents sentenced i: ibusing wife

Staff Writer (http://www.newsindiatimes.com/author/ruchi) · July 26, 2018

ttp://www.newsindiatimes.com/wp-content/uploads/2017/01/crime.jpg)Indian American Devir Kalsi, :
iupinder Kalsi, 62, pleaded guilty last week to beating and holding ▮▮▮▮▮▮ against her will.

l three were arrested last year on several charges for the assault.

:cording to a FOX 13 reports, Gaind said that the abuse took a violent turn last September when her in-
isband's request.

:vir had been abusing ▮▮▮▮ for many years and she said, "his parents also got involved, they have ph}
ey didn't let me call the police. They tried to murder me. They physically beat me so hard. His father g

his defendant involved hersel[ ]it by striking the victim in the l[ ]d and back with an open hand ag[ ]ctim suffered multiple bruises to her head, neck and torso," Prosecutor Christine Brown said in court.

[ ]cording to the police report, Kalsi and ▮▮▮ got into a heated argument on a Friday night when he st[ ]s parents joined in.

[ ]ring the attack, ▮▮▮l was not allowed to contact the police. However, she was able to call her parent[ ]

first, no one came to the door, but when he heard ▮▮▮l screaming, he forced his way in.

▮▮▮▮▮ and her 18-month-old child were both hit in the face and put in separate rooms.

[ ]ind now has full custody of her child.

[ ]l three have gotten 24 months probation followed by community service and Kalsi's parents will be d[ ]

EXHIBIT #15

INDIAN COUNTRY SUMMARY - HUMAN RIGHTS WATCH
(JANUARY 2018)

India

Vigilante violence aimed at religious minorities, marginalized communities, and critics of the government—often carried out by groups claiming to support the ruling Bharatiya Janata Party (BJP)—became an increasing threat in India in 2017. The government failed to promptly or credibly investigate the attacks, while many senior BJP leaders publicly promoted Hindu supremacy and ultra-nationalism, which encouraged further violence. Dissent was labeled anti-national, and activists, journalists, and academics were targeted for their views, chilling free expression. Foreign funding regulations were used to target nongovernmental organizations (NGOs) critical of government actions or policies.

Lack of accountability for past abuses committed by security forces persisted even as there were new allegations of torture and extrajudicial killings, including in the states of Uttar Pradesh, Haryana, Chhattisgarh, and Jammu and Kashmir.

Supreme Court rulings in 2017 strengthened fundamental rights, equal rights for women, and accountability for security forces violations. In August, the court declared the right to individual privacy "intrinsic" and fundamental under the country's constitution, and emphasized the constitution's protections, including free speech, rule of law, and "guarantees against authoritarian behaviour."

That month, the court also ended the practice of "triple *talaq*," allowing Muslim men the right to unilaterally and instantaneously divorce their wives.

In July, the court ordered an investigation into 87 alleged unlawful killings by government forces in Manipur state from 1979 to 2012.

Violent Protests, Impunity for Security Forces

In the first 10 months of 2017, there were 42 reported militant attacks in the state of Jammu and Kashmir in which 184 people were killed, including 44 security force personnel. Several were killed or injured as government forces attempted to contain violent protests.

In May, the army gave a commendation to an officer who used a bystander unlawfully as a "human shield" to evacuate security personnel and election staff from a mob in Jammu and Kashmir's Budgam district.

In a setback for accountability for security force abuses, the Armed Forces Tribunal in July suspended the life sentences of five army personnel who were convicted in 2014 for a 2010 extrajudicial killing of three villagers in the Machil sector in Jammu and Kashmir.

The government failed to review and repeal the abusive Armed Forces Special Powers Act (AFSPA), in force in Jammu and Kashmir and in parts of India's northeastern region, which gives soldiers who commit violations effective immunity from prosecution. At time of writing, the government had yet to comply with a Supreme Court ruling civilian authorities should investigate all allegations of violations by troops.

Several parts of India witnessed violent protests in 2017. In August, at least 38 people were killed during protests in Haryana and Punjab led by supporters of a popular spiritual guru, after he was convicted of raping two female followers. In June, the West Bengal state government's decision to make Bengali language mandatory in all schools triggered protests in Darjeeling district over the longstanding demand for a separate Gorkhaland state, killing eight. Five farmers were fatally shot in June in Madhya Pradesh state, allegedly by police, during protests demanding debt relief and better prices.

In April, 26 paramilitary soldiers from the Central Reserve Paramilitary Force were killed in an ambush by Maoists in Chhattisgarh's Sukma district.

In June, Manjula Shetye died in a Mumbai prison after six prison staff allegedly beat and raped her. The case drew attention to mistreatment in custody, but police reforms remained stalled.

Treatment of Dalits, Tribal Groups, and Religious Minorities

Mob attacks by extremist Hindu groups affiliated with the ruling BJP against minority communities, especially Muslims, continued throughout the year amid rumors that they sold, bought, or killed cows for beef. Instead of taking prompt legal action against the attackers, police frequently filed complaints against the victims under laws banning cow slaughter. As of November, there had been 38 such attacks, and 10 people killed during the year.

In July, even after Prime Minister Narendra Modi finally condemned such violence, an affiliate organization of the BJP, the Rashtriya Swayamsevak Sangh (RSS), announced plans to recruit 5,000 "religious soldiers" to "control cow smuggling and love jihad." So-called love jihad, according to Hindu groups, is a conspiracy among Muslim men to marry Hindu women and convert them to Islam.

Two people died in caste clashes between Dalits and members of an upper caste community in Uttar Pradesh in April and May. Between April and July, 39 people reportedly died from being trapped in toxic sewage lines, revealing how the inhuman practice of "manual scavenging"—disposal of human waste by communities considered low-caste—continues because of the failure to implement laws banning the practice.

In November, following a two-week official visit to India, the United Nations special rapporteur on the human rights to safe drinking water and sanitation, Léo Heller, called on the government to incorporate a human rights perspective into its national programs on water and sanitation, including the flagship Swachh Bharat Mission. As part of his preliminary findings, he said the government's emphasis on constructing toilets to end open defecation should not "involuntarily contribute to violating fundamental rights of others," including specific castes engaged in manual scavenging, or marginalized people, including ethnic minorities and those living in remote rural areas.

Tribal communities remained vulnerable to displacement because of mining, dams, and other large infrastructure projects.

Freedom of Expression

Authorities in India continued to use sedition and criminal defamation laws against government critics. In June, police in Madhya Pradesh state arrested 15 Muslims on sedition charges for allegedly celebrating Pakistan's victory over India in a cricket match, despite Supreme Court directions that sedition allegations must involve actual violence or incitement to violence. After a public outcry, the police dropped the sedition case but charged them with disturbing communal harmony. Also, in June, the Karnataka state assembly punished two editors for articles that allegedly defamed two of its members.

In March, authorities in Maharashtra state charged a journalist for spying and criminal trespass for reporting that officers improperly used subordinates for personal work, filming on army premises without permission, and using a hidden camera.

Journalists faced increasing pressure to self-censor due to threat of legal action, smear campaigns and threats on social media, and even threats of physical attacks. In September, unidentified gunmen shot dead publisher and editor Gauri Lankesh, a vocal critic of militant Hindu nationalism, outside her home in Bengaluru city.

State governments resorted to blanket internet shutdowns either to prevent violence or social unrest, or to respond to an ongoing law and order problem. By November, they had imposed 60 internet shutdowns, 27 of these in Jammu and Kashmir. In August, the government issued rules to govern temporary shutdown of the internet and telecommunications services in the event of "a public emergency or public safety [issue]." However, the rules do not specify what the government considers to be a public emergency, or a threat.

Civil Society and Freedom of Association

Activists and human rights defenders faced harassment including under the Foreign Contribution Regulation Act (FCRA), which governs access to foreign funding for NGOs.

In April, the government canceled the FCRA license of the Public Health Foundation of India (PHFI), one of country's largest public health advocacy groups, accusing it of diverting foreign funds to lobby parliamentarians, media, and the government.

Although FCRA may be revoked if the groups violate procedures laid down in the law, the government's political motivations became evident after the Centre for Promotion of Social Concerns (CPSC) challenged the government's decision in the Delhi High Court. A January 2017 government affidavit in response accused CPSC of using foreign funding to share information with United Nations special rapporteurs and foreign embassies, "portraying India's human rights record in negative light." In November 2016, India's National Human Rights Commission questioned the government's decision not to renew the FCRA for CPSC and concluded: "Prima-facie it appears FCRA license non-renewal is neither legal nor objective."

Women's and Girls' Rights

Multiple high-profile cases of rape across the country during the year once again exposed the failures of the criminal justice system. Nearly five years after the government amended laws and put in place new guidelines and policies aimed at justice for survivors of rape and sexual violence, girls and women continue to face barriers to reporting such crimes, including humiliation at police stations and hospitals; lack of protection; and degrading "two-finger" tests by medical professionals to make characterizations about whether the victim was "habituated to sex."

Rape survivors also lack adequate support services including health care, quality legal assistance, and compensation. While women and girls should have access to safe abortions if they become pregnant after rape, several rape victims have had to petition courts in 2017, including in Delhi and Chandigarh, seeking safe abortion when denied by doctors.

In a setback for women's rights, in July the Supreme Court passed several directives on section 498A of the penal code—the anti-dowry law—to curb what it said was "abuse" of the law, directing police not to make arrests until complaints are verified by family welfare committees, bodies the court recommended be comprised of members of civil society, not police.

Children's Rights

The murder of a 7-year-old boy in a private school in Haryana state in September highlighted that child sexual abuse is disturbingly common in homes, schools, and residential care facilities.

In a deadly outcome resulting from state corruption and neglect, over 60 children died in a public hospital in Uttar Pradesh state in August when a private supplier cut off the oxygen supply after government officials failed to pay long-pending dues.

Children's education was frequently disrupted in areas facing conflict and violent protests. Clashes between protesters and security forces in Jammu and Kashmir state that began in July 2016, continued to simmer throughout 2017, leading to frequent closing of schools and colleges. In May 2017, a student was killed by paramilitary forces inside a government school in Anantnag district during a violent protest.

Schools and colleges also faced disruptions in Darjeeling district in West Bengal state after violent protests and strikes erupted in June over demands for a separate Gorkhaland state.

In October, the Supreme Court ruled that sex with a girl younger than 18 was unlawful, regardless of whether she is married or not, saying the exception for married girls was arbitrary and discriminatory.

Sexual Orientation and Gender Identity

In August, the Supreme Court, in its ruling that privacy is a fundamental right, gave hope to lesbian, gay, bisexual, and transgender (LGBT) people in India by stating that section 377 of India's penal code, which effectively criminalizes same-sex relationships between consenting adults, had a chilling effect on "the unhindered fulfilment of one's sexual orientation, as an element of privacy and dignity."

In July, a parliamentary committee submitted a report examining the draft Transgender Persons (Protection of Rights) Bill, introduced in parliament in August 2016. The report recommended that the bill adopt a 2014 Supreme Court ruling, guaranteeing transgender people the right to self-determine their gender identity. The committee also recommended the bill recognize transgender people's right to marriage, partnership, divorce, and adoption.

No date has been set for the Supreme Court to hear a set of curative petitions, filed in 2014, challenging the 2013 ruling that reinstated section 377 after a High Court had struck it down in 2009.

Rights of Persons with Disabilities

In April, India enacted a new mental health law that provides for mental health care and services for everyone and decriminalizes suicide. However, disability rights groups say much remains to be done to ensure that the law is properly enforced.

Death Penalty

There were no executions in 2017 but nearly 400 prisoners remained on death row. The number of people sentenced to death nearly doubled from 2015 to 2016, from 70 to 136. Most crimes for which capital punishment was handed down included murder, and murder involving sexual violence.

Foreign Policy

In May, India did not attend China's Belt and Road Initiative (BRI) summit in Beijing, citing sovereignty and procedural issues. The initiative is China's major development campaign to build infrastructure connecting it to countries across Asia and beyond.

Despite concerns over China's influence, India intervened in Nepal to persuade the government to adopt inclusive policies that accommodated minority communities in the southern part of the country.

India continued to abstain, and even played a negative role, in country-specific resolutions at the UN Human Rights Council (UNHRC) and General Assembly.

In September, Prime Minister Modi visited Burma amid a growing humanitarian crisis as more than 600,000 Rohingya Muslims in Rakhine State fled to Bangladesh in the face of ethnic cleansing by Burmese security forces following attacks by a Rohingya militant group. India committed to providing aid for large-scale infrastructure and socio-economic development projects in Rakhine State, but did not call on the government to check abuses by its security forces or to amend its discriminatory citizenship law that effectively keeps the Rohingya stateless. At home, BJP leaders threatened to deport Rohingya refugees, saying they were illegal immigrants.

Key International Actors

In May, at India's Universal Periodic Review at the UNHRC, countries raised numerous human rights issues and reminded India to fulfil its past commitments to ratify human rights conventions, including the Convention against Torture. Several countries, including the US, Norway, South Korea, Czech Republic, Switzerland, Canada, Germany, and Sweden raised concerns over restrictions on civil society and called on India to ensure freedom of association.

During Modi's visit to the United States in June, a US-India joint statement reiterated cooperation on increasing trade and combating terrorism, including calling upon Pakistan to ensure that its territory is not used to launch terrorist attacks on other countries. There was not even a token mention of pressing human rights issues in India, including limits on free speech and attacks on religious minorities.

China's attempt to extend an unpaved road on the Doklam Plateau in June, part of the disputed territory between China and Bhutan, led to a three-month military standoff between India and China. India, competing with China for influence in the region, saw this as a move by China to extend its control. In August, both sides agreed to de-escalate tensions ahead of September's BRICS (Brazil, Russia, India, China, and South Africa) Summit in Xiamen, China.

EXHIBIT #16

INDIA 2017/2018 ANNUAL REPORT - AMNESTY INTERNATIONAL

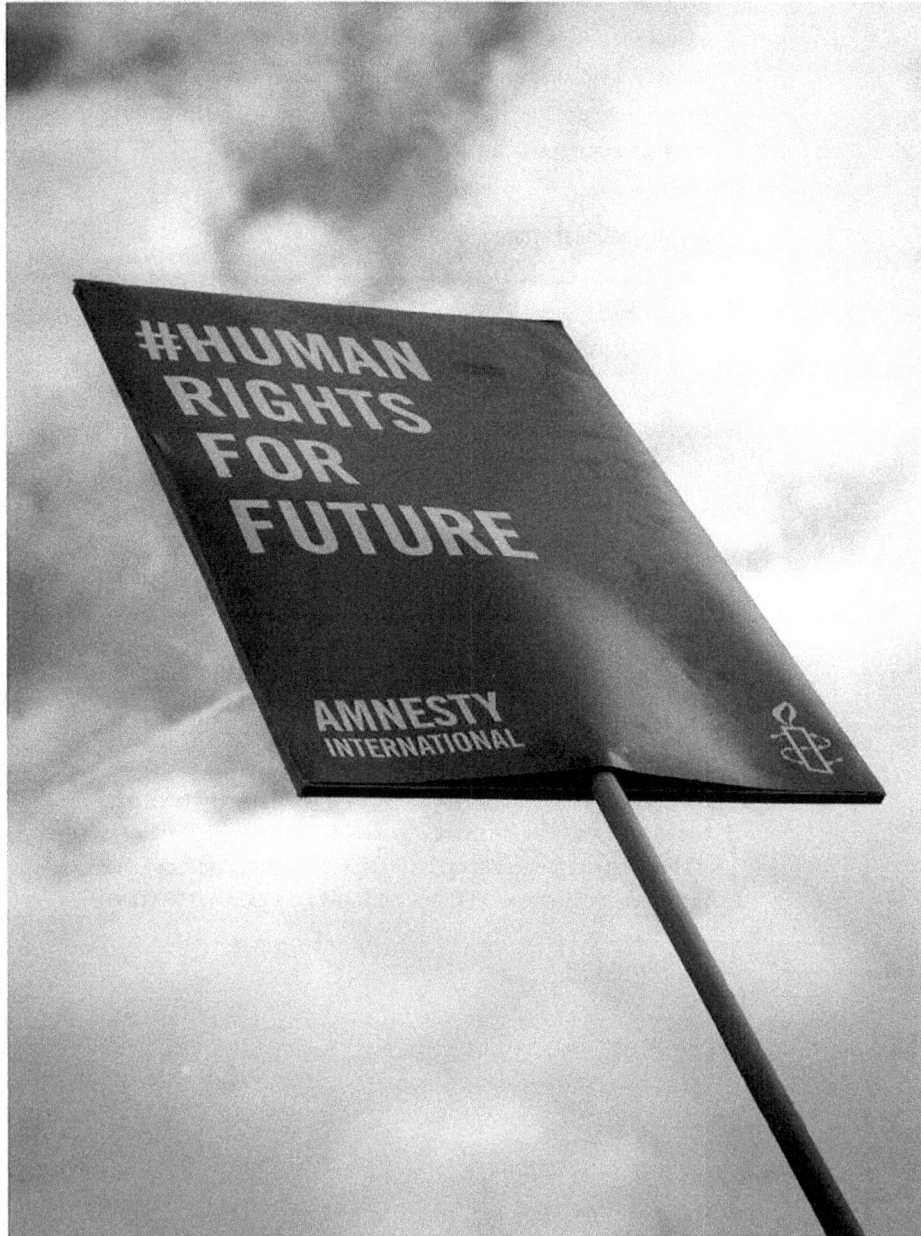

INDIA 2017/2018

← Back to India

INDIA 2017/2018

Religious minority groups, particularly Muslims, faced increasing demonization by hardline Hindu groups, pro-government media and some state officials. Adivasi communities continued to be displaced by industrial projects, and hate crimes against Dalits remained widespread. Authorities were openly critical of human rights defenders and organizations, contributing to a climate of hostility against them. Mob violence intensified, including by vigilante cow protection groups. Press freedom and free speech in universities came under attack. India failed to respect its human rights commitments made before the UN Human Rights Council. The Supreme Court and High Courts delivered several progressive judgments, but some rulings undermined human rights. Impunity for human rights abuses persisted.

Abuses by armed groups

In January, three road construction workers were killed in an attack on a military camp by suspected members of the Jamaat-ud-Dawa armed group in Akhnoor, in the state of Jammu and Kashmir (J&K). The United Liberation Front of Asom (Independent) claimed responsibility for detonating seven bombs across Assam state on 26 January; no casualties were reported. In July, suspected members of the Lashkar-e-Taiba armed group attacked a bus carrying Hindu pilgrims in Botengoo, J&K, killing eight people and injuring

17.

Suspected armed group members in J&K threatened and attacked political workers and ransacked the homes of state police personnel. Armed groups in northeastern states were suspected of carrying out abductions and unlawful killings. The Communist Party of India (Maoist) armed group was suspected of killing suspected police "informants" in several states.

Caste-based discrimination and violence

Official statistics released in November stated that more than 40,000 crimes against Scheduled Castes were reported in 2016. Several incidents were reported of members of dominant castes attacking Dalits for accessing public and social spaces or for perceived caste transgressions.

In May, two Dalit men were killed, several injured, and dozens of Dalit homes burned by dominant caste men in Saharanpur, Uttar Pradesh, following a clash between members of the communities. In September, S. Anitha, a 17-year-old Dalit girl who had campaigned against the introduction of a uniform national exam for admission to medical colleges, committed suicide, sparking protests in Tamil Nadu. Protesters said the exam would disadvantage students from marginalized backgrounds.

Activists said that at least 90 Dalits employed as manual scavengers died during the year while cleaning sewers, despite the practice being prohibited. Many of those killed were illegally employed by government agencies. In August, the Delhi state government said that people who employed manual scavengers would be prosecuted for manslaughter. In November, the UN Special Rapporteur on safe drinking water and sanitation expressed concern that the government's emphasis on building new toilets as part of its Clean India Mission could prolong manual scavenging.

Children's rights

In November, statistics were published stating that over 106,000 cases of violence against children were reported in 2016. In June, India ratified two key ILO conventions on child labour. Activists remained critical of amendments to child labour laws which allowed children to work in family enterprises.

According to national survey data released in March, nearly 36% of children aged below five were underweight, and more than 38% were short for their age. In September, 70 children died at a hospital in Gorakhpur, Uttar Pradesh, allegedly because of disruption to the oxygen supply. The share of public spending on health remained low at 1.2% of GDP. Spending on government programmes to provide nutrition and pre-school education to children under six remained inadequate.

Communal and ethnic violence

Dozens of hate crimes against Muslims took place across the country. At least 10 Muslim men were lynched and many injured by vigilante cow protection groups, many of which seemed to operate with the support of members of the ruling Bharatiya Janata Party (BJP). Some arrests were made, but no convictions were reported. In September, Rajasthan police cleared six men suspected of killing Pehlu Khan, a dairy farmer who had named the suspects before he died. Some BJP officials made statements which appeared to justify the attacks. In September, the Supreme Court said that state governments were obligated to compensate victims of cow vigilante violence.

A special investigation team set up in 2015 to reinvestigate closed cases related to the 1984 Sikh massacre closed 241 cases and filed charges in 12 others. In August, the Supreme Court set up a panel comprising two former judges to examine the decisions to close the cases.

In March, mobs carried out with impunity a string of racist attacks against black African students in Greater Noida, Uttar Pradesh. In June, three people were killed in Darjeeling, West Bengal, in violent clashes between police and protesters demanding a separate state of Gorkhaland.

Freedom of expression

Journalists and press freedom came under increasing attack. In September, journalist Gauri Lankesh, an outspoken critic of Hindu nationalism and the caste system, was shot dead outside her home in Bengaluru by unidentified gunmen. The same month, journalist Shantanu Bhowmick was beaten to death near Agartala while covering violent political clashes. In September, photojournalist Kamran Yousuf was arrested in J&K for allegedly instigating people to throw stones at security forces, under a law which does not meet international human rights standards. In November, journalist Sudip Datta Bhowmik was shot dead, allegedly by a paramilitary force member, at a paramilitary camp near Agartala. In December, a French film-maker conducting research for a documentary on the Kashmir conflict was detained for three days in J&K, allegedly for violating visa regulations.

Journalists continued to face criminal defamation cases filed by politicians and companies. In June, the Karnataka legislature sentenced two journalists to one year's imprisonment each for allegedly writing defamatory articles about members of the state assembly.

Repressive laws were used to stifle freedom of expression. In June, 20 people were arrested for sedition in Madhya Pradesh and Rajasthan, following complaints that they had cheered the Pakistan cricket team's victory over India. In July, 31 Dalit activists were arrested and detained for a day in Lucknow for organizing a press conference about caste-based violence. State governments banned books, and the central film certification board denied the theatrical release of certain films, on vague and overly broad grounds. In November, five state governments banned the release of *Padmaavat*, a Hindi period film, on the grounds that it would "hurt community s[c]   ments".

Freedom of expression in universities remained under threat. The student body of the Hindu nationalist organization Rashtriya Swayamsevak Sangh used threats and violence to block events and talks at some universities. In June, eight Lucknow University students were arrested and detained for 20 days for protesting against the Uttar Pradesh Chief Minister. In September, Uttar Pradesh police personnel baton-charged students, mostly women, protesting against sexual assault at Banaras Hindu University.

In August, India's Supreme Court ruled in a landmark judgment that the right to privacy was part of the constitutional right to life and personal liberty.

Human rights defenders

In January, the Home Ministry said that it had refused to renew the foreign funding licence of the NGO known as People's Watch because it had allegedly portrayed India's human rights record in a "negative light" internationally.

In March, GN Saibaba, an activist and academic, was convicted with four others and sentenced to life imprisonment by a Maharashtra court for being a member of and supporting a banned Maoist group. The conviction was based primarily on letters, pamphlets and videos, and used the provisions of the Unlawful Activities Prevention Act, a law which does not meet international human rights standards.

The same month, Jailal Rathia, an Adivasi activist, died in Raigarh, Chhattisgarh, after allegedly being poisoned by members of a land mafia he was campaigning against. In April, Varsha Dongre, an official at Raipur Central Jail in Chhattisgarh, was transferred after she posted on Facebook that she had seen police torturing Adivasi girls.

In May, four men were arrested in Chennai and held in administrative detention for more than three months for attempting to stage a memorial for Tamils killed in the civil war in Sri Lanka. The same month, the Odisha state police arrested Kuni Sikaka, an Adivasi activist opposing bauxite mining in the Niyamgiri hills, and released her only after presenting her to journalists as a surrendered Maoist.

In August, activist Medha Patkar and three others protesting against inadequate rehabilitation for families affected by the Sardar Sarovar dam project (see below) were arrested on fabricated charges and detained for more than two weeks.

Indigenous Peoples' rights

In November, statistics were published stating that over 6,500 crimes were committed against Scheduled

Tribes in 2016. Indigenous Adiv... communities continued to face displ... ment by industrial projects. The government acquired land for coal mining under a special law without seeking the free, prior and informed consent of Adivasis. In July, an Environment Ministry panel said that coal mines seeking to increase production capacity by up to 40% did not have to consult affected communities.

In September, activists protested against the inauguration of the Sardar Sarovar dam in Gujarat, saying that some 40,000 displaced families, including many Adivasi families, had not received adequate reparation. In June, 98 Adivasis in Raigarh, Chhattisgarh, tried to file criminal cases under the Scheduled Castes and Scheduled Tribes (Prevention of Atrocities) Act, alleging that they had been forced into selling their land to agents of private companies, following intimidation and coercion. The police accepted the complaints but refused to register criminal cases.

Jammu and Kashmir

In April, eight people were killed by security forces, some of them by the use of excessive force, following protests during a by-election for a parliamentary seat. One voter, Farooq Ahmad Dar, was beaten by army personnel, strapped to the front of an army jeep and driven around for over five hours, seemingly as a warning to protesters. In May, the officer suspected of being responsible received an army commendation for his work in counter-insurgency operations. In July, the J&K State Human Rights Commission directed the state government to pay Farooq Dar 100,000 INR (around USD1,500) as compensation. In November, the state government refused to pay.

Impunity for human rights abuses persisted. In June, a military court set up under the paramilitary Border Security Force acquitted two soldiers of killing 16-year-old Zahid Farooq Sheikh in 2010. The force had successfully prevented the case from being prosecuted in a civilian court. In July, the Supreme Court refused to reopen 215 cases in which over 700 members of the Kashmiri Pandit community were killed in J&K in 1989, citing the passage of time. The same month, an appellate military court suspended the life sentences of five army personnel convicted by a court-martial of the extrajudicial executions of three men in Machil in 2010. In November, the State Human Rights Commission repeated a directive issued to the state government in 2011 to investigate over 2,000 unmarked graves.

Security forces continued to use inherently inaccurate pellet-firing shotguns during protests, blinding and injuring several people. Authorities frequently shut down internet services, citing public order concerns.

Police and security forces

In January, four Adivasi women in Dhar, Madhya Pradesh, said they had been gang-raped by police personnel. In March, Adivasi villagers in Sukma, Chhattisgarh, accused security force personnel of gang-raping a 14-year-old Adivasi girl. In September, two paramilitary personnel were arrested on suspicion of killing a woman and raping and throwing acid on her friend in Mizoram in July.

In April, a senior officer of the paramilitary Central Reserve Police Force alleged in writing to his commanding authorities that multiple security agencies had killed two suspected armed group members in an extrajudicial execution in Assam. The officer was transferred. In July, the Supreme Court directed the Central Bureau of Investigation to investigate more than 80 alleged extrajudicial executions by police and security force personnel in Manipur between 1979 and 2012. The court ruled that cases should not go uninvestigated merely because of the passage of time.

In June, the Madhya Pradesh police shot dead five farmers who were among protesters in Mandsaur demanding better prices for crops. In August, at least 38 people were killed, some of them by the use of excessive force, when they were fired on by police during protests in Haryana following the conviction for rape of a self-styled "godman", or guru.

Refugees' and migrants' rights

An estimated 40,000 Rohingya people in India were at risk of mass expulsion. They included more than 16,000 who were recognized as refugees by UNHCR, the UN refugee agency. In August, the Home Ministry wrote to state governments asking them to identify "illegal immigrants", including Rohingya. In September, the Ministry said that all Rohingya in India were "illegal immigrants", and claimed to have evidence that some Rohingya had ties to terrorist organizations. In October, in response to a petition filed by two Rohingya refugees, the Supreme Court temporarily deferred expulsions.

In September, the Home Ministry said that it would grant citizenship to about 100,000 Chakma and Hajong refugees who had fled to India from Bangladesh in the 1960s.

Torture and other ill-treatment

Between January and August, 894 deaths in judicial custody and 74 deaths in police custody were recorded. In February, Uma Bharti, a central government minister, said she had ordered rape suspects to be tortured when she was Chief Minister of Madhya Pradesh. In August, Manjula Shetye, a woman prisoner at the Byculla jail in Mumbai, died after being allegedly beaten and sexually assaulted by officials for complaining about food in the prison. A team of parliamentarians that visited Byculla jail reported that prisoners were routinely beaten. In November, a committee set up by the Delhi High Court said that 18 prisoners in Tihar jail in New Delhi had been beaten after they had objected to their pillow covers being taken.

In September, during India's UN UPR process before the UN Human Rights Council, the government accepted for the third time recommendations to ratify the UN Convention against Torture, which it signed in 1997. India's Law Commission released a report in October recommending that the government ratify the

Convention and enact a law criminalizing torture.

Women's rights

In November, statistics were published showing that over 338,000 crimes against women were registered in 2016, including over 110,000 cases of violence by husbands and relatives. Responding to petitions in courts seeking to criminalize marital rape, the central government stated that doing so would "destabilize the institution of marriage".

In August, the Supreme Court banned the practice of triple talaq (Islamic instant divorce), declaring that it was arbitrary and unconstitutional. However, in other cases, court rulings undermined women's autonomy. In July, the Supreme Court weakened a law enacted to protect women from violence in their marriages, by requiring that complaints be initially assessed by civil society "family welfare committees". In October, the Supreme Court suggested that it would review its judgment. The same month, it ruled that sexual intercourse by a man with his wife, if she was under 18, would amount to rape.

Several rape survivors, including girls, approached courts for permission to terminate pregnancies over 20 weeks, as required under Indian law. Courts approved some abortions, but refused others. In August, the central government instructed states to set up permanent medical boards to decide such cases promptly.

GET THE AMNESTY INTERNATIONAL REPORT 2017/18

Choose language ⌄

DOWNLOAD PDF

EXHIBIT #17

INDIA TRAVEL ADVISORY - U.S. DEPARTMENT OF STATE
(JANUARY 10, 2018)

India Travel Advisory

Travel Advisory
January 10, 2018

India - Level 2:
Exercise Increased
Caution

C T U O

Exercise increased caution in India due to **crime and terrorism.** Some areas have increased risk. Read the entire Travel Advisory.

Do not travel to:

- The state of Jammu and Kashmir (except the eastern Ladakh region and its capital, Leh) due to **terrorism and civil unrest**.

- Within 10 km of the India-Pakistan border due to **the potential for armed conflict.**

Indian authorities report rape is one of the fastest growing crimes in India. Violent crime, such as sexual assault, has occurred at tourist sites and in other locations.

Terrorist or armed groups are active in East Central India, primarily in rural areas. Terrorists may attack with little or no warning, targeting tourist locations, transportation hubs, markets/shopping malls, and local government facilities.

The U.S. government has limited ability to provide emergency services to U.S. citizens in rural areas from eastern Maharashtra and northern Telangana through western West Bengal as U.S. government employees must obtain special authorization to travel to these areas.

Read the Safety and Security section on the country information page.

If you decide to travel to India:

- Do not travel alone, particularly if you are a

woman. Visit our website for Women Travelers.

- Review your personal security plans, and remain alert to your surroundings.

- Enroll in the Smart Traveler Enrollment Program (STEP) to receive Alerts and make it easier to locate you in an emergency.

- Follow the Department of State on Facebook ⍗ and Twitter⍗.

- Review the Crime and Safety Reports for India.

- U.S. citizens who travel abroad should always have a contingency plan for emergency situations. Review the Traveler's Checklist.

State of Jammu and Kashmir

Terrorist attacks and violent civil unrest are possible in the state of Jammu and Kashmir. Avoid all travel to this state (with the exception of visits to the eastern Ladakh region and its capital, Leh). Sporadic violence occurs particularly along the Line of Control (LOC) separating India and Pakistan, and in tourist destinations in the Kashmir Valley: Srinagar, Gulmarg, and Pahalgam. The Indian government prohibits foreign tourists from visiting certain areas along the LOC.

Visit our website for Travel to High-Risk Areas.

India-Pakistan Border

India and Pakistan maintain a strong military presence on both sides of the border. The only official India-Pakistan border crossing point for persons who are not citizens of India or Pakistan is in the state of Punjab between Atari, India, and Wagah, Pakistan. The border crossing is usually open, but confirm the current status of the border crossing prior to commencing travel. A Pakistani visa is required to enter Pakistan. Only U.S. citizens residing in India may apply for a Pakistani visa in India. Otherwise apply for a Pakistani visa in your country of residence before traveling to India.

Visit our website for Travel to High-Risk Areas.

Northeastern States

Incidents of violence by ethnic insurgent groups, including bombings of buses, trains, rail lines, and markets, occur occasionally in the northeast.

U.S. government employees are prohibited from traveling to the states of Assam, Arunachal Pradesh, Mizoram, Nagaland, Meghalaya, Tripura, and Manipur without special authorization from the U.S. Consulate General in Kolkata.

Visit our website for Travel to High-Risk Areas.

East Central and Southern India

Maoist extremist groups, or "Naxalites," are active in a large swath of India from eastern Maharashtra and northern Telangana through western West Bengal, particularly in rural parts of Chhattisgarh and Jharkhand and on the borders of Telangana, Andhra Pradesh, Maharashtra, Madhya Pradesh, Uttar Pradesh, Bihar, West Bengal, and Odisha. The Naxalites have conducted frequent terrorist attacks on local police, paramilitary forces, and government officials.

Due to the fluid nature of the threat, all U.S. government travelers to states with Naxalite activity must receive special authorization from the U.S. consulate responsible for the area to be visited. U.S. officials traveling only to the capital cities in these states do not need prior authorization.

Visit our website for Travel to High-Risk Areas.

EXHIBIT #18

2018 TRAFFICKING IN PERSON REPORT: INDIA - U.S. DEPARTMENT OF STATE

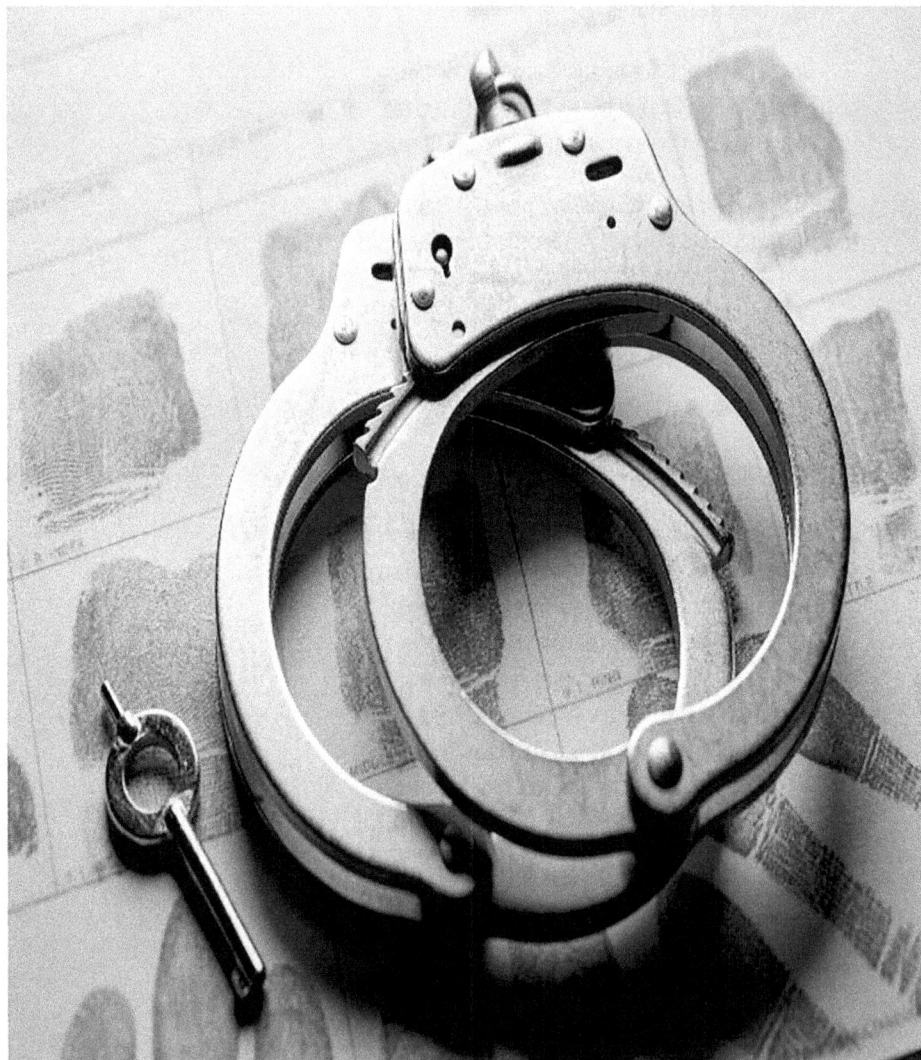

were unable to confirm the form of trafficking of the other potential victims. The national police commissioner maintained detailed procedures for police to use to identify, contact, and deal with possible trafficking victims to provide them with assistance. The government continued to distribute information on the EU-issued "Guidelines for the Identification of Victims of Trafficking" and NGO-developed interview guidelines to government employees most likely to come into contact with trafficking victims. The Directorate of Immigration had written procedures to identify trafficking victims and provide them with information and resources, including during the interview process for asylum-seekers. Immigration and police officers maintained a pocket checklist to identify potential victims and inform them of available services. The government did not have a national referral mechanism, but police maintained standardized referral procedures that required police to contact welfare services in the municipality and the Ministry of Welfare (MOW) to coordinate victim care and placement. NGOs stated these procedures worked effectively in practice but required further clarification on the roles and responsibilities, including guidance on where to refer victims. Government-funded NGOs provided equal assistance and support to official and potential victims; the MOW provided services to two potential victims and four potential victims received assistance from the women's shelter, compared to one victim in 2016. The government held 10 sessions on victim identification and assistance for approximately 400 officials.

The government maintained its two-year agreement signed in December 2016 to provide funding for an NGO-run domestic abuse shelter to provide emergency shelter to female trafficking victims and their children. The 2018 state budget allocated 76 million krona ($730,140) to the domestic abuse shelter, compared with 71 million krona ($682,100) for 2017. The MOW provided the shelter with an additional 300,000 krona ($2,880) for the provision of services for trafficking victims, compared to 350,000 krona ($3,360) in 2017. The shelter maintained a team of specialists to manage cases involving possible trafficking victims. Victims had access to free legal, medical, psychological, and financial assistance, whether or not they stayed at the shelter or cooperated with authorities. Municipal social service agencies provided services and financial assistance to trafficking victims, and the MOW reimbursed the municipalities for all associated expenses. In 2016, the government refunded 22.3 million krona ($214,240) to municipal governments for expenses related to "foreign citizens in distress," which may have included trafficking victims. The government allocated 77 million krona ($739,740) in the 2018 state budget to a separate NGO offering psychological services to individuals in prostitution and trafficking victims, compared to 71 million krona ($682,100) in 2017. The government in collaboration with several NGOs opened a center offering free comprehensive services to abuse victims, including trafficking victims, as a two-year pilot project and allocated 50 million krona ($480,350). There were no specialized care available for male victims, though they could access general social services and receive referrals to NGOs providing food, shelter, legal advice, and health care. Municipal and state child protection services were responsible for assisting unaccompanied children, including child trafficking victims.

Witness protection for trafficking victims was not mandated by law, but the government could provide it. In previous years, an NGO reported victims of forced marriage, which may involve forced labor or sex trafficking crimes, generally did not contact police or press charges due to fear of traffickers and because cases can be difficult to prove. Victims could file civil suits

against traffickers or seek restitution from the government, but no victims did so during the reporting period. Any foreign trafficking victim could obtain a nine-month residence permit. An additional one-year renewable residence permit was available to victims who cooperated with law enforcement or who faced retribution or hardship in their home countries; however, victims with either temporary residence permit could not apply for a permit to work legally in the country. Police reported that investigations often stall because foreign victims leave the country to seek employment. The government did not report issuing any temporary residence permits in 2017, compared to one in 2016.

PREVENTION

The government maintained efforts to prevent trafficking. MOI led the steering group that met once a month to coordinate interagency anti-trafficking efforts. The Directorate of Labor (DOL) maintained a three-member team to respond to suspected trafficking cases and educate government employees on trafficking and identifying possible victims. DOL monitored the operations of companies that hired foreign "posted workers" by reviewing hiring contracts, checking paychecks against bank statements, and conducting targeted visits to talk to employees and supervisors. The government's 2013-2016 national action plan expired during the previous reporting period; the government reported a new action plan was in development. The government organized an awareness raising conference for approximately 200 government officials and civil society, including police, prosecutors, and labor unions. Police continued to enforce laws against purchasing commercial sex but did not report efforts to reduce the demand for forced labor.

TRAFFICKING PROFILE

As reported over the past five years, Iceland is a destination and transit country for women subjected to sex trafficking and men and women subjected to labor trafficking. Women from Eastern Europe, the Baltics, and South America are subjected to sex trafficking, often in nightclubs and bars. Men and women from the Baltics, Eastern Europe, South America, and East Asia are subjected to forced labor in construction, tourism, and restaurants. Foreign "posted workers" are at particular risk of forced labor as the traffickers pay them in their home countries and contract them to work for up to 183 days in Iceland to avoid taxes and union fees, limiting tax authorities' and union officials' ability to monitor their work conditions and pay. Traffickers also subject women to domestic servitude, forced labor, and sex trafficking and men to forced labor; NGOs note these cases rarely come to the attention of police. Traffickers reportedly exploit the visa-free regime in the Schengen Zone and the European Economic Area to bring victims to Iceland for up to three months and move them out of the country before they must register with local authorities.

INDIA: TIER 2

The Government of India does not fully meet the minimum standards for the elimination of trafficking; however, it is making significant efforts to do so. The government demonstrated increasing efforts compared to the previous reporting period; therefore India remained on Tier 2. The government demonstrated increasing efforts by nearly tripling the number of victims identified and increasing its budget for shelter programs for female and child trafficking victims. The government's inter-ministerial committee met during the reporting period to discuss and revise a draft anti-trafficking bill and India's border guard force on the India-Nepal border conducted several awareness activities on human trafficking for students and border communities. However, the government did not meet the minimum standards in several key areas. Overall victim protection remained inadequate and inconsistent, and the government sometimes penalized victims through arrests for crimes committed as a result of being subjected to human trafficking. The government's conviction rate and the number of investigations, prosecutions, and convictions was disproportionately low relative to the scale of trafficking in India, particularly with respect to bonded and forced labor. Despite reports of some officials complicit in trafficking, the government did not report investigating such allegations.

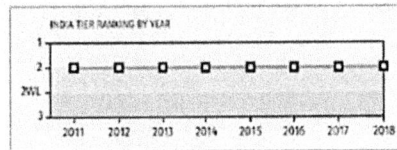

INDIA TIER RANKING BY YEAR

RECOMMENDATIONS FOR INDIA

Increase prosecutions and convictions for all forms of trafficking, including forced and bonded labor, and of officials allegedly complicit in trafficking, respecting due process; establish and fully resource anti-human trafficking units (AHTUs) in all districts, including by providing additional dedicated, trained staff and by clarifying the mandate of AHTUs; significantly increase efforts to identify victims proactively to include disseminating and implementing standard operating procedures (SOPs) to harmonize victim identification and referral, and training officials on their use; cease the penalization of trafficking victims; protect victim confidentiality and privacy, including on government-issued identification documents; improve central and state government implementation of protection programs and compensation schemes to ensure trafficking victims receive benefits, release certificates, and compensation funds; develop and adopt a national action plan to combat trafficking; eliminate all recruitment fees charged to workers and raise awareness among workers that they are not required to pay for a job; promptly disburse government funding for shelters and develop monitoring mechanisms to ensure quality of care; continue to increase the transparency of government efforts to combat trafficking and provide disaggregated data on efforts to criminally investigate, prosecute, and punish sex and labor trafficking; lift the ban on female labor migration to certain countries to discourage migration through undocumented channels; provide funding for states to establish fast-track courts that deal with all forms of human trafficking; and provide anti-trafficking training or guidance for diplomatic personnel to prevent their engagement in or facilitation of trafficking crimes, and to provide personnel the tools to identify and assist trafficking victims in their work.

PROSECUTION

The government maintained law enforcement efforts. Indian law criminalized sex trafficking and some forms of labor trafficking. Section 370 of the Indian Penal Code (IPC) criminalized slavery, servitude, and most forms of sex trafficking and prescribed penalties ranging from seven years to life imprisonment, which were sufficiently stringent and, with respect to sex trafficking,

commensurate with those prescribed for other serious crimes, such as rape. Inconsistent with international law, Section 370 required a demonstration of force, fraud, or coercion to constitute a child sex trafficking offense, and therefore did not criminalize all forms of child sex trafficking. However, Sections 372 and 373 of the IPC criminalized the exploitation of children through prostitution without requiring a demonstration of such means, thereby addressing this gap. These sections prescribed penalties of up to ten years imprisonment and a fine, which were also sufficiently stringent and commensurate with those prescribed for other serious crimes, such as rape. Section 370 criminalized government officials' involvement in human trafficking and prescribed penalties up to life imprisonment. Bonded labor was specifically criminalized under the Scheduled Castes and Scheduled Tribes (Prevention of Atrocities) Act, which prescribed sufficiently stringent penalties of up to five years imprisonment, and the Bonded Labor System (Abolition) Act (BLSA), which prescribed penalties of up to three years imprisonment, which were not sufficiently stringent. The Juvenile Justice Act and other sections of the IPC criminalized many forms of forced labor; however, these provisions were unevenly enforced and some of their prescribed penalties were not sufficiently stringent, allowing for only fines or short prison sentences. The government frequently used the Immoral Traffic Prevention Act (ITPA) and various provisions of the IPC, which prescribed penalties that were sufficiently stringent and commensurate with other serious crimes such as rape, to prosecute sex trafficking.

During the reporting period, the National Crimes Record Bureau (NCRB) issued the 2016 Crime in India Report, the most recent law enforcement data available. The 2016 report utilized different sections of law from previous years' reports by including additional sections of the penal code relevant to human trafficking and removing ITPA data from the reported totals for human trafficking, thereby making past data incomparable. The 2016 report also included IPC section 367 in its aggregated trafficking data despite this section covering crimes broader than trafficking; the government did not report if it had disaggregated non-trafficking crimes from the data. In 2016, police investigated 5,217 trafficking cases and the government completed the prosecution of 587 cases. Of these cases, courts convicted traffickers in 163 cases and acquitted individuals in 424 cases. The acquittal rate for trafficking cases increased from 65 percent in 2015 to 72 percent in 2016. The government did not publish the categorization of the cases between sex or labor trafficking. The NCRB did not include cases of bonded labor in the overall human trafficking statistics, but did separately report 114 investigations and 13 prosecutions of cases in 2016 under the BLSA. This was an increase from 77 investigations and seven case prosecutions in 2015. However, the courts' convictions under the BLSA remained notably low at only three in 2016 (compared to four in 2015), although bonded labor offenders may also be charged and convicted under other laws. The government did not report sentences for convictions. A senior police official noted at least one state did not report conviction data to the NCRB because of concern over the integrity of local data. Despite the overall increase in trafficking cases reported by the NCRB, NGOs continued to comment the figures did not reflect the large scale of human trafficking crimes in India, as many cases were not registered by police or were settled at the complaint stage. Inconsistent application of the law across jurisdictions, corruption among some officials, and a lack of awareness or capacity in some parts of the country resulted in incidents of inaction on trafficking crimes by police and prosecutors.

In February 2018, the Union Cabinet, chaired by the prime minister, approved the Trafficking in Persons (Prevention, Protection and Rehabilitation) Bill for introduction in the Parliament. If passed, the government reported the bill would address the issue of trafficking from the "point of view of prevention, rescue and rehabilitation," criminalize aggravated forms of trafficking, and create a national anti-trafficking bureau to comply with a December 2015 Supreme Court directive to establish an anti-trafficking investigative agency. The creation of such an agency was pending the passage of the anti-trafficking bill, although the Ministry of Women and Child Development (MWCD) had allocated 832 million Indian rupees (INR) ($13.1 million) to the Ministry of Home Affairs (MHA) for the agency. AHTUs continued to serve as the primary investigative force for human trafficking crimes. In the previous reporting period, MHA released funds to establish a total of 270 AHTUs out of the more than 600 districts. MHA reported 264 AHTUs were operational throughout the country during the reporting period, an increase of five compared with the previous reporting period. Some NGOs reported significant cooperation with AHTUs on investigations and police referral of victims to NGOs for rehabilitation services. However, other NGOs noted some AHTUs continued to lack clear mandates and were not solely dedicated to anti-trafficking, which created confusion with other district- and state-level police units and in some cases impeded their ability to proactively investigate cases. Some police offices reportedly used AHTU resources and personnel for non-trafficking cases. Coordination across states remained a significant challenge in cases where the alleged trafficker was located in a different state from the victim. NGOs noted some police offices were overburdened, underfunded, and lacked the necessary resources, such as vehicles and computers, to combat trafficking effectively. NGOs noted some prosecutors and judges did not have sufficient resources to properly prosecute and adjudicate cases. State and local governments partnered with NGOs and international organizations to train police, border guards, public prosecutors, railway police, and social welfare and judicial officers. MHA provided roughly 191,000 INR ($3,000) for Telangana and Andhra Pradesh to organize a judicial colloquium in December 2017 for 130 judges and prosecutors on sex trafficking.

Official complicity in human trafficking occurred at varying levels of government. The government did not report comprehensive data on investigations, prosecutions, or convictions of government officials complicit in human trafficking offenses. The 2016 Crime in India Report, the most recent law enforcement data available, stated under the corruption act and related IPC sections, there were 4,764 officials charged, 1,071 officials convicted, and 1,947 officials acquitted in 2016; the government did not report whether any of the cases were related to human trafficking. Some corrupt law enforcement officers reportedly protected suspected traffickers and brothel owners from law enforcement action, received bribes from sex trafficking establishments and sexual services from victims, and tipped off sex and labor traffickers on forthcoming raids. Media quoted a Delhi government official as stating Delhi's red-light area had become a hub for human trafficking, especially of girls, and alleging the involvement of police, politicians, and local government officials. There were no reports of investigations into such cases of complicity for the second consecutive year.

PROTECTION
The government increased efforts to protect victims. The NCRB reported the government's identification of 22,955 victims in 2016, compared with 8,281 in 2015. The NCRB reported 11,212 of the victims were exploited in forced labor, 7,570 exploited in sex trafficking, 3,824 exploited in an unspecified manner, and 349 exploited in forced marriage, although it is unclear if the forced marriage cases directly resulted in forced labor or sex trafficking. The government did not disaggregate the type of exploitation experienced by the age, gender, or nationality of the victim and included a small number of non-trafficking crimes in its overall victim demographic numbers; thus the following information included 162 more persons than the total number of trafficking victims identified. The government identified 8,651 boys, 7,238 women, 5,532 girls, and 1,696 men as trafficking victims. Of the victims, 22,932 were Indian, 38 Sri Lankan, 38 Nepali, 36 Bangladeshi, and 73 were various other nationalities, including Thai and Uzbek. A 2009 MHA non-binding directive advised state officials to use SOPs for proactive victim identification and referral to protection services; however, it is unclear if all 29 states employed such SOPs. Some NGOs noted police did not use SOPs and were not proactive in their identification of potential victims; instead, police reportedly relied on NGOs to identify and report the location of the victim to the police for rescue. In December 2017, after consultations with civil society, the National Human Rights Commission created and published SOPs for combating human trafficking. These SOPs included information on the definition of trafficking, myths and misconceptions about trafficking, a screening tool to help identify potential victims, steps to rescue a victim including providing immediate care and support to the victim, and information on rehabilitation programs and restitution. MWCD's SOPs for cases of missing children, created in the previous reporting period, continued to mandate the transfer of cases not resolved within four months to an AHTU. MWCD and MHA continued to implement TrackChild, a system to identify missing children nationally. MWCD continued to support the national Childline hotline, an emergency phone service for children in need of assistance, including trafficking victims. State- and district-level law enforcement continued to carry out operations to rescue and rehabilitate missing and exploited children, some of whom may have been subjected to forced labor or sex trafficking. Some state- and district-level law enforcement actively partnered with NGOs to identify, rescue, and provide rehabilitation services to victims; however, other police officers reportedly undertook rescue operations without further investigating or charging suspects.

MWCD continued to fund NGO- and government-run shelter and rehabilitation services for women and children through the *Ujjawala* program, specifically for female sex trafficking victims, and the *Swadhar Greh* program, for women in difficult circumstances. The central government's budget for the *Ujjawala* program increased from 203 million INR ($3.2 million) in 2016-2017 to 350 million INR ($5.5 million) in 2017-2018 and the *Swadhar Greh* budget decreased from 840 million INR ($13.2 million) to 750 million INR ($11.8 million). NGOs continued to report the number of government shelters was insufficient and overcrowding compromised victim rehabilitation. Both government- and NGO-run shelters faced shortages of financial resources and trained personnel, particularly of counselors and medical staff. NGOs relied primarily on donor contributions to provide victim services, although some received government funds. The disbursal of government funding to NGOs was sometimes delayed for multiple years and corruption reportedly drained some resources intended for victim care. Some victims waited months for transfer from temporary "transit homes" to shelters that provide long-term care due to shortages of government funds, shelter staff, or police escorts. Government child welfare committees placed child victims in private shelters or in government juvenile justice homes, some of which may have housed child victims with children accused of crimes. Children largely received the same government services as adults. Media reported allegations that some privately-run children's homes subjected children to trafficking. During the reporting period, police in Tamil Nadu charged the director of an unregistered children's home under trafficking and juvenile justice laws.

In May 2016, the central government revised its program for the rehabilitation of bonded laborers to increase compensation and include female sex trafficking and child forced labor victims as eligible to receive restitution and assistance. In June 2017, the Ministry of Labor and Employment (MoLE) disseminated a memo to local and state governments clarifying parts of the 2016 program and outlining additional modifications. The memo clarified district administrations could provide immediate monetary assistance up to 20,000 INR ($310) to a victim released from bonded labor regardless of the status of a related court case. However, the release of the overall restitution amounts (between 100,000 INR [$1,570] and 300,000 INR [$4,710] based on the victim's demographics) remained contingent on the conviction of the trafficker or administrative processes that may take several years to conclude. Media and NGOs reported a small number of victims received initial monetary assistance; however, media also reported the inaction of districts and states on bonded labor in part due to a lack of funds. State governments were required to provide victims with immediate monetary assistance from state budgets and then request reimbursement from the central government. Judges could also order victim restitution through other government compensation programs. While these programs were also mostly based on the conviction of the trafficker, in August 2017 before a trial took place a judge ordered restitution of 300,000 INR ($4,710) to a child sex trafficking victim under the 2012 Prevention of Children Against Sexual Offenses Act's compensation fund. Rescued bonded laborers were entitled to "release certificates" enabling them to receive government-funded services. Many victims received certificates at or soon after their rescue, especially in areas where there was significant coordination between the government and NGOs. Other victims experienced lengthy delays before obtaining the certificates. The government did not provide adult male trafficking victims, other than bonded labor victims, any protection services. Government-run hospitals provided emergency medical services to victims, although long waiting lists made it difficult to obtain surgery and other procedures and NGOs often had to pay for victims' emergency medical treatment. In August 2017, the district government of Jashpur, Chhattisgarh initiated a pilot program to provide ten female trafficking survivors a location and equipment to open a bakery. In March 2018, the President of the Republic of India awarded the bakery and the survivors the Nari Shakti Puraskar (Women Empowerment Award) and launched an NGO-run three-month course to build the confidence of trafficking survivors, assess their skills and educational levels, and connect them with the government-run Skill India program for vocational training. Media reported the government aimed to provide vocational training to 500,000 survivors in the future.

Foreign victims received the same access to shelter and services as Indian nationals. Government policy on foreign victims dictated their return to their country of origin at the earliest possible time. Authorities detained foreign sex trafficking victims to government aftercare homes until repatriation and did not permit them to work in the local economy. The repatriation of foreign victims could take years due to a number of constraints, including some victims' lack of identity documents. NGOs stated

children who could not identify their home state or country were unable to be returned to their families or place of origin. The governments of India and Bangladesh continued to implement their 2015 Memorandum of Understanding (MOU) on human trafficking, including through coordination on repatriation; Bangladeshi NGOs reported the average Bangladeshi victim was repatriated within six months.

To protect both Indian and foreign national victims during trial, prosecutors may request the victim be permitted to testify by video or behind a screen, the proceeding be closed to the media and public, and irrelevant and potentially harmful questions be barred; it is unknown if these protections were used for trafficking victims during the reporting period. In 2009, MHA provided guidelines to all state governments encouraging police not to charge victims for crimes committed while subjected to human trafficking, including foreign women and child victims for immigration violations. However, in certain cases, the government continued to penalize victims as a result of inconsistent identification and screening efforts, including sex trafficking victims arrested for prostitution and foreign trafficking victims charged with immigration violations. In 2014, the government began denying travel of trafficking victims and their family members, including by confiscating the passports of Indians who received a visa from a foreign government indicating the person was a trafficking victim in the foreign country or was a family member of a victim. The government revised this policy in 2015 to allow these victims and their families to renew their passports and travel if documentation of the victim's trafficking experience was provided and the Indian government determined the person to be a trafficking victim. However, some victims continued to cite lengthy delays, requests from the government for private or otherwise sensitive information, and inconsistent application of the policy when attempting to renew their passports. In 2016 and 2017, the government stamped the passports of some recipients of the foreign government's visas, for both trafficking victims and their eligible family members, identifying them as trafficking victims involved in a particular investigation, civil, or criminal case. While the stamp requested authorities permit the visa holder to travel without hindrance, some NGOs familiar with this practice noted it made some victims fearful of reprisal and penalization and served as a deterrent to victims interacting with authorities.

PREVENTION

The government maintained overall efforts to prevent human trafficking. The government's inter-ministerial committee, chaired by the secretary of the MWCD and including civil society organizations and relevant government ministries, met during the reporting period to discuss and revise the draft anti-trafficking bill. The government did not have a national action plan to combat trafficking; however, it did have a national plan of action for children, launched in a previous reporting period, which outlined efforts to prevent and protect children from trafficking and to conduct research and analysis. In January 2018, the government reported help desks had been established in 33 major railway stations to provide immediate support to unaccompanied children, who may be missing, abandoned, or runaways and who may be vulnerable to exploitation, including trafficking. Sashastra Seema Bal (SSB), India's border guard force on the India-Nepal border, conducted several awareness activities on human trafficking for students and border communities in September 2017. SSB hosted a workshop, organized a painting competition to raise awareness in 39 schools, and commissioned two vehicles to create an awareness caravan for border districts with speakers and awareness materials. Some state governments had state-level action plans, task forces, and MOUs to combat trafficking and conducted anti-trafficking awareness campaigns or made in-kind contributions to NGO-run campaigns. West Bengal police continued to implement regular awareness events with students, teachers, and administrators, including in four new districts in early 2018.

The government registered foreign recruitment agencies and Indian migrant workers through the eMigrate online system. The government required migrant workers going to 17 specific countries, including the Middle East, to receive emigration clearance before their departure. Among other steps, clearance required Indian overseas missions to verify employment agreements for unskilled and farm workers and all female migrant workers. The government banned female migrant workers under age 30 from working in the 17 countries. The UN and members of civil society continued to argue any ban on migration increased the likelihood of migrating illegally and therefore heightened their vulnerability to human trafficking. MEA provided counseling and other resources to those considering migrant work at five resource centers in Chennai, Gurgaon, Hyderabad, Kochi, and Lucknow. In July 2017, India's Cabinet approved revised guidelines for the MEA's Indian Community Welfare Fund (ICWF) to expand the fund's geographic use from 43 Indian missions to all Indian missions abroad and the scope of services to include awareness measures and hotlines for migrant workers in distress, in addition to continuing the services of shelter, legal assistance, and repatriation. The ICWF was primarily funded through overseas consular fees. The government had MOUs on human trafficking with Bahrain, Bangladesh, and the United Arab Emirates, and in January 2018, India and Cambodia signed a MOU on the prevention of human trafficking and the rescue and repatriation of victims. The government permitted licensed foreign employment recruiters to charge migrant workers up to 20,000 INR ($310) for worker-paid recruitment fees and costs; however, observers stated migrant workers were frequently charged more than the maximum and obtained loans to pay the recruiters, thereby increasing their debt and vulnerability to labor trafficking. The government prohibited the role of unregulated and unregistered sub-agents; however, sub-agents reportedly continued to operate widely with impunity. MEA reportedly worked with the Central Bureau of Investigation to address cases of recruitment fraud and trafficking allegations and revoked recruitment licenses, but it did not report how many licenses it revoked during the reporting period.

Within India, some states regulated aspects of the informal labor sector, including seven state governments that stipulated a minimum wage for domestic work. In October 2017, MoLE solicited public input on the formulation of a national domestic worker policy. The government amended the Child Labor (Abolition) Act in August 2016 to ban employment of children below the age of 14. The amended law also prohibited the employment of children between the ages of 14 and 18 in hazardous work except in mines; however, the law permitted employment of children in family-owned enterprises, involving nonhazardous activities, after school hours. Indian civil society continued to express concern that these changes amounted to legalizing some forms of child labor that would subsequently increase the vulnerability of children to trafficking. According to Indian child labor organizations, the number of labor inspectors was inadequate for the scope of work and inspectors could only inspect private farms or residences if a complaint had been filed.

The central government's May 2016 revision of the bonded laborers rehabilitation program provided for the reimbursement of 450,000 INR ($7,060) per district for a census of bonded labor. In its June 2017 memo, MoLE outlined modifications to this provision, including that the central government will advance 50 percent of the amount required for conducting the surveys to the state and that five evaluation studies per year may be conducted. The government did not report if any state had conducted such surveys.

Despite India being a destination for child sex tourism, the government did not report measures to reduce child sex tourism. In January 2018, the government of Andhra Pradesh appointed a panel of legal experts and civil society to make recommendations on which laws could be used to prosecute buyers of sex. The government did not report additional efforts to reduce the demand for commercial sex acts or forced labor. The Indian military conducted training on trafficking for its personnel before deployment on peacekeeping or similar missions. The government did not provide information about any anti-trafficking training provided to its diplomatic personnel.

TRAFFICKING PROFILE
As reported over the past five years, India is a source, destination, and transit country for men, women, and children subjected to forced labor and sex trafficking. Forced labor constitutes India's largest trafficking problem; men, women, and children in debt bondage—sometimes inherited from previous generations—are forced to work in brick kilns, rice mills, embroidery factories, and agriculture. Most of India's trafficking problem is internal, and those from the most disadvantaged social strata—lowest caste Dalits, members of tribal communities, religious minorities, and women and girls from excluded groups—are most vulnerable. Within India, some are subjected to forced labor in sectors such as construction, steel, garment, and textile industries, wire manufacturing for underground cables, biscuit factories, pickling, floriculture, fish farms, and ship breaking. Workers within India who mine for sand are potentially vulnerable to human trafficking. Thousands of unregulated work placement agencies reportedly lure adults and children under false promises of employment into sex trafficking or forced labor, including domestic servitude.

In addition to bonded labor, some children are subjected to forced labor as factory and agricultural workers, carpet weavers, domestic servants, and beggars. Begging ringleaders sometimes maim children to earn more money. Some NGOs and media report girls are sold and forced to conceive and deliver babies for sale. The "Provident Funds" or "Sumangali" scheme in Tamil Nadu, in which employers pay young women a lump sum, used for education or a dowry, at the end of multi-year labor contracts may amount to conditions of forced labor. Separatist groups, such as the Maoists in Bihar, Chhattisgarh, Jharkhand, Maharashtra, West Bengal, and Odisha, force some children to act as spies and couriers, plant improvised explosive devices, and fight against the government, although reportedly to a lesser degree than previous years.

Experts estimate millions of women and children are victims of sex trafficking in India. Traffickers use false promises of employment or arrange sham marriages within India or Gulf states and subject women and girls to sex trafficking. In addition to traditional red light districts, women and children increasingly endure sex trafficking in small hotels, vehicles, huts, and private residences. Traffickers increasingly use websites, mobile applications, and online money transfers to facilitate commercial sex. Children continue to be subjected to sex trafficking in religious pilgrimage centers and by foreign travelers in tourist destinations. Many women and girls, predominately from Nepal and Bangladesh, and from Europe, Central Asia, Africa, and Asia, including Rohingya and other minority populations from Burma, are subjected to sex trafficking in India. Prime destinations for both Indian and foreign female trafficking victims include Kolkata, Mumbai, Delhi, Gujarat, Hyderabad, and along the India-Nepal border; Nepali women and girls are increasingly subjected to sex trafficking in Assam, and other cities such as Nagpur and Pune. Some corrupt law enforcement officers protect suspected traffickers and brothel owners from law enforcement efforts, take bribes from sex trafficking establishments and sexual services from victims, and tip off sex and labor traffickers to impede rescue efforts.

Some Indian migrants who willingly seek employment in construction, domestic work, and other low-skilled sectors in the Middle East and, to a lesser extent, other regions, face forced labor, often following recruitment fraud and exorbitant recruitment fees charged by labor brokers. Girls from northeast India were reportedly vulnerable to human trafficking as they transited Burma on fake Burmese passports to circumvent the Indian government's required emigration clearance to migrate for work to certain countries. Some Bangladeshi migrants are subjected to forced labor in India through recruitment fraud and debt bondage. Some Nepali, Bangladeshi, and Afghan women and girls are subjected to both labor and sex trafficking in major Indian cities. Following the 2015 Nepal earthquakes, Nepali women who transit through India are increasingly subjected to trafficking in the Middle East and Africa. Some boys from Bihar and Uttar Pradesh are subjected to forced labor in embroidery factories in Nepal. Burmese Rohingya, Sri Lankan Tamil, and other refugee populations continue to be vulnerable to sex trafficking and forced labor in India.

INDONESIA: TIER 2

The Government of Indonesia does not fully meet the minimum standards for the elimination of trafficking; however, it is making significant efforts to do so. The government demonstrated increasing efforts compared to the previous reporting period; therefore Indonesia remained on Tier 2. The government demonstrated increasing efforts by investigating, prosecuting, and convicting more traffickers, and identifying more victims compared to the previous year. It also repatriated and provided services to more Indonesian victims from overseas; implemented new regulations to prevent trafficking in the fishing industry; negotiated initiatives with the private sector to reduce vulnerability of Indonesian overseas workers; and conducted training for officials. The government convicted an immigration official under the 2007 anti-trafficking law and sentenced him to six years in prison in June 2017. However, the government did not meet the minimum standards in several key areas. Endemic corruption among officials remained, which impeded anti-trafficking efforts and enabled many traffickers to operate with impunity. The 2007 anti-trafficking law included a requirement of demonstrated force, fraud, or coercion to constitute a child sex trafficking crime, which is inconsistent with international law. Officials' lack of familiarity with trafficking indicators and anti-trafficking laws impaired proactive victim identification among vulnerable populations and hindered law enforcement efforts.

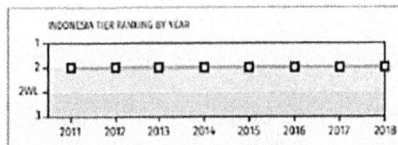

RECOMMENDATIONS FOR INDONESIA

Investigate, prosecute, and convict corrupt public officials that willfully ignore, facilitate, or engage in trafficking crimes; amend the 2007 law to remove the required demonstration of force, fraud, or coercion to constitute child sex trafficking; increase efforts to effectively monitor labor recruitment agencies and brokers and investigate, prosecute, and convict traffickers; refine procedures to identify potential victims among vulnerable groups, including returning migrant workers, persons in prostitution, and fishing vessel crewmembers; train marine ministry staff and labor inspectors on victim identification and referral procedures; provide anti-trafficking training for judges, prosecutors, police, and social workers; take steps to eliminate recruitment fees charged to workers by labor recruiters; proactively offer identified victim reintegration services; promote safe and legal migration with trafficking prevention measures; increase resources for the anti-trafficking task force and improve its coordination across ministries; establish a data collection system to track anti-trafficking efforts at all levels of law enforcement; train hospital staff and other health care providers about provisions guaranteeing government-funded care for trafficking victims; and create a national protocol that clarifies roles for prosecuting trafficking cases outside victims' home provinces.

PROSECUTION

The government increased law enforcement efforts. The 2007 anti-trafficking law criminalized all forms of labor trafficking and sex trafficking of adults and prescribed penalties of three to 15 years imprisonment, which were sufficiently stringent and, with respect to sex trafficking, commensurate with those prescribed for other serious crimes, such as rape. Inconsistent with international law, the law required a demonstration of force, fraud, or coercion to constitute a child sex trafficking offense, and therefore did not criminalize all forms of child sex trafficking.

Corrupt officials reportedly continued to facilitate the issuance of false documents, accepted bribes to allow brokers to transport undocumented migrants across borders, protected venues where sex trafficking occurred, practiced weak oversight of recruitment agencies, and thwarted law enforcement and judicial processes to hold traffickers accountable. However, the government did convict an immigration official under the 2007 anti-trafficking law and sentenced him to six years in prison in June 2017.

The government ratified the ASEAN Convention against Trafficking in Persons, Especially Women and Children, through passage of Law No.12/2017. The Law expanded the government's authority to prosecute suspects for illegal recruitment and provided a legal basis for Indonesian law enforcement agencies to collaborate with other ASEAN countries.

Officials reported ineffective coordination among police, witnesses, prosecutors, and judges continued to hinder the government's ability to investigate, prosecute, and convict traffickers, especially when cases involved numerous jurisdictions or other countries. The national police anti-trafficking unit did

EXHIBIT #19

2017 HUMAN RIGHTS REPORT: INDIA - U.S. DEPARTMENT OF STATE

INDIA 2017 HUMAN RIGHTS REPORT

EXECUTIVE SUMMARY

India is a multiparty, federal, parliamentary democracy with a bicameral legislature. The president, elected by an electoral college composed of the state assemblies and parliament, is the head of state, and the prime minister is the head of the government. Under the constitution the 29 states and seven union territories have a high degree of autonomy and have primary responsibility for law and order. Voters elected President Ram Nath Kovind in July to a five-year term, and Narendra Modi became prime minister following the victory of the National Democratic Alliance coalition led by the Bharatiya Janata Party in the 2014 general elections. Observers considered these elections, which included more than 551 million participants, free and fair despite isolated instances of violence.

Civilian authorities maintained effective control over the security forces.

The most significant human rights issues included police and security force abuses, such as extrajudicial killings, disappearances, torture, arbitrary arrest and detention, rape, harsh and life-threatening prison conditions, and lengthy pretrial detention. Widespread corruption; reports of political prisoners in certain states; and instances of censorship and harassment of media outlets, including some critical of the government continued. There were government restrictions on foreign funding of some nongovernmental organizations (NGOs), including on those with views the government stated were not in the "national interest," thereby curtailing the work of these NGOs. Legal restrictions on religious conversion in eight states; lack of criminal investigations or accountability for cases related to rape, domestic violence, dowry-related deaths, honor killings, sexual harassment; and discrimination against women and girls remained serious problems. Violence and discrimination based on religious affiliation, sexual orientation, and caste or tribe, including indigenous persons, also persisted due to a lack of accountability.

A lack of accountability for misconduct at all levels of government persisted, contributing to widespread impunity. Investigations and prosecutions of individual cases took place, but lax enforcement, a shortage of trained police officers, and an overburdened and underresourced court system contributed to a small number of convictions.

Separatist insurgents and terrorists in the state of Jammu and Kashmir, the northeast, and the Maoist-affected areas committed serious abuses, including killings and torture of armed forces personnel, police, government officials, and of civilians, and recruitment and use of child soldiers.

Section 1. Respect for the Integrity of the Person, Including Freedom from:

a. Arbitrary Deprivation of Life and Other Unlawful or Politically Motivated Killings

There were reports the government and its agents committed arbitrary or unlawful killings, including extrajudicial killings of suspected criminals and insurgents.

During the year the South Asian Terrorism Portal, run by the nonprofit Institute for Conflict Management, reported the deaths of 111 civilians, 15 security force members, and 210 terrorists or insurgents as of June 2. Data from the institute also showed 317 fatalities from terrorist violence were recorded in the state of Jammu and Kashmir through August, compared with 329 for 2016.

There were 108 reported deaths as a result of "encounter killings"--a term used to describe any encounter between the security or police forces and alleged criminals or insurgents that resulted in a death--documented countrywide by the Investigation Division of the National Human Rights Commission (NHRC), according to Ministry of Home Affairs 2016-17 data.

On June 6, police killed six individuals during a protest in Madhya Pradesh. The Madhya Pradesh government appointed a one-member commission to investigate police action and paid 10 million rupees ($160,000) to each of the victims' families. By year's end the investigation had not concluded.

Reports of custodial death cases, in which prisoners or detainees were killed or died in police custody, continued. Decisions by central and state authorities not to prosecute police or security officials despite reports of evidence in certain cases remained a problem. The National Crime Records Bureau (NCRB) reported 92 cases of custodial deaths nationwide in 2016 with Maharashtra reporting the highest number of cases at 16. Madhya Pradesh and Gujarat reported 11 cases, and Uttar Pradesh, nine cases. According to a media report, in response to a "Right to Information" (RTI) petition, the NHRC stated that 74 persons died in police custody from January 1 through August 2.

On July 24, the Supreme Court sought an update from the government's Central Bureau of Investigation (CBI) and the Madhya Pradesh state government on a

Country Reports on Human Rights Practices for 2017
United States Department of State • Bureau of Democracy, Human Rights and Labor

249 | P a g e

court-monitored investigation into the October 2016 killings of eight suspected members of the outlawed Students' Islamic Movement of India after they allegedly killed a guard and escaped from a high security prison. In November 2016 the NHRC issued a formal complaint against the state government, police, and prison authorities, expressing doubt that the men were killed while attempting to escape, classifying them instead as custodial deaths. A relative of one of the deceased, in her petition to the Supreme Court, criticized the Madhya Pradesh government for only appointing only a one-person investigative commission.

On October 25, a special CBI court brought charges against 16 law enforcement officers for their alleged involvement in the encounter deaths of Sohrabuddin Sheikh and Tulsiram Prajapati. A joint Rajasthan and Gujarat antiterrorist squad allegedly killed Sheikh on a highway near Ahmedabad in November 2005; later, police allegedly killed his wife Kausar Bi and Tulsiram Prajapati, a key witness in the case. According to the CBI, charges were not brought against those accused who had applications pending in the Bombay High Court or the Supreme Court.

On March 25, the High Court of Madras directed the Tamil Nadu government to pay one million rupees ($16,000) to the family of a man named Ramesh, known as "Nambu," who died in 2010 after reportedly being tortured while in police custody on suspicion of theft. The court also imposed a fine of 50,000 rupees ($800) on the municipal administration secretary of the Tamil Nadu government for failing to provide compensation to the family of the victim. A probe into the case by the additional director general of police confirmed in July that Nambu was subjected to "ill treatment" during his illegal detention and died as a result of this treatment.

Three individuals died in separate incidents due to alleged torture while in Telangana state police custody. On April 7, Mohan Krishna died on the way to a hospital after he returned from Begumpet police station in Hyderabad, where he was detained and questioned in a case of alleged sexual harassment of a minor. On April 21, a man identified as "Ganesh" died on the way to a hospital after he was interrogated in the Hayathnagar police station near Hyderabad for "suspicious movement" on the road. On March 18, Bhim Singh died in a Hyderabad police station after being detained for questioning following an altercation. In all these instances, police denied that detainees were tortured, citing previous illnesses as the cause of death.

The Armed Forces Special Powers Act (AFSPA) remained in effect in Nagaland, Manipur, Assam, and parts of Mizoram, and a version of the law was in effect in the state of Jammu and Kashmir. The government also declared Meghalaya's

Country Reports on Human Rights Practices for 2017
United States Department of State • Bureau of Democracy, Human Rights and Labor

250 | P a g e

border areas adjoining Assam and three districts in Arunachal Pradesh as "disturbed" for two more months from August through October. While the Nagaland government demanded the AFSPA be lifted in the state, the central government extended it through December.

Under the AFSPA, a central government designation of a state or union territory as a "disturbed area" authorizes security forces in the state to use deadly force to "maintain law and order" and arrest any person "against whom reasonable suspicion exists" without informing the detainee of the grounds for arrest. The law also provides security forces immunity from civilian prosecution for acts committed in regions under the AFSPA, although in 2016 the Supreme Court concluded that every death caused by the armed forces in a disturbed area, whether a common person or a terrorist, should be thoroughly investigated, adding that the law must be equally applied.

There was considerable public support for repeal of the AFSPA, particularly in areas that experienced a significant decrease in insurgent attacks. Human rights organizations also continued to call for the repeal of the law, citing numerous alleged human rights violations over the years. On July 14, the Supreme Court directed the CBI to set up a five-member team to examine at least 87 of 1,528 alleged killings by police, army, and paramilitary forces between 1979 and 2012 in Manipur. This order was in response to a petition filed by victims' families and NGOs. According to rights activists, until mid-December the CBI had not summoned any victims or witnesses and was still collecting documents related to the killings from the courts and the government of Manipur. The Supreme Court judgment stated the CBI must file formal charges by December 31.

The NGO Commonwealth Human Rights Initiative noted in its 2016 report that of 186 complaints of human rights violations reported against the armed forces in states under the AFSPA, between 2012 and 2016, 49.5 percent were from the state of Jammu and Kashmir. The data supplied by the Ministry of Home Affairs under the RTI Act did not, however, indicate whether complaints were deemed to have merit.

On June 27, the Gujarat High Court granted bail to Atul Vaidya, one of 24 individuals convicted in the 2002 Gulbarg Society killings, when a rioting mob killed 69 individuals during communal unrest. The Gujarat government did not allow the Supreme Court-appointed special investigation to appeal to the Supreme Court to enhance the sentences awarded to some of the 24 persons convicted or to challenge the acquittal of 14 others accused. On October 5, the Gujarat High Court

Country Reports on Human Rights Practices for 2017
United States Department of State • Bureau of Democracy, Human Rights and Labor

251 | P a g e

dismissed Zakia Jafri's plea, upholding a lower court's verdict exonerating senior Gujarat government officials, citing lack of prosecutable evidence following her allegations of "a larger conspiracy" behind the 2002 riots. The court allowed Jafri to appeal in higher courts.

Nongovernmental forces, including organized insurgents and terrorists, committed numerous killings and bombings in the state of Jammu and Kashmir, the northeastern states, and Maoist-affected areas (see section 1.g.). Maoists in Jharkhand and Bihar continued to attack security forces and key infrastructure facilities such as roads, railways, and communication towers. On April 24, Maoist insurgents attacked a convoy in Chhattisgarh, killing 25 Central Reserve Police Force personnel and critically injuring six.

b. Disappearance

There were allegations police failed to file required arrest reports for detained persons, resulting in hundreds of unresolved disappearances. Police and government officials denied these claims. The central government reported that state government screening committees informed families about the status of detainees. There were reports, however, that prison guards sometimes required bribes from families to confirm the detention of their relatives.

Disappearances attributed to government forces, paramilitary forces, and insurgents occurred in areas of conflict during the year (see section 1.g.).

c. Torture and Other Cruel, Inhuman, or Degrading Treatment or Punishment

The law prohibits torture, but NGOs reported torture occurred during the year.

Police beatings of prisoners resulted in custodial deaths (see section 1.a.).

The law does not permit authorities to admit coerced confessions into evidence, but NGOs and citizens alleged authorities used torture to coerce confessions. In some instances authorities submitted these confessions as evidence in capital cases. Authorities allegedly also used torture as a means to extort money or as summary punishment. According to human rights experts, the government continued to try individuals arrested and charged under the repealed Prevention of Terrorism Act and Terrorist and Disruptive Activities Act. Under the repealed laws, authorities treated a confession made to a police officer as admissible evidence in court.

Country Reports on Human Rights Practices for 2017
United States Department of State • Bureau of Democracy, Human Rights and Labor

On June 19, Abhay Singh, an antiques dealer, died while in custody in Odisha, allegedly following seven days of torture. Police took Singh into custody on May 30 to investigate the theft of a mobile phone, subsequently charged him with drug trafficking, and transported him to a hospital on June 10 where his health reportedly deteriorated. The NHRC and Odisha State Human Rights Commission (SHRC) ordered the state human rights protection cell of police to investigate and submit a report. At year's end there were no updates to the case.

On July 18, a 19-year-old lower-caste man reportedly committed suicide at Engadiyur in Kerala's Thrissur District a day after he was released from police custody for not having proper motor vehicle registration papers. His father and friends alleged instead that he died from injuries sustained from police brutality while in custody, and a postmortem report confirmed he had injuries consistent with torture. Based on the complaint by the victim's father, a case was filed against several police officers under the Criminal Procedure Code and the Scheduled Caste/Scheduled Tribes Prevention of Atrocities Act. Two police officers were suspended for the death, and the case was transferred to the Crime Bureau for further investigation.

There were continued reports that police raped female and male detainees. The government authorized the NHRC to investigate rape cases involving police officers. By law the NHRC may also request information about cases involving the army and paramilitary forces, but it has no mandate to investigate those cases. NGOs claimed the NHRC underestimated the number of rapes committed in police custody. Some rape victims were unwilling to report crimes due to social stigma and the possibility of retribution, compounded by a perception of a lack of oversight and accountability, especially if the perpetrator was a police officer or other official. There were reports police officials refused to register rape cases.

Prison and Detention Center Conditions

Prison conditions were frequently life threatening, most notably due to inadequate sanitary conditions and medical care and extreme overcrowding. Prisons did not meet international standards.

Physical Conditions: Prisons were often severely overcrowded, and food, medical care, sanitation, and environmental conditions often were inadequate. Potable water was often unavailable. Prisons and detention centers remained underfunded,

Country Reports on Human Rights Practices for 2017
United States Department of State • Bureau of Democracy, Human Rights and Labor

253 | P a g e

understaffed, and lacking sufficient infrastructure. Prisoners were physically mistreated.

According to the NCRB *Prison Statistics India 2015* report, there were 1,401 prisons in the country with an authorized capacity of 366,781 persons. The actual incarcerated population was 419,623. Persons awaiting trial accounted for more than two-thirds of the prison population. The law requires detention of juveniles in rehabilitative facilities, although at times authorities detained them in adult prisons, especially in rural areas. Authorities often detained pretrial detainees along with convicted prisoners. In Uttar Pradesh occupancy at most prisons was two and sometimes three times the permitted capacity, according to an adviser appointed by the Supreme Court.

In November 2016 the Commonwealth Human Rights Initiative launched two reports on the "alarming conditions" in prisons. According to the reports, those awaiting trial included 67 percent of the country's prison population, and independent monitors regularly inspected less than 1 percent of prisons.

According to the NCRB *Prison Statistics India 2015* report, overcrowding was most severe in Dadra and Nagar Haveli at 277 percent of capacity, while Chhattisgarh prisons were at 234 percent of capacity and Delhi prisons, at 227 percent of capacity. On August 8, Minister of State for Home Affairs Hansraj Gangaram Ahir quoted NCRB data to inform the lower house of parliament that 149 out of 1,401 jails in the country had an overcrowding rate of more than 200 percent at the end of 2015.

In March, Minister of State for Home Affairs Ahir informed the lower house of parliament that there were 4,391 female jail staff for a population of 17,834 female prisoners as of 2015.

On September 26, police submitted charges in a local court against six prison officials for the death of Manjula Shetye, a female convict in Mumbai. On July 8, Mumbai police arrested six prison officials who allegedly assaulted Shetye following her complaint about inadequate food. Her death resulted in violent protests by 200 prison inmates, who were later charged with rioting. On July 31, the Bombay High Court ordered an inquiry into the cause of Shetye's death. A government doctor who signed the death certificate was suspended.

Country Reports on Human Rights Practices for 2017
United States Department of State • Bureau of Democracy, Human Rights and Labor

254 | P a g e

<u>Administration</u>: Authorities permitted visitors some access to prisoners, although some family members claimed authorities denied access to relatives, particularly in conflict areas, including the state of Jammu and Kashmir.

On August 4, through an alternative dispute resolution mechanism, the Tamil Nadu State Legal Services Authority released 570 pretrial detainees (in nine Central Prisons and five Special Prisons for women in Tamil Nadu) who had been detained for longer than the minimum term prescribed for their alleged crimes.

<u>Independent Monitoring</u>: The NHRC received and investigated prisoner complaints of human rights violations throughout the year, but civil society representatives believed few prisoners filed complaints due to fear of retribution from prison guards or officials. On May 26, the NHRC ordered an investigation into torture allegations by 21 inmates on trial in a jail in Bhopal.

Authorities permitted prisoners to register complaints with state and national human rights commissions, but the authority of the commissions extended only to recommending that authorities redress grievances. Government officials reportedly often failed to comply with a Supreme Court order instructing the central government and local authorities to conduct regular checks on police stations to monitor custodial violence.

In many states the NHRC made unannounced visits to state prisons, but NHRC jurisdiction does not extend to military detention centers. An NHRC special rapporteur visited state prisons to verify that authorities provided medical care to all inmates. The rapporteur visited prisons on a regular basis throughout the year but did not release a report to the public or the press.

d. Arbitrary Arrest or Detention

The law prohibits arbitrary arrest and detention, but both occurred during the year. Police also used special security laws to postpone judicial reviews of arrests. Pretrial detention was arbitrary and lengthy, sometimes exceeding the duration of the sentence given to those convicted.

According to human rights NGOs, some police used torture, mistreatment, and arbitrary detention to obtain forced or false confessions. In some cases police reportedly held suspects without registering their arrests and denied detainees sufficient food and water.

Country Reports on Human Rights Practices for 2017
United States Department of State • Bureau of Democracy, Human Rights and Labor

255 | P a g e

Role of the Police and Security Apparatus

The 29 states and seven union territories have primary responsibility for maintaining law and order, with policy oversight from the central government. Police are under state jurisdiction. The Ministry of Home Affairs controls most paramilitary forces, the internal intelligence bureaus, and national law enforcement agencies, and provides training for senior officials from state police forces. According to Human Rights Watch (HRW), cases of arbitrary arrest, torture, and forced confessions by security forces remained common. Police continued to be overworked, underpaid, and subjected to political pressure, in some cases contributing to corruption. The HRW 2017 India country report found that officials were rarely prosecuted for crimes committed because the law made it "difficult, if not impossible" to prosecute public officials.

The effectiveness of law enforcement and security forces varied widely throughout the country. According to the law, courts may not hear a case against a police officer unless the central or state government first authorizes prosecution. Nonetheless, NGOs reported that in many instances police refused to register victim's complaints, termed "first information reports" (FIR), on crimes reported against officers, effectively preventing victims from pursuing justice. Additionally, NGOs reported that victims were sometimes reluctant to report crimes committed by police due to fear of retribution. There were cases of officers at all levels acting with impunity, but there were also cases of security officials held accountable for illegal actions. Military courts investigated cases of abuse by the armed forces and paramilitary forces. Authorities tried cases against law enforcement officers in public courts but sometimes did not adhere to due process. Authorities sometimes transferred officers after convicting them of a crime.

The NHRC recommended the Criminal Investigations Department of the state police investigate all deaths taking place during police pursuits, arrests, or escape attempts. Many states did not follow this nonbinding recommendation and continued to conduct internal reviews at the discretion of senior officers.

While NHRC guidelines call for state governments to report all cases of deaths from police actions to the NHRC within 48 hours, state governments did not consistently adhere to those guidelines. The NHRC also called for state governments to provide monetary compensation to families of victims, but the state governments did not consistently adhere to this practice. Authorities did not require the armed forces to report custodial deaths to the NHRC.

Country Reports on Human Rights Practices for 2017
United States Department of State • Bureau of Democracy, Human Rights and Labor

256 | P a g e

On July 27, the Armed Forces Tribunal suspended the life sentences of five army personnel involved in the 2010 killing of three civilians from the state of Jammu and Kashmir. The civilians were reportedly killed in a staged encounter and later accused of being foreign militants.

Arrest Procedures and Treatment of Detainees

Police may detain an individual without charge for up to 30 days, although an arrested person must be brought before a judge within 24 hours of arrest. Lengthy arbitrary detention remained a significant problem due to overburdened and under resourced court systems and a lack of legal safeguards.

Arraignment of detainees must occur within 24 hours unless authorities hold the suspect under a preventive detention law. State authorities invoked preventive detention laws, most frequently in Delhi but also in the states of Gujarat, Maharashtra, Uttar Pradesh, Punjab, and Jammu and Kashmir.

Authorities must promptly inform persons detained on criminal charges of the charges against them and of their right to legal counsel. By law a magistrate may authorize the detention of an accused person for a period of no more than 90 days prior to filing charges. Under standard criminal procedure, authorities must release the accused on bail after 90 days if charges are not filed. The law also allows police to summon individuals for questioning, but it does not grant police prearrest investigative detention authority. There were incidents in which authorities allegedly detained suspects beyond legal limits.

The law also permits authorities to hold a detainee in judicial custody without charge for up to 180 days (including the 30 days in police custody). The Unlawful Activities Prevention Act (UAPA), which gives authorities the ability to detain persons without charge in cases related to insurgency or terrorism, makes no bail provisions for foreign nationals and allows courts to deny bail in the case of detained citizens. It presumes the accused to be guilty if the prosecution can produce evidence of the possession of arms or explosives, or the presence of fingerprints at a crime scene, regardless of whether authorities demonstrate criminal intent. State governments also reportedly held persons without bail for extended periods before filing formal charges under the UAPA.

The law permits preventive detention in certain cases. The National Security Act allows police to detain persons considered security risks anywhere in the country, except the state of Jammu and Kashmir, without charge or trial for as long as one

Country Reports on Human Rights Practices for 2017
United States Department of State • Bureau of Democracy, Human Rights and Labor

257 | P a g e

year. The law allows family members and lawyers to visit national security detainees and requires authorities to inform a detainee of the grounds for detention within five days, or 10 to 15 days in exceptional circumstances.

The Public Safety Act, which applies only in the state of Jammu and Kashmir permits state authorities to detain persons without charge or judicial review for up to two years without visitation from family members. Authorities allowed detainees access to a lawyer during interrogation, but police in the state of Jammu and Kashmir allegedly routinely employed arbitrary detention and denied detainees access to lawyers and medical attention.

Accused individuals have a right to free legal assistance, including for their first hearing after arrest. The constitution specifies that the state should furnish legal aid to provide that opportunities for securing justice are not denied to any citizen by reason of economic or other disabilities, but authorities did not assess this need systematically.

There were reported cases in which police denied suspects the right to meet with legal counsel as well as cases in which police unlawfully monitored suspects' conversations and violated confidentiality rights. By law authorities must allow family members access to detainees, but this was not always observed.

Arbitrary Arrest: The law prohibits arbitrary arrest or detention, but in some cases police reportedly continued to arrest citizens arbitrarily. There were reports of police detaining individuals for custodial interrogation without identifying themselves or providing arrest warrants.

Pretrial Detention: The Center for Constitutional Right, Research and Advocacy (CCRRA) in Kochi, Kerala, reported certain prisoners with mental disabilities in the Kerala central prison considered "not fit for trial" had awaited trial for 10 to 26 years. According to the NGO, the prisoners in some cases were in detention far longer than their potential sentences. In 2013 CCRRA's founder filed a writ petition with the Kerala High Court for the release of those prisoners. The court responded by issuing an order directing the state government to provide adequate medical treatment to the accused to render them fit for trial. The case was pending in the Kerala High Court at year's end.

The government continued efforts to reduce lengthy detentions and alleviate prison overcrowding by using "fast track" courts, which specified trial deadlines, provided directions for case management, and encouraged the use of bail. Some

Country Reports on Human Rights Practices for 2017
United States Department of State • Bureau of Democracy, Human Rights and Labor

258 | Page

NGOs criticized these courts for failing to uphold due process and requiring detainees unable to afford bail remain in detention.

NCRB data from 2015 showed most individuals awaiting trial spent more than three months in jail before they could secure bail, and nearly 65 percent spent between three months and five years before being released on bail. The NCRB's 2016 report did not include updated statistics.

e. Denial of Fair Public Trial

The law provides for an independent judiciary, but judicial corruption was widespread. For example, in May, *The Hindu* newspaper reported on the case of five judges facing impeachment proceedings for a variety of offenses, including allegations of corruption.

The judicial system remained seriously overburdened and lacked modern case management systems, often delaying or denying justice. According to 2015-16 data released by the Supreme Court, there was a 43 percent vacancy of judges in the country's 24 high courts.

There were developments related to the 2010 killing of Amit Jethwa, an RTI activist. In June the Gujarat High Court ordered a retrial after concluding that Dinu Solanki, a member of parliament at the time he was accused of ordering Jethwa's killing, had tampered with witnesses after 105 out of 195 witnesses turned hostile during the trial. On October 30, the Supreme Court cancelled Solanki's bail and directed him to surrender to police. The court also ordered the trial to be held on a day-to-day basis and directed that Solanki not be in Gujarat unless required in the case.

Trial Procedures

The law provides for public trials, except in proceedings that involve official secrets or state security. Defendants enjoy the presumption of innocence, except as described under UAPA conditions, and may choose their counsel. The state provides free legal counsel to defendants who cannot afford it, but circumstances often limited access to competent counsel, and an overburdened justice system resulted in lengthy delays in court cases, with disposition sometimes taking more than a decade.

Country Reports on Human Rights Practices for 2017
United States Department of State • Bureau of Democracy, Human Rights and Labor

259 | P a g e

While defendants have the right to confront accusers and present their own witnesses and evidence, defendants sometimes did not exercise this right due to lack of proper legal representation. Defendants have the right not to testify or confess guilt. Courts must announce sentences publicly, and there are effective channels for appeal at most levels of the judicial system.

Political Prisoners and Detainees

There were reports of political prisoners and detainees. NGOs reported the state of Jammu and Kashmir held political prisoners and temporarily detained individuals under the Public Safety Act (PSA). More than 650 such cases were registered by the Jammu and Kashmir state government under the PSA through June and referred to the Jammu and Kashmir High Court.

Civil Judicial Procedures and Remedies

Individuals, or NGOs on behalf of individuals or groups, may file public-interest litigation (PIL) petitions in any high court or directly to the Supreme Court to seek judicial redress of public injury. Grievances may include a breach of public duty by a government agent or a violation of a constitutional provision. NGOs credited PIL petitions with making government officials accountable to civil society organizations in cases involving allegations of corruption and partiality.

In January 2016 the Bombay High Court addressed a two-fold rise in reported custodial death and police torture cases from 2014 to 2015 and directed the Maharashtra government to submit a report to the court. The court also criticized the government for its failure to install closed-circuit television cameras in police stations. In January the Maharashtra government allocated 27.5 million rupees ($440,000) to install closed-circuit television cameras in 25 of the 91 police stations in Mumbai in the first phase of implementation of a court order to install them in all police stations.

f. Arbitrary or Unlawful Interference with Privacy, Family, Home, or Correspondence

While the constitution does not contain an explicit right to privacy, the Supreme Court has found such a right implicit in other constitutional provisions. In August the Supreme Court ruled that privacy is a "fundamental right" in a case involving government collection of biographical information. The law, with some exceptions, prohibits arbitrary interference. The government generally respected

Country Reports on Human Rights Practices for 2017
United States Department of State • Bureau of Democracy, Human Rights and Labor

260 | P a g e

this provision, although at times authorities infringed upon the privacy rights of citizens. The law requires police to obtain warrants to conduct searches and seizures, except in cases in which such actions would cause undue delay. Police must justify warrantless searches in writing to the nearest magistrate with jurisdiction over the offense.

The law hindered transparency and accountability with regard to electronic surveillance. According to a government report quoting NCRB provisional data for 2016, Minister of State for Home Affairs Ahir cited 30 registered cases in violation of the law in 2016 compared with nine in 2015.

Both the central and state governments intercepted communications under legal authority. The Group of Experts on Privacy convened in 2012 by the Government of India Planning Commission, the most recent review available, noted that the differences between two provisions of law had created an unclear regulatory regime that was, according to the report, "inconsistent, nontransparent, prone to misuse, and does not provide remedy or compensation to aggrieved individuals."

The UAPA provides an additional legal basis for warrantless searches. The UAPA also allows use of evidence obtained from intercepted communications in terrorist cases. In the states of Jammu and Kashmir, Punjab, and Manipur, security officials have special authorities to search and arrest without a warrant.

The Chhattisgarh Special Public Security Act (CSPSA) of 2005 allows police to detain a person without charge for as long as 90 days. Opponents argued the law, which authorizes detention of individuals with a "tendency to pose an obstacle to the administration of law," infringed upon privacy and free speech. The government detained two journalists under the CSPSA, accusing them of complicity in a deadly attack on police by Naxalite insurgents; some media reports indicated authorities imprisoned the journalists because of their reporting. A local court acquitted one of the two journalists in July 2016. On February 27, the Supreme Court granted bail to Santosh Yadav, a freelance journalist from Chhattisgarh's Bastar District jailed under the CSPSA and the Unlawful Activities Prevention Act (UAPA) for alleged links with Maoist insurgents.

g. Abuses in Internal Conflict

The country's armed forces, the security forces of individual states, and paramilitary forces engaged in armed conflict with insurgent groups in several northeastern states, and with Maoist insurgents in the north, central, and eastern

Country Reports on Human Rights Practices for 2017
United States Department of State • Bureau of Democracy, Human Rights and Labor

261 | P a g e

parts of the country--although the intensity of these conflicts continued to decrease significantly. Army and central security forces remained stationed at conflict areas in the northeast.

The use of force by all parties to the conflicts resulted in deaths and injuries to both conflict participants and civilians. There were reports government security forces committed extrajudicial killings, including staging encounter killings to conceal the deaths of captured militants. Human rights groups claimed police refused to release bodies in cases of alleged "encounters." Authorities did not require the armed forces to report custodial deaths to the NHRC.

In July the SHRC directed the state of Jammu and Kashmir to pay one million rupees ($16,000) as compensation to a textile worker who was tied to the front bumper of a military jeep by an army major and used as a human shield against demonstrators in central Kashmir in May. Media reported Major Nitin Gogoi used the victim to prevent an angry mob from attacking military personnel during a parliamentary by-election on April 9. Human rights activists also criticized Army Chief General Bipin Rawat's statement backing Gogoi's actions. Gogoi was also awarded the army chief's commendation card for his action and was not individually punished.

The central and state governments and armed forces investigated complaints and punished some violations committed by government forces. Authorities arrested and tried insurgents under terrorism-related legislation.

There were few investigations and prosecutions of human rights violations arising from internal conflicts. NGOs claimed that due to AFSPA immunity provisions, authorities did not hold the armed forces responsible for the deaths of civilians killed in the state of Jammu and Kashmir in previous years.

Killings: Various domestic and international human rights organizations continued to express serious concern at the use of pellet guns by security forces for crowd control purposes in the state of Jammu and Kashmir. In 143 instances in which pellet guns were reportedly used across 12 districts of the Kashmir Valley through July 31, one civilian was killed and 36 were injured. By comparison in 2016 777 instances of pellet gun use across the state of Jammu and Kashmir, mostly during violent protests following the July 2016 killing of Hizbul Mujahideen terrorist Burhan Wani, left at least 15 civilians dead and 396 injured. In a report during the year, Amnesty International detailed cases of 88 individuals in the country whose eyesight was damaged by metal pellets fired by the state of Jammu and Kashmir

Country Reports on Human Rights Practices for 2017
United States Department of State • Bureau of Democracy, Human Rights and Labor

262 | P a g e

police and the Central Reserve Police Force in the years 2014-17. Both national and international media sources and NGOs have reported on the harm, both physical and psychological, to individuals injured by pellet guns.

In Maoist-affected areas, there were reports of abuses by security forces and insurgents. On March 29, two tribal-affiliated citizens died in Assam's Chirang District after an encounter with security forces. The two were believed to be members of a banned armed insurgent group called the National Democratic Front of Bodoland. In a report filed by the Assam Police, the security forces stated they came under heavy fire from the group and that retaliatory fire from the security forces killed the two men. An inquiry conducted by the inspector general of the Central Reserve Police Force (CRPF), however, stated that the two men, already in police custody, were taken to a nearby village, shot, and killed. The report also found that security forces planted arms and ammunition, including a hand grenade with Chinese markings, as incriminating evidence. The CRPF refused to make the inspector general's report public, although a pirated, online version was available.

On March 12, Maoist insurgents killed 13 paramilitary personnel near the Bheji village of Sukma in Chhattisgarh. On April 25, Maoist insurgents killed 25 paramilitary personnel and injured six others, also in Chhattisgarh. The soldiers were providing security for road construction at the time of the attack.

Abductions: Human rights groups maintained that military, paramilitary, and insurgent forces abducted numerous persons in Manipur, Jharkhand, and Maoist-affected areas. Human rights activists alleged cases of prisoners tortured or killed during detention. During the year media outlets reported cases of abduction by insurgent groups in Manipur. According to media reports, in May militants abducted three Kuki tribal members in Manipur and killed two of them. No one claimed responsibility for the incident. United NGOs Mission Manipur reported 291 cases of extrajudicial killing, rape, and disappearance committed by security forces, including Assam Rifles, Manipur Police, and the army as of June.

Physical Abuse, Punishment, and Torture: There were reports government security forces tortured, raped, and mistreated insurgents and alleged terrorists in custody and injured demonstrators.

Child Soldiers: Insurgent groups reportedly used children to attack government entities. The Ministry of Home Affairs reported Maoist groups conscripted boys and girls ages six to 12 into specific children's units (Bal Dasta and Bal Sangham) in the states of Bihar, Jharkhand, Chhattisgarh, and Odisha. The Maoist groups

Country Reports on Human Rights Practices for 2017
United States Department of State • Bureau of Democracy, Human Rights and Labor

263 | Page

used the children in combat and intelligence-gathering roles. Insurgents trained children as spies and couriers, as well as in the use of arms, planting explosives, and intelligence gathering.

Although the United Nations was not able to verify all allegations of child soldiers, reports submitted to parliament contained similar allegations. Recruitment of children by Maoist armed groups allegedly continued. Observers reported children as young as age 12 were members of Maoist youth groups and allied militia. The children reportedly handled weapons and improvised explosive devices (IEDs). Maoists reportedly held children against their will and threatened severe reprisals, including the killing of family members, if the children attempted to escape. The government claimed, based on statements of several women formerly associated with Maoist groups, that sexual violence, including rape and other forms of abuse, was a practice in some Maoist camps. NGOs quoting police contacts stated that children employed by Maoist groups in Jharkhand were made to carry IED triggers with them. Police did not engage the children to retrieve these triggering devices.

According to government sources, Maoist armed groups used children as human shields in confrontations with security forces. Attacks on schools by Maoists continued to affect children's access to education in affected areas. There were continued reports on the use of schools as military barracks and bases. The deployment of government security forces near schools remained a concern. There were reports armed groups recruited children from schools in Chhattisgarh.

Other Conflict-related Abuse: The Internal Displacement Monitoring Center estimated that conflicts, violence, and natural disasters in the country displaced 2.8 million persons in 2016.

In August, Minister of State for Home Affairs Ahir informed parliament's lower house there were approximately 62,000 registered Kashmiri migrant families in the country. The Jammu and Kashmir state government reported threats to Kashmiri Pandits (Hindus) in the Kashmir Valley during the year. Tens of thousands of Kashmiri Pandits have fled the Kashmir Valley to Jammu, Delhi, and other areas in the country since 1990 because of conflict and violent intimidation, including destruction of houses of worship, sexual abuse, and theft of property, by Kashmiri separatists.

During the year the state of Jammu and Kashmir allotted apartments to 31 Kashmiri Pandit migrant families who did not leave the valley during the 1990s.

Country Reports on Human Rights Practices for 2017
United States Department of State • Bureau of Democracy, Human Rights and Labor

264 | P a g e

These flats were constructed under a program approved by the central government for rehabilitation of Kashmiri migrants.

In the central and eastern areas, armed conflicts between Maoist insurgents and government security forces over land and mineral resources in tribal forest areas continued. According to the South Asian Terrorism Portal's existing conflict map, Maoist-affected states included Madhya Pradesh, Maharashtra, Karnataka, Kerala, Tamil Nadu, Andhra Pradesh, Telangana, Odisha, Chhattisgarh, Jharkhand, West Bengal, Bihar, Uttar Pradesh, and Assam. Human rights advocates alleged the government's operations sought not only to suppress the Maoists but also to force tribal populations from their land, allowing for purchase by the private sector.

Internally displaced person (IDP) camps continued to operate in Chhattisgarh for tribal persons displaced during the 2005 fighting between Maoists and the subsequently disbanded state-sponsored militia Salwa Judum.

Throughout the year there were reports by media organizations and academic institutions of corporations' abuses against tea workers, including violations of the law. In some cases violent strikes resulted from companies withholding medical care required by law. Other reports indicated workers had difficulty accessing clean water, with open sewage flowing through company housing areas.

On January 6, the NHRC found that Chhattisgarh police personnel in Bijapur District raped 16 tribal women in 2015. The NHRC directed state authorities to compensate the victims and initiate action against the perpetrators. The NHRC also began an investigation into details of the sexual assault allegations, which the victims reported in January 2016. There was no update on the status of the investigation or delivery of compensation by year's end.

Section 2. Respect for Civil Liberties, Including:

a. Freedom of Expression, Including for the Press

The constitution provides for freedom of speech and expression, but it does not explicitly mention freedom of the press. The government generally respected these rights, although there were instances in which the government allegedly pressured or harassed media outlets critical of the government.

Freedom of Expression: Individuals routinely criticized the government publicly and privately. According to HRW, however, sedition and criminal defamation

Country Reports on Human Rights Practices for 2017
United States Department of State • Bureau of Democracy, Human Rights and Labor

265 | P a g e

laws were sometimes used to prosecute citizens who criticized government officials or opposed state policies. In certain cases local authorities arrested individuals under laws against hate speech for expressions of political views. Freedom House asserted the view that freedom of expression is eroding in the country, noting the government's silence regarding direct attacks on free speech. In some instances the government reportedly withheld public-sector advertising from outlets that criticized the government, causing some outlets to practice self-censorship. According to media watchdog The Hoot's *India Freedom Report* detailing cases between January 2016 and April 2017, "there was an overall sense of shrinking liberty not experienced in recent years." The report detailed 54 alleged attacks on journalists, at least three cases of television news channels being banned, 45 internet shutdowns, and 45 sedition cases against individuals and groups.

On March 12, a graduate student from Periyar University in Tamil Nadu state was apprehended by police while distributing pamphlets in support of continuing protests against government oil exploration projects at Neduvasal in Pudukottai District and Kadiramangalam in Thanjavur District. Police invoked a provision of the Goondas Act, which allows preventive detention of a habitual offender for up to one year without the possibility of bail. Chief Minister Edappadi K. Palaniswami, who also holds the home portfolio, defended the student's detention, saying that she "was causing disturbances to the public by taking part in various protests."

On September 13, Akhil Gogoi, an RTI activist and president of the anticorruption organization Krishak Mukti Sangram Samiti, was arrested in Assam on charges of sedition a day after he gave a speech criticizing various policies of the ruling Bharatiya Janata Party (BJP). Additionally, Gogoi was labelled a Maoist by the government. His case continued at year's end.

Press and Media Freedom: Independent media generally expressed a wide variety of views. The law prohibits content that could harm religious sentiments or provoke enmity among groups, and authorities invoked these provisions to restrict print media, broadcast media, and publication or distribution of books.

On June 5, CBI officials searched the offices and residence of NDTV founder Prannoy Roy due to fraud allegations. NDTV called the raids "a blatant political attack on the freedom of the press." Other news agencies characterized the raids as political in light of NDTV's critical reports of BJP leadership. The Editors Guild of India expressed concern about the raids and called on the CBI to uphold due

Country Reports on Human Rights Practices for 2017
United States Department of State • Bureau of Democracy, Human Rights and Labor

266 | P a g e

process of law and freedom of expression for media. On September 11, *Hindustan Times* (HT) owner Shobhana Bhartia announced editor in chief Bobby Ghosh's exit from the media outlet. Ghosh had been critical of BJP leadership, including Prime Minister Modi, and was the creator of HT's "Hate Tracker" regarding violence against Muslims; Dalits; women; lesbian, gay, bisexual, transgender, and intersex individuals (LGBTI); and other discriminated groups.

On November 5, cartoonist G. Bala was arrested for posting a cartoon critical of Tamil Nadu Chief Minister Edappadi K. Palaniswami and other state government officials on his Facebook page. Bala's cartoon suggested officials were preoccupied with enriching themselves rather than addressing the problems of citizens. Police confirmed Bala was arrested and charged with publishing obscene materials in electronic form and printing defamatory material. He was granted bail on November 6.

The government maintained a monopoly on AM radio stations, limiting broadcasting to the state-owned All India Radio (AIR), and restricted FM radio licenses for entertainment and educational content. Widely distributed private satellite television provided competition for Doordarshan, the government-owned television network. There have been some accusations of political interference in the state-owned broadcasters. On August 15, the Chief Minister of Tripura, Manik Sarkar, alleged that Doordarshan and AIR refused to broadcast his Independence Day remarks. State governments banned the import or sale of some books due to material government censors deemed inflammatory or could provoke communal or religious tensions.

Violence and Harassment: Some journalists and media persons reportedly experienced violence and harassment in response to their reporting. During the year a subcommittee of the Press Council of India issued a report to the government on the protection and preservation of the freedom of the press and integrity of journalists; the report highlighted that at least 80 journalists had been killed since 1990 and only one conviction had been made.

Online and mobile harassment, particularly of female journalists, was prevalent, with some female activists and journalists reporting that they receive thousands of abusive tweets from "trolls" every week. The HT launched an antitrolling campaign to call attention to this problem.

The Committee to Protect Journalists (CPJ) expressed concern over attacks on journalists. For example, according to the CPJ, supporters of a legislator

Country Reports on Human Rights Practices for 2017
United States Department of State • Bureau of Democracy, Human Rights and Labor

267 | P a g e

associated with the ruling Telugu Desam Party allegedly chased and attacked a reporter with a local Telugu newspaper in Andhra Pradesh on February 5. The attack, which was recorded anonymously on video, was allegedly in retribution for an investigative report published in a local journal, which accused the legislator and his brother of illegally mining sand and defaulting on bank loans.

On September 5, senior journalist and activist Gauri Lankesh was shot and killed by three assailants at her home in Bengaluru. The Karnataka government instituted a Special Investigation Team to probe the killing. On September 11, UN High Commissioner for Human Rights Zeid Ra'ad al-Hussein highlighted the killing of Lankesh as a journalist who addressed the corrosive effect of sectarianism and hatred. No arrests were made, and the investigation continued at year's end.

On September 20, television journalist Shantau Bhowmik was beaten and stabbed to death while reporting on a clash between police and the Indigenous People's Front of Tripura. The National Union of Journalists India and others have condemned Bhowmik's death and called for a journalist protection act to provide safety for journalists.

In an October 3 report, Reporters without Borders reported that journalist Deeksha Sharma received messages threatening her with rape and death. The report also included threats against *Asian News International*'s Abhay Kumar, *The Hindu's* Mohammad Ali, *Firstpost's* Debobrat Ghose, and NDTV's Sonal Mehrotra Kapoor, among others.

Censorship or Content Restrictions: In June the Union Ministry of Information and Broadcasting denied permission to screen three films at a film festival in Kerala. Films screened at festivals do not require certification by the Central Board of Film Certification (CBFC), but they need a censor exemption from the ministry. The three films were about protests at the Jawaharlal Nehru University, the unrest in Kashmir, and the suicide of doctoral student activist Rohith Vemula.

In July the CBFC refused to approve a documentary on Nobel Laureate Economist Amartya Sen for public viewing. According to media reports, the CBFC objected to sections in the documentary where Sen used the terms "cow," "Gujarat," "Hindu India," and "Hindutva." The maker of the documentary, Suman Ghosh, refused to accede to the CBFC instruction to mute these four terms.

Libel/Slander Laws: In April the BJP filed a complaint against Delhi Chief Minister Arvind Kejriwal for accusing the National Election Commission of

Country Reports on Human Rights Practices for 2017
United States Department of State • Bureau of Democracy, Human Rights and Labor

268 | P a g e

manipulating voting machines, the use of which Kejriwal's Aam Aadmi Party had contested and lost, in the Punjab state elections.

National Security: In some cases government authorities cited laws protecting national interest to restrict media content. For example, on April 26, the state of Jammu and Kashmir ordered internet service providers to block 22 social media and instant messaging sites, including Facebook, WhatsApp, and Twitter, for one month after persistent street demonstrations. This was the first time the state government banned individual social media websites rather than restricting internet and data services.

Nongovernmental Impact: In a statement released in June 2016, UN special rapporteurs on human rights expressed the view that Foreign Contribution Regulation Act (FCRA) "provisions were increasingly being used...to silence organizations involved in advocating civil, political, economic, social, environmental, or cultural priorities, which may differ from those backed by the [g]overnment." The statement highlighted the suspension of foreign banking licenses for NGOs including Greenpeace India, Lawyers Collective, and the Sabrang Trust. In May, HRW urged UN member countries to call on India to stop targeting NGOs and others who criticized the government or its policies.

Internet Freedom

There were some government restrictions on access to the internet, disruptions of access to the internet, and censorship of online content. There were also reports the government occasionally monitored users of digital media, such as chat rooms and person-to-person communications. The law permits the government to block internet sites and content and criminalizes sending messages the government deems inflammatory or offensive. Both central and state governments have the power to issue directions for blocking, intercepting, monitoring, or decrypting computer information.

In 2015 the Supreme Court struck down a provision of information technology law that had resulted in a significant number of arrests between 2012 and 2015 for content published on social media. The Supreme Court upheld other provisions authorizing the government to block certain online content. One provision gives the government authority to issue orders to block online content "in the interest of sovereignty and integrity of India, defense of India, security of the State, and friendly relations with foreign states or public order" without court approval.

On August 7, the central Ministry of Communications announced new rules allowing the government to shut telephone and internet services temporarily during a "public emergency" or for "public safety." Experts noted these rules meant internet shutdowns could be carried out in a more organized manner but raised concerns over arbitrary censorship. According to HRW from January to June, the government temporarily shut the internet 20 times in different locations across the country. In 2016 there were 31 reported shutdowns.

Internet access and services were frequently curtailed during several weeks of violence and curfew in the state of Jammu and Kashmir and occasionally in other parts of the country, including in Haryana during large-scale demonstrations by the Dera Sacha Sauda religious sect in August. The government claimed that it was sometimes necessary to restrict access to the internet to prevent violence fueled by social media. According to HRW authorities sometimes failed to follow legal procedures and in some instances ordered shutdowns unnecessarily.

In July media watchdog The Hoot reported internet shutdowns had risen from eight in the first half of 2016 to 23 in the first half of the year.

In July and August, the central government's Ministry of Electronics and Information Technology, based on a complaint filed by the State of Jammu and Kashmir Police, reportedly asked Twitter to block 248 accounts, tweets, and hashtags in view of threats posed by them. The ministry requested that a list of 115 accounts and tweets, which were found "propagating objectionable contents," be blocked "in the interest of the public order as well as for preventing any cognizable offense...."

Persons continued to be charged with posting offensive or derogatory material on social media. For example, the BJP filed charges against Delhi Chief Minister Arvind Kejriwal for posting election-related material on Facebook. An individual was arrested in Madhya Pradesh on charges of hurting religious sentiments by posting a picture of a holy man buying meat. Following Hindu nationalist Yogi Adityanath's appointment as chief minister of Uttar Pradesh, several critics were reportedly charged over their social media posts.

The Central Monitoring System (CMS) continued to allow governmental agencies to monitor electronic communications in real time without informing the subject or a judge. The CMS is a mass electronic surveillance data-mining program installed by the Center for Development of Telematics, a government-owned telecommunications technology development center. The CMS gives security

Country Reports on Human Rights Practices for 2017
United States Department of State • Bureau of Democracy, Human Rights and Labor

270 | P a g e

agencies and income tax officials centralized access to the telecommunication network and the ability to hear and record mobile, landline, and satellite telephone calls and Voice over Internet Protocol, to read private emails and mobile phone text messages, and to track geographical locations of individuals in real time. Authorities can also use it to monitor posts shared on social media and track users' search histories on search engines, without oversight by courts or parliament. This monitoring facility was available to nine security agencies, including the Intelligence Bureau, the Research and Analysis Wing, and the Home Affairs Ministry.

In August, Minister of State in the Ministry of Communications Manoj Singh informed parliament's upper house that the government decided to set up the CMS to automate the process of lawful interception and monitoring of telecommunications. The law governing interception and monitoring provides an oversight mechanism to prevent unauthorized interceptions. Punishment for unauthorized interception includes fines and/or a maximum prison sentence of three years.

Freedom House, in its 2016 India Country Report, rated the country "partly free" with respect to internet user rights, including accessibility, limits on content, and violations of individual rights. According to Freedom House, internet freedom declined slightly in 2016, offsetting gains made in 2014 and 2015. The NGO reported the number of network shutdowns ordered by local authorities increased. The report documented incidents of physical attacks on internet users for content posted online and stated at least 17 individuals were arrested for information circulated on WhatsApp, including group administrators based on content shared by other group members.

Authorities may hold search engines liable for displaying prohibited content, and the government sometimes requested user data from internet companies. According to Facebook's April transparency report, the government made 7,289 data requests in the second half of 2016, and Facebook complied with 52 percent of those requests. Google also highlighted an increase in government requests for user data in its most recent transparency report. From January 1 through June 30, Twitter reported 261 account information requests from the government--a 55-percent increase over the previous six months--and 102 requests for accounts to be removed.

Academic Freedom and Cultural Events

The government occasionally applied restrictions on the travel and activities of visiting foreign experts and scholars; however, in most cases the government supported and issued visas for international academic conferences and exchanges.

Police in Telangana and Andhra Pradesh filed cases against lower-caste Dalit academician Kancha Ilaiah Shepherd after complaints were received from Vysya caste groups that his book, *Samajika Smugglurlu Komatollu*, portrayed the community in a negative light. On September 12, Hyderabad police registered three cases following complaints lodged by Vysya caste associations and Ilaiah against each other. Ilaiah also complained of receiving abusive calls and death threats. On September 19, the Andhra Pradesh Crime Investigation Department filed a case against Ilaiah on the charge of "promoting enmity between different groups based on religion, place, and through other means." Andhra Pradesh Director General of Police N. Sambasiva Rao stated police were examining if there was a need to ban the book.

b. Freedoms of Peaceful Assembly and Association

The law provides for the freedoms of peaceful assembly and association, and the government generally respected those rights.

Freedom of Peaceful Assembly

The law provides for freedom of assembly. Authorities often required permits and notification before parades or demonstrations, and local governments generally respected the right to protest peacefully, except in the state of Jammu and Kashmir, where the state government sometimes denied permits to separatist political parties for public gatherings, and security forces sometimes reportedly detained and assaulted members of political groups engaged in peaceful protest (see section 1.g.). During periods of civil unrest in the state of Jammu and Kashmir, authorities used the law to ban public assemblies or impose curfews.

Security forces, including local police, often disrupted demonstrations and used excessive force when attempting to disperse protesters.

From January 17-23, thousands of protesters assembled in Chennai and other parts of Tamil Nadu demanding legalization of the traditional Tamil sport Jallikattu, a form of bullfighting, which was banned in 2014. Some protesters alleged police used disproportionate force to disband peaceful gatherings on January 23, leading to widespread unrest with pockets of violence across the state.

Country Reports on Human Rights Practices for 2017
United States Department of State • Bureau of Democracy, Human Rights and Labor

272 | P a g e

There were restrictions on the organization of international conferences. Authorities required NGOs to secure approval from the Ministry of Home Affairs before organizing international conferences. Authorities routinely granted permission, although in some cases the approval process was lengthy. Some human rights groups claimed this practice provided the government with tacit control over the work of NGOs and constituted a restriction on freedoms of assembly and association.

Freedom of Association

The law provides for freedom of association. While the government generally respected that right, the government's increased regulation of NGO activities that receive foreign funding has caused concern. In certain cases, for example, the government required "prior approval" for some NGOs to receive foreign funds, and in other instances canceled or declined to renew FCRA registrations. According to media reports, the government took action to suspend foreign banking licenses or freeze accounts of NGOs that allegedly received foreign funding without the proper clearances or illegally combined foreign and domestic funding streams. Some human rights organizations claimed these actions were sometimes used to target specific NGOs.

In March the NGO Compassion International, which had been placed on the government's prior approval list, closed its operations due to the inability to transfer funds to its implementing partners. The human rights NGO The Lawyer's Collective was unable to reregister after its FCRA registration was cancelled in 2016. According to media reports, on April 10, the Ministry of Home Affairs also cancelled the license of the Public Health Foundation of India (PHFI), a public health advocacy group. The PHFI filed a request with the government for reinstatement of its license, which continued under government review at year's end.

In July, Minister of State for Home Affairs Kiren Rijiju told parliament's lower house more than 1,000 NGOs were barred from receiving foreign aid after they were found to have "misutilized" such funds. He said more than 2,000 NGOs have been asked to validate their existing bank accounts designated for receiving funds from abroad. All organizations that received financial aid from abroad must be registered under FCRA.

Country Reports on Human Rights Practices for 2017
United States Department of State • Bureau of Democracy, Human Rights and Labor

273 | P a g e

NGOs continued to express concern regarding the government's enforcement of the FCRA, provisions of which bar some foreign-funded NGOs from engaging in activities the government believed were not in the "national or public interest," curtailing the work of some civil society organizations. Some NGOs expressed concern over politically motivated enforcement of the law to intimidate organizations that address social issues or criticize the government or its policies, arguing that the law's uses of broad and vague terms such as "public interest" and "national interest" have left it open to abuse. Some multi-national and domestic companies also stated in some instances the law made it difficult to comply with government-mandated corporate social responsibility obligations due to lengthy and complicated registration processes.

Experts also reported that it was increasingly difficult to secure FCRA registrations for new NGOs. Although the law imposes a limit of 90 days for application processing, FCRA applications were sometimes pending months longer.

In April 2016 the UN special rapporteur on freedom of assembly and association published a legal analysis asserting that the FCRA did not conform to international law, principles, and standards. In June 2016 the UN special rapporteurs on human rights defenders, freedom of expression, and freedom of assembly and association called on the government to repeal the FCRA.

c. Freedom of Religion

See the Department of State's *International Religious Freedom Report* at www.state.gov/religiousfreedomreport/.

d. Freedom of Movement

The law provides for freedom of internal movement, foreign travel, emigration, and repatriation. The government generally respected these rights. In 2015 the implementation of a land boundary agreement between India and Bangladesh enfranchised more than 50,000 previously stateless residents, providing access to education and health services.

The country hosts a large refugee population, including 108,005 Tibetan refugees and approximately 63,000 from Sri Lanka. The government generally allows the Office of the High Commissioner for Refugees (UNHCR) to assist the 36,000 asylum seekers and refugees from noncontiguous countries and Burma. In some

Country Reports on Human Rights Practices for 2017
United States Department of State • Bureau of Democracy, Human Rights and Labor

274 | P a g e

cases refugees and asylum seekers under UNHCR's mandate have faced challenges regularizing their status through long-term visas and residence permits.

<u>Abuse of Migrants, Refugees, and Stateless Persons</u>: The law does not contain the term "refugee," treating refugees as any other foreigners. Undocumented physical presence in the country is a criminal offense. Persons without documentation were vulnerable to forced returns and abuse.

The courts appropriately protected refugees and asylum seekers in accordance with the constitution.

Refugees reported exploitation by nongovernment actors, including assaults, gender-based violence, frauds, and labor exploitation. Also, problems of domestic violence, sexual abuse, and early and forced marriage continued. Gender-based violence and sexual abuse were common in camps for Sri Lankans. Most urban refugees worked in the informal sector or in occupations such as street vending, where they suffered from police extortion, nonpayment of wages, and exploitation.

On August 9, Minister of State for Home Affairs Kiren Rijiju stated in parliament that Rohingya were "illegal immigrants in India and as per law they stand to be deported." A Home Ministry spokesperson later clarified that the government was trying to identify how many refugees were in the country and asking states to develop plans proactively.

<u>In-country Movement</u>: The central government relaxed restrictions on travel by foreigners to Arunachal Pradesh, Nagaland, Mizoram, Manipur, and parts of Jammu and Kashmir, excluding foreign nationals from Pakistan, China, and Burma. The Ministry of Home Affairs and state governments required citizens to obtain special permits upon arrival when traveling to certain restricted areas.

<u>Foreign Travel</u>: The government may legally deny a passport to any applicant for engaging in activities outside the country "prejudicial to the sovereignty and integrity of the nation."

The trend of delaying issuance and renewal of passports to citizens from the state of Jammu and Kashmir continued, sometimes up to two years. The government reportedly subjected applicants born in the state of Jammu and Kashmir, including children born to military officers deployed in the state, to additional scrutiny and police clearances before issuing them passports.

Country Reports on Human Rights Practices for 2017
United States Department of State • Bureau of Democracy, Human Rights and Labor

275 | Page

Internally Displaced Persons (IDPs)

Authorities located IDP settlements throughout the country, including those containing groups displaced by internal armed conflicts in the state of Jammu and Kashmir, Maoist-affected areas, the northeastern states (see section 1.g.), and Gujarat. The 2016 annual report of the Internal Displacement Monitoring Center asserted that longstanding regional conflicts had displaced at least 796,000 persons. Estimating precise numbers of those displaced by conflict or violence was difficult, because the government does not monitor the movements of displaced persons, and humanitarian and human rights agencies had limited access to camps and affected regions. While authorities registered residents of IDP camps, an unknown number of displaced persons resided outside camps. Many IDPs lacked sufficient food, clean water, shelter, and health care (see section 1.g., Other Conflict-related Abuse).

Paramilitary operations against Maoists displaced members of the Gotti Koya tribe in the Dandakaranya forests in Chhattisgarh, who migrated to the neighboring Khammam and Bhupalapalli Districts in Telangana. Following the bifurcation of Andhra Pradesh to form the new state of Telangana in 2014, the state governments transferred parts of Khammam District with Gotti Koya settlements to Andhra Pradesh.

NGOs estimated the number of IDPs in Chhattisgarh at 50,000 and in Telangana and Andhra Pradesh combined at 27,000. The Chhattisgarh government reportedly did not acknowledge IDPs in Andhra Pradesh and Telangana camps as Chhattisgarh residents, and the Andhra Pradesh and Telangana governments reportedly provided them basic support, including food rations and education for children. Telangana forest authorities, however, reportedly destroyed several settlements of the Gotti Koya in Bhupalpally District on the charge that they were engaging in unsustainable farming practices by cutting down trees. On April 21, several Gotti Koya huts were burned, and on September 16, 36 huts were pulled down as a woman tied herself to a tree in an effort to stop authorities from carrying out the operation. On October 13, the Hyderabad High Court directed the Telangana government not to displace the Gotti Koya tribal members or demolish their dwelling units.

National policy or legislation did not address the issue of internal displacement resulting from armed conflict or from ethnic or communal violence. Responsibility for the welfare of IDPs was generally the purview of state governments and local authorities, allowing for gaps in services and poor

Country Reports on Human Rights Practices for 2017
United States Department of State • Bureau of Democracy, Human Rights and Labor

276 | P a g e

accountability. The central government provided limited assistance to IDPs, but they had access to NGOs and human rights organizations, although neither access nor assistance was standard for all IDPs or all situations.

In May the Mizoram state government, which had previously refused to accept the repatriation of Bru refugees, submitted a plan to the Ministry of Home Affairs to repatriate more than 20,000 Brus, including 11,500 minors. Bru IDPs were lodged in six relief camps in North Tripura District. The ministry approved the Mizoram plan in July. The repatriation process could not start until August, because Bru IDPs raised new demands about land, security, and resettlement.

Protection of Refugees

Refoulement: Media reported instances of the government detaining Rohingya in the states of West Bengal and Manipur. After serving the allotted time for illegal entry into the country, the government reportedly sought to return some Rohingya to Burma. During negotiations the Burmese government claimed there was no record of the individuals ever having Burmese citizenship. In most cases the Indian government kept the persons in detainment.

Access to Asylum: Absent a legal framework, the government sometimes granted asylum on a situational basis on humanitarian grounds in accordance with international law. This approach resulted in varying standards of protection for different refugee and asylum seeker groups. The government recognized refugees from Tibet and Sri Lanka and honored UNHCR decisions on refugee status determination for individuals from other countries.

UNHCR did not maintain an official presence in the country, but the government permitted UNHCR staff access to refugees in urban centers and allowed it to operate in Tamil Nadu to assist with Sri Lankan refugee repatriation. UNHCR registered asylum seekers and conducted refugee status determination for refugees from noncontiguous countries and Burma. Authorities did not permit UNHCR direct access to Sri Lankan refugee camps, Tibetan settlements, or asylum seekers in Mizoram; but it permitted asylum seekers from Mizoram to travel to New Delhi to meet UNHCR officials. UNHCR did not have access to asylum seekers in Mizoram. The government generally permitted NGOs, international humanitarian organizations, and foreign governments access to Sri Lankan refugee camps and Tibetan settlements but generally denied access to asylum seekers in Mizoram.

Country Reports on Human Rights Practices for 2017
United States Department of State • Bureau of Democracy, Human Rights and Labor

277 | P a g e

After the end of the Sri Lankan civil war, the government ceased registering Sri Lankans as refugees. The Tamil Nadu government assisted UNHCR by providing exit permission for Sri Lankan refugees to repatriate voluntarily.

The benefits provided to Sri Lankan Tamil refugees by the state government of Tamil Nadu were applicable only within Tamil Nadu. NGOs working with Sri Lankan refugees in Tamil Nadu reported a decreased willingness within the state government to assist on refugee issues since the death of the previous chief minister.

Refugees outside Delhi faced added expense and time to register their asylum claims.

Employment: The government granted work authorization to many UNHCR-registered refugees, and others found employment in the informal sector. Some refugees reported discrimination by employers.

Access to Basic Services: Although the country generally allowed recognized refugees and asylum seekers access to housing, primary and secondary education, health care, and the courts, access varied by state and by population. Refugees were able to access public services. In most cases where refugees were denied access, it was due to a lack of knowledge of refugee rights by the service provider. In many cases UNHCR was able to intervene successfully and advocate for refugee access. The government allowed UNHCR-registered refugees and asylum seekers to apply for long-term visas that would provide work authorization and access to higher education. For undocumented asylum seekers, UNHCR provided a letter upon registration indicating the person was under consideration for UNHCR mandate refugee status.

The government did not fully complete a 2012 Ministry of Home Affairs directive to issue long-term visas to Rohingya. These visas would allow refugees to access formal employment in addition to education, health services, and bank accounts.

Government services such as mother-child health programs were available. Refugees were able to request protection from police and courts as needed.

Sri Lankan refugees were permitted to work in Tamil Nadu. Police, however, reportedly summoned refugees back into the camps on short notice, particularly during sensitive political times such as elections, and required refugees or asylum seekers to remain in the camps for several days.

Country Reports on Human Rights Practices for 2017
United States Department of State • Bureau of Democracy, Human Rights and Labor

278 | P a g e

The government did not accept refugees for resettlement from other countries.

Stateless Persons

By law parents confer citizenship, and birth in the country does not automatically result in citizenship. Any person born in the country on or after January 26, 1950, but before July 1, 1987, obtained Indian citizenship by birth. A child born in the country on or after July 1, 1987, obtained citizenship if either parent was an Indian citizen at the time of the child's birth. Authorities considered those born in the country on or after December 3, 2004, citizens only if at least one parent was a citizen and the other was not illegally present in the country at the time of the child's birth. Authorities considered persons born outside the country on or after December 10, 1992, citizens if either parent was a citizen at the time of birth, but authorities did not consider those born outside the country after December 3, 2004, citizens unless their birth was registered at an Indian consulate within one year of the date of birth. Authorities could also confer citizenship through registration under specific categories and via naturalization after residing in the country for 12 years. Tibetans reportedly sometimes faced difficulty acquiring citizenship despite meeting the legal requirements.

According to UNHCR and NGOs, the country had a large population of stateless persons, but there were no reliable estimates. Stateless populations included Chakmas and Hajongs, who entered the country decades ago from present-day Bangladesh, and groups affected by the 1947 partition of the subcontinent into India and Pakistan.

Approximately 70,000 stateless Bangladeshi Chakma persons lived in Arunachal Pradesh. During the year the Supreme Court ordered the central government and the Arunachal Pradesh state government to consider citizenship for Chakma and Hajong refugees who have lived in the state for almost 50 years. In the early 1960s, Buddhist Chakmas and Hajongs fled persecution from former East Pakistan (Bangladesh) and approximately 15,000 settled in the Changlang District of Arunachal Pradesh.

Children born in Sri Lankan refugee camps received Indian birth certificates. While Indian birth certificates alone do not entitle refugees to Indian citizenship, refugees may present Indian birth certificates to the Sri Lankan High Commission to obtain a consular birth certificate, which entitles them to pursue Sri Lankan citizenship later. According to the Organization for Eelam Refugees'

Country Reports on Human Rights Practices for 2017
United States Department of State • Bureau of Democracy, Human Rights and Labor

279 | P a g e

Rehabilitation, approximately 16,000 of 27,000 Sri Lankan refugee children born in the refugee camps have presented birth certificates to the Sri Lankan High Commission in Chennai. During the year the Sri Lankan High Commission in Chennai issued approximately 2,400 consular birth certificates.

UNHCR and refugee advocacy groups estimated that between 25,000 and 28,000 of the approximately 100,000 Sri Lankan Tamil refugees living in Tamil Nadu were "hill country" Tamils. While Sri Lankan law allows "hill country" refugees to present affidavits to secure Sri Lankan citizenship, UNHCR believed that until the Sri Lankan government processes the paperwork, such refugees were at risk of becoming stateless.

Section 3. Freedom to Participate in the Political Process

The constitution provides citizens the ability to choose their government in free and fair periodic elections held by secret ballot and based on universal and equal suffrage.

Elections and Political Participation

Recent Elections: The Election Commission of India is an independent constitutional body responsible for administering all elections at the central and state level throughout the country. During the year a national electoral college elected President Ramnath Kovind to a five-year term. The seven states of Uttar Pradesh, Gujarat, Punjab, Uttarakhand, Goa, Himachal Pradesh, and Manipur held elections for their state assemblies. Observers considered these elections, which included more than 300 million participants, free and fair, despite very isolated instances of violence.

Political Parties and Political Participation: The constitution provides for universal voting rights for all citizens age 18 and above. There were no restrictions placed on the formation of political parties or on individuals of any communities from participating in the election process. The election law bans the use of government resources for political campaigning, and the Election Commission effectively enforced the law. The commission's guidelines ban opinion polls 48 hours prior to an election, and exit poll results may not be released until completion of the last phase (in a multiphase election).

Participation of Women and Minorities: The law reserves one-third of the seats in local councils for women. Religious, cultural, and traditional practices and ideas

Country Reports on Human Rights Practices for 2017
United States Department of State • Bureau of Democracy, Human Rights and Labor

prevented women from proportional participation in political office. Nonetheless, women held many high-level political offices, including positions as ministers, members of parliament, and state chief ministers. No laws limit participation of women or members of minorities in the political process, and they did participate.

The constitution stipulates that to protect historically marginalized groups and provide for representation in the lower house of parliament, each state must reserve seats for Scheduled Castes and Scheduled Tribes in proportion to their population in the state. Only candidates belonging to these groups may contest elections in reserved constituencies. Members of minority populations previously served as prime minister, vice president, cabinet ministers, Supreme Court justices, and members of parliament.

Some Christians and Muslims were identified as Dalits, but the government limited reservations for Dalits to Hindus, Sikhs, and Jains.

Section 4. Corruption and Lack of Transparency in Government

The law provides criminal penalties for corruption by officials at all levels of government. Officials frequently engaged, however, in corrupt practices with impunity. There were numerous reports of government corruption during the year.

Corruption: Corruption was present at all levels of government. According to Crime in India 2016 data, the CBI registered 673 corruption-related cases. NGOs reported the payment of bribes to expedite services, such as police protection, school admission, water supply, or government assistance. Civil society organizations drew public attention to corruption throughout the year, including through demonstrations and websites that featured stories of corruption.

Media reports, NGOs, and activists reported links between contractors, militant groups, and security forces in infrastructure projects, narcotics trafficking, and timber smuggling in the northeastern states. These reports alleged ties among politicians, bureaucrats, security personnel, and insurgent groups. In Manipur and Nagaland, allegations of bribes paid to secure state government jobs were prevalent, especially in police and education departments.

Corruption sometimes hampered government programs to investigate allegations of government corruption. On February 14, V. K. Sasikala, general secretary of the Tamil Nadu ruling party, All India Anna Dravida Munntra Kazhagam-Amma, was convicted of corruption after the Supreme Court restored the trial court verdict

Country Reports on Human Rights Practices for 2017
United States Department of State • Bureau of Democracy, Human Rights and Labor

281 | P a g e

in a 21-year-old case. Additionally, by law Sasikala was barred from contesting any election for six years following her prison term.

In 2015 the Supreme Court ordered the CBI to take over a Madhya Pradesh state government investigation of fraud within the Professional Examination Board, a state government body that conducts school entrance and government service exams. Arrests in the case since the investigation began in 2013 included more than 2,000 individuals. In August 2016 the CBI filed formal complaints against 60 individuals and filed charges against a student candidate and an impersonator. The Madhya Pradesh High Court granted bail to some of the accused. The CBI was also investigating the deaths of 48 individuals over the span of five years, including a journalist who reported on the alleged fraud. On February 13, the Supreme Court cancelled the admission of more than 600 Madhya Pradesh medical students who they believed used examination malpractice to pass.

On April 10, the Anticorruption Bureau (ACB) registered a complaint against Eknath Khadse, the former Maharashtra agriculture and revenue minister, his wife, son-in-law, and an aide in Pune for alleged corruption in a land deal. On March 8, the state government informed the court that the ACB would take over investigations from the local police. Khadse had resigned as a minister in June 2016 when the allegations surfaced. There was no update on the case by year's end.

Financial Disclosure: The law mandates asset declarations for all officers in the Indian Administrative Services. Both the Election Commission and the Supreme Court upheld mandatory disclosure of criminal and financial records for election candidates.

Section 5. Governmental Attitude Regarding International and Nongovernmental Investigation of Alleged Abuses of Human Rights

Most domestic and international human rights groups generally operated without government restriction, investigating and publishing their findings on human rights cases. In some circumstances groups faced restrictions. Government officials were generally responsive to NGO requests. There were more than three million NGOs in the country advocating for social justice, sustainable development, and human rights. The government generally met with domestic NGOs, responded to their inquiries, and took action in response to their reports or recommendations. The NHRC worked cooperatively with numerous NGOs. Several NHRC committees had NGO representation. Human rights monitors in the state of

Country Reports on Human Rights Practices for 2017
United States Department of State • Bureau of Democracy, Human Rights and Labor

282 | P a g e

Jammu and Kashmir were able to document human rights violations, but security forces, police, and other law enforcement authorities reportedly restrained or harassed them at times.

Representatives of certain international human rights NGOs sometimes faced difficulties obtaining visas and reported that occasional official harassment and restrictions limited their public distribution of materials.

On July 10, the Supreme Court rejected the relief plea of activists Teesta Setalvad, Javed Anand, and their colleagues associated with Citizens for Justice and Peace from charges of corruption and misappropriation of funds. Police authorities in Gujarat charged the activists with embezzling 1.5 million rupees ($24,000) collected to build a memorial to victims of the 2002 Gujarat riots. The activists alleged authorities filed the case in retaliation for their work on behalf of the riot victims.

The United Nations or Other International Bodies: The government continued to limit access by the United Nations to the northeastern states and Maoist-controlled areas.

Government Human Rights Bodies: The NHRC is an independent and impartial investigatory and advisory body, established by the central government, with a dual mandate to investigate and remedy instances of human rights violations and to promote public awareness of human rights. It is directly accountable to parliament but works in close coordination with the Ministry of Home Affairs and the Ministry of Law and Justice. It has a mandate to address official violations of human rights or negligence in the prevention of violations, intervene in judicial proceedings involving allegations of human rights violations, and review any factors (including acts of terrorism) that infringe on human rights. The law authorizes the NHRC to issue summonses and compel testimony, produce documentation, and requisition public records. The NHRC also recommends appropriate remedies for abuses in the form of compensation to the victims of government killings or their families. It has neither the authority to enforce the implementation of its recommendations nor the power to address allegations against military and paramilitary personnel.

Human rights groups claimed these limitations hampered the work of the NHRC. Some human rights NGOs criticized the NHRC's budgetary dependence on the government and its policy of not investigating abuses more than one year old. Some claimed the NHRC did not register all complaints, dismissed cases

Country Reports on Human Rights Practices for 2017
United States Department of State • Bureau of Democracy, Human Rights and Labor

283 | Page

arbitrarily, did not investigate cases thoroughly, rerouted complaints back to the alleged violator, and did not adequately protect complainants.

Twenty-four of 29 states have human rights commissions, which operated independently under the auspices of the NHRC. In six states the position of chairperson remained vacant. Some human rights groups alleged local politics influenced state committees, which were less likely to offer fair judgments than the NHRC.

In the course of its nationwide evaluation of state human rights committees, the Human Rights Law Network (HRLN) observed most state committees had few or no minority, civil society, or female representatives. The HRLN claimed the committees were ineffective and at times hostile toward victims, hampered by political appointments, understaffed, and underfunded.

The Jammu and Kashmir commission does not have the authority to investigate alleged human rights violations committed by members of paramilitary security forces. The NHRC has jurisdiction over all human rights violations, except in certain cases involving the army. The NHRC has authority to investigate cases of human rights violations committed by Ministry of Home Affairs paramilitary forces operating under the AFSPA in the northeast states and in the state of Jammu and Kashmir.

Section 6. Discrimination, Societal Abuses, and Trafficking in Persons

Women

Rape and Domestic Violence: The law criminalizes rape in most cases, although marital rape is not illegal when the woman is over the age of 15. Official statistics pointed to rape as the country's fastest growing crime, prompted at least in part by the increasing willingness of victims to report rapes, although observers believed the number of rapes still remained vastly underreported.

Law enforcement and legal recourse for rape victims were inadequate, overtaxed, and unable to address the problem effectively. Police officers sometimes worked to reconcile rape victims and their attackers, in some cases encouraging female rape victims to marry their attackers. NGO Lawyers Collective noted the length of trials, lack of victim support, and inadequate protection of witnesses and victims remained major concerns. Doctors continued to carry out the invasive "two-finger test" to speculate on sexual history, despite the Supreme Court's holding that the

Country Reports on Human Rights Practices for 2017
United States Department of State • Bureau of Democracy, Human Rights and Labor

284 | P a g e

test violated a victim's right to privacy. In 2015 the government introduced new guidelines for health professionals for medical examinations of victims of sexual violence. It included provisions regarding consent of the victim during various stages of examination, which some NGOs claimed was an improvement to recording incidents.

Women in conflict areas, such as in the state of Jammu and Kashmir, the northeast, Jharkhand, and Chhattisgarh, as well as vulnerable Dalit or tribal women, were often victims of rape or threats of rape. National crime statistics indicated Dalit women were disproportionately victimized compared with other caste affiliations.

Domestic violence continued to be a problem. Acid attacks against women caused death and permanent disfigurement. During the year Chhattisgarh became the first state to establish one-stop crisis centers for women in distress, called "Sakhi centers," in all its 27 districts, supported with federal funds from the Ministry of Women and Child Development. These centers provide medical, legal, counseling, and shelter services for women facing various types of violence, but primarily domestic violence related to dowry disputes and sexual violence. The NCRB estimated the conviction rate for crimes against women to be 18.9 percent.

In 2015 the Supreme Court directed all private hospitals to provide medical assistance to victims of acid attacks. Implementation of the policy began in Chennai in 2016. In April the government announced that acid attack victims were to be included in the provisions of the Rights of Persons with Disabilities Act 2016.

In July 2016 the central government launched a revised Central Victim Compensation Fund scheme to reduce disparities in compensation for victims of crime including rape, acid attacks, crime against children, and human trafficking.

Female Genital Mutilation/Cutting (FGM/C): No national law addresses the practice of FGM/C. According to human rights groups and media reports, between 70 and 90 percent of Dawoodi Bohras, a population of approximately one million concentrated in Maharashtra, Gujarat, Rajasthan, and Delhi, practiced FGM/C.

On June 26, the Supreme Court sought responses from the national government and the states of Gujarat, Maharashtra, Rajasthan, and Delhi following a public interest litigation (PIL) petition seeking a ban on FGM/C. In May national

Country Reports on Human Rights Practices for 2017
United States Department of State • Bureau of Democracy, Human Rights and Labor

285 | P a g e

Minister for Women and Child Development Maneka Gandhi said FGM/C should be a criminal offense.

Other Harmful Traditional Practices: The law forbids the provision or acceptance of a dowry, but families continued to offer and accept dowries, and dowry disputes remained a serious problem. NCRB data showed authorities arrested 19,973 persons for dowry deaths in 2015.

"Sumangali schemes" affected an estimated 120,000 young women. These plans, named after the Tamil word for "happily married woman," are a form of bonded labor in which young women or girls work to earn money for a dowry to be able to marry. The promised lump-sum compensation ranged from 80,000 to 100,000 rupees ($1,300 to $1,600), which is normally withheld until the end of three to five years of employment. Compensation, however, sometimes went partially or entirely unpaid. While in bonded labor, employers reportedly subjected women to serious workplace abuses, severe restrictions on freedom of movement and communication, sexual abuse, sexual exploitation, sex trafficking, and being killed. The majority of sumangali-bonded laborers came from the Scheduled Castes (SC) and, of those, employers subjected Dalits, the lowest-ranking Arunthathiyars, and migrants from the northern part of the country, to particular abuse. Authorities did not allow trade unions in sumangali factories, and some sumangali workers reportedly did not report abuses due to fear of retribution. A 2014 case study by NGO Vaan Muhil described health problems among workers and working conditions reportedly involving physical and sexual exploitation. In 2016 the Madras High Court ordered the Tamil Nadu government to evaluate the legality of sumangali schemes. It is unclear whether the state has complied with the court order.

Most states employed dowry prohibition officers. A 2010 Supreme Court ruling makes it mandatory for all trial courts to charge defendants in dowry-death cases with murder.

So-called honor killings remained a problem, especially in Punjab, Uttar Pradesh, and Haryana. These states also had low female birth ratios due to gender-selective abortions. On August 21, the Supreme Court sought suggestions from NGO Shakti Vahini and khap panchayats on ways to prevent harassment and killings of young couples in the name of family honor. The most common justification for the killings cited by the accused or by their relatives was that the victim married against her family's wishes.

Country Reports on Human Rights Practices for 2017
United States Department of State • Bureau of Democracy, Human Rights and Labor

286 | P a g e

In a case of suspected honor killing in Telangana, police found a lower-caste Dalit man M. Madhukar dead from injuries on March 13. Dalit rights organizations rejected the police contention that it was a case of suicide and asserted the family members of an upper-caste girl were involved in his death. On April 6, the Hyderabad High Court ordered another autopsy on the body following protests and allegations that a local member of parliament was involved in a cover-up operation. There were no updates to the case at year's end.

There were reports women and girls in the "devadasi" system of symbolic marriages to Hindu deities were victims of rape or sexual abuse at the hands of priests and temple patrons, a form of sex trafficking. NGOs suggested families forced some SC girls into prostitution in temples to mitigate household financial burdens and the prospect of marriage dowries. Some states have laws to curb prostitution or sexual abuse of women and girls in temple service. Enforcement of these laws remained lax, and the problem was widespread. Some observers estimated more than 450,000 women and girls engaged in temple-related prostitution.

There was no federal law addressing accusations of witchcraft; however, authorities may use other legal provisions as an alternative for a victim accused of witchcraft. Bihar, Odisha, Chhattisgarh, Rajasthan, Assam, and Jharkhand have laws criminalizing those who accuse others of witchcraft. Most reports stated villagers and local councils usually banned those accused of witchcraft from the village.

Sexual Harassment: Sexual harassment remains a serious problem. Authorities required all state departments and institutions with more than 50 employees to operate committees to prevent and address sexual harassment, often referred to as "eve teasing."

Coercion in Population Control: There were reports of coerced and involuntary sterilization.

Some women reportedly were pressured to have tubal ligations, hysterectomies, or other forms of sterilization because of the payment structures for health workers and insurance payments for private facilities. This pressure appeared to affect disproportionately poor and lower-caste women. In September 2016 the Supreme Court ordered the closure of all sterilization camps within three years.

Country Reports on Human Rights Practices for 2017
United States Department of State • Bureau of Democracy, Human Rights and Labor

287 | P a g e

The country continued to have deaths related to unsafe abortion, maternal mortality, and coercive family planning practices, including coerced or unethical sterilization and policies restricting access to entitlements for women with more than two children. Policies and guideline initiatives penalizing families with more than two children remained in place in seven states, but some authorities did not enforce them. Certain states maintained government reservations for government jobs and subsidies for adults with no more than two children and reduced subsidies and access to health care for those who have more than two.

Rajasthan, one of 11 states to adopt a two-child limit for elected officials at the local level, was the first to adopt the law in 1992. Despite efforts at the state level to reverse or amend the law, it remained unchanged during the year. According to NGO Lawyers Collective, such policies often induced families to carry out sex-selection for the second birth to assure they have at least one son, without sacrificing future eligibility for political office.

Although national health officials noted the central government did not have the authority to regulate state decisions on population issues, the central government creates guidelines and funds state level reproductive health programs. A Supreme Court decision deemed the national government responsible for providing quality care for sterilization services at the state level. Almost all states also introduced "girl child promotion" schemes, intended to counter sex selection, some of which required a certificate of sterilization for the parents to collect benefits.

The government has promoted female sterilization as a form of family planning for decades and, as a result, female sterilization made up 86 percent of all contraceptive use in the country. Despite recent efforts to expand the range of contraceptive choices, the government sometimes promoted permanent female sterilization to the exclusion of alternate forms of contraception.

Estimates on maternal mortality and contraceptive prevalence are available at: www.who.int/reproductivehealth/publications/monitoring/maternal-mortality-2015/en/.

Discrimination: The law prohibits discrimination in the workplace and requires equal pay for equal work, but employers often paid women less than men for the same job, discriminated against women in employment and credit applications, and promoted women less frequently than men.

Country Reports on Human Rights Practices for 2017
United States Department of State • Bureau of Democracy, Human Rights and Labor

288 | P a g e

Many tribal land systems, including in Bihar, deny tribal women the right to own land.

In January 2016 the Bihar government approved a 35-percent quota for women in state government jobs at all levels.

Gender-biased Sex Selection: According to the latest census (2011), the national average male-female sex ratio at birth was 1,000 to 943. The law prohibits prenatal sex selection, but authorities rarely enforced it.

Children

Birth Registration: The law establishes state government procedures for birth registration. UNICEF estimated authorities registered 58 percent of national births each year. Children lacking citizenship or registration may not be able to access public services, enroll in school, or obtain identification documents later in life.

Education: The constitution provides for free education for all children from ages six to 14, but the government did not always comply with this requirement. The NGO Pratham's 2016 *Annual Survey of Education* noted that in the states of Uttar Pradesh, Bihar, Manipur, West Bengal, and Madhya Pradesh, female student attendance rates ranged between 50 to 60 percent.

According to the *National Survey of Out of School Children 2014* report, 28 percent of children with disabilities ages six to 13 did not attend school.

Child Abuse: The law prohibits child abuse, but it does not recognize physical abuse by caregivers, neglect, or psychological abuse as punishable offenses. Although banned, teachers often used corporal punishment. The government often failed to educate the public adequately against child abuse or to enforce the law.

In May humanitarian aid organization World Vision India conducted a survey of 45,844 children between the ages of 12 and 18 across 26 states and found that one in every two children was a victim of sexual abuse. The Counsel to Secure Justice reported nearly 30 percent of child sexual abuse cases involved incest and 99 percent of overall child sexual abuse cases were not reported.

The government sponsored a toll-free 24-hour helpline for children in distress working with 640 partners in 402 locations.

Country Reports on Human Rights Practices for 2017
United States Department of State • Bureau of Democracy, Human Rights and Labor

289 | P a g e

Early and Forced Marriage: The law sets the legal age of marriage for women at 18 and men at 21, and it empowers courts to annul child marriages. It also sets penalties for persons who perform, arrange, or participate in such marriages. Authorities did not consistently enforce the law nor address rape of girls forced into marriage. The law does not characterize a marriage between a girl below age 18 and a boy below age 21 as "illegal," but it recognizes such unions as voidable. According to international and local NGOs, procedural limitations effectively left married minors with no legal remedy in most situations.

The law establishes a full-time child-marriage prohibition officer in every state to prevent and police child marriage. These individuals have the power to intervene when a child marriage is taking place, document violations of the law, file charges against parents, remove children from dangerous situations, and deliver them to local child-protection authorities.

In May Karnataka amended existing legislation to declare every child marriage illegal and empowered police to take specific action.

On July 20, Minister of State for Women and Child Development Krishna Raj informed the upper house of parliament that 2015-16 data from NFHS-4 revealed a decline in the percentage of women between ages 20 and 24 married before age 18.

Sexual Exploitation of Children: The law prohibits child pornography and sets the legal age of consent at 18. It is illegal to pay for sex with a minor, to induce a minor into prostitution or any form of "illicit sexual intercourse," or to sell or buy a minor for the purposes of prostitution. Violators are subjected to 10 years' imprisonment and a fine.

Special Courts to try child sexual abuse cases existed in all six Delhi courts. Civil society groups observed, however, that large caseloads severely limited judges' abilities to take on cases in a timely manner.

Child Soldiers: No information was available on how many persons under age 18 were serving in the armed forces. NGOs estimated there were at least 2,500 children associated with insurgent armed groups in Maoist-affected areas as well as child soldiers in insurgent groups in the state of Jammu and Kashmir. There were allegations government-supported, anti-Maoist village defense forces recruited children (see section 1.g., Child Soldiers).

Country Reports on Human Rights Practices for 2017
United States Department of State • Bureau of Democracy, Human Rights and Labor

290 | Page

<u>Displaced Children</u>: Displaced children, including refugees, IDPs, and street children, faced restrictions on access to government services (see also section 2.d.).

<u>Institutionalized Children</u>: Lax law enforcement and a lack of safeguards encouraged an atmosphere of impunity in a number of group homes and orphanages.

The Calcutta Research Group reported police sometimes separated families detained at the India-Bangladesh border in the state of West Bengal by institutionalizing children in Juvenile Justice Homes with limited and restricted access to their families.

<u>International Child Abductions</u>: The country is not a party to the 1980 Hague Convention on the Civil Aspects of International Child Abduction. See the Department of State's *Annual Report on International Parental Child Abduction* at travel.state.gov/content/childabduction/en/legal/compliance.html.

Anti-Semitism

Jewish groups from the 4,650-member Jewish community cited no reports of anti-Semitic acts during the year.

Trafficking in Persons

See the Department of State's *Trafficking in Persons Report* at www.state.gov/j/tip/rls/tiprpt/.

Persons with Disabilities

The constitution does not explicitly mention disability. The law provides equal rights for persons with a variety of disabilities, and the Rights of Persons with Disabilities Act 2016 increased the number of recognized disabilities, including Parkinson's disease and acid attacks. The law set a two-year deadline for the government to provide persons with disabilities with unrestricted free access to physical infrastructure and public transportation systems.

The law also reserves 3 percent of all educational places for persons with disabilities, and 4 percent of government jobs. In June 2016 the Supreme Court directed the government to extend the 4-percent reservation to all government posts. In June a government panel decided that private news networks must

Country Reports on Human Rights Practices for 2017
United States Department of State • Bureau of Democracy, Human Rights and Labor

291 | P a g e

accompany public broadcasts with sign language interpretations and closed captions to accommodate persons with disabilities better. The government allocated funds to programs and NGO partners to increase the number of jobs filled.

Despite these efforts, problems remained. Private-sector employment of persons with disabilities remained low, despite governmental incentives.

Discrimination against persons with disabilities in employment, education, and access to health care was more pervasive in rural areas, and 45 percent of the country's population of persons with disabilities was illiterate. There was limited accessibility to public buildings. A PIL file was pending in the Supreme Court on accessibility to buildings and roads.

A Department of School Education and Literacy program provided special educators and resource centers for students with disabilities. Mainstream schools remained inadequately equipped with teachers trained in inclusive education, resource material, and appropriate curricula.

The Ministry of Health and Family Welfare estimated of the individuals with mental disabilities, 25 percent were homeless.

Patients in some mental-health institutions faced food shortages, inadequate sanitary conditions, and lack of adequate medical care. HRW reported women and girls with disabilities occasionally were forced into mental hospitals against their will.

In June 2016 the Supreme Court directed the government to extend the 4-percent reservation to all government posts.

National/Racial/Ethnic Minorities

The constitution prohibits caste discrimination. The registration of castes and tribes continued for the purpose of affirmative action programs, as the government implemented programs to empower members of the low castes. Discrimination based on caste remained prevalent particularly in rural areas.

The term "Dalit," derived from the Sanskrit for "oppressed" or "crushed," refers to members of what society regarded as the lowest Hindu castes, the Scheduled Castes (SC). Many SC members continued to face impediments to social

Country Reports on Human Rights Practices for 2017
United States Department of State • Bureau of Democracy, Human Rights and Labor

292 | Page

advancement, including education, jobs, access to justice, freedom of movement, and access to institutions and services. According to the 2011 census, SC members constituted 17 percent (approximately 200 million persons) of the population.

Although the law protects Dalits, there were numerous reports of violence and significant discrimination in access to services, such as health care, education, temple attendance, and marriage. Many Dalits were malnourished. Most bonded laborers were Dalits. Dalits who asserted their rights were often victims of attacks, especially in rural areas. As agricultural laborers for higher-caste landowners, Dalits reportedly often worked without monetary remuneration. Reports from the UN Committee on the Elimination of Racial Discrimination described systematic abuse of Dalits, including extrajudicial killings and sexual violence against Dalit women. Crimes committed against Dalits reportedly often went unpunished, either because authorities failed to prosecute perpetrators or because victims did not report crimes due to fear of retaliation.

NGOs reported widespread discrimination, including prohibiting Dalits from walking on public pathways, wearing footwear, accessing water from public taps in upper-caste neighborhoods, participating in some temple festivals, bathing in public pools, or using certain cremation grounds. In Gujarat, for example, Dalits were reportedly denied entry to temples and denied educational and employment opportunities.

NGOs reported that Dalit students were sometimes denied admission to certain schools because of their caste or were required to present caste certification prior to admission. There were reports that school officials barred Dalit children from morning prayers, asked Dalit children to sit in the back of the class, or forced them to clean school toilets while denying them access to the same facilities. There were also reports that teachers refused to correct the homework of Dalit children, refused to provide midday meals to Dalit children, and asked Dalit children to sit separately from children of upper-caste families.

In April the supporters of Bhim Army, a lower-caste Dalit advocacy group in Uttar Pradesh, reportedly faced violence at the hands of organized upper-caste Thakur landlords in Uttar Pradesh. More than 50 Dalit houses were reportedly burned and many individuals injured in the violence. In May thousands of Dalits, led by the Bhim Army, staged a demonstration against the violence. As confrontations between the communities escalated, police arrested several Bhim Army activists, including leader Chandrshekhar Azad. State police reportedly did not detain upper-caste participants.

Country Reports on Human Rights Practices for 2017
United States Department of State • Bureau of Democracy, Human Rights and Labor

293 | P a g e

The federal and state governments continued to implement programs for members of lower caste groups to provide better-quality housing, quotas in schools, government jobs, and access to subsidized foods. Critics claimed many of these programs suffered from poor implementation and/or corruption.

Manual scavenging--the removal of animal or human waste by Dalits--continued in spite of its legal prohibition. NGO activists claimed elected village councils employed a majority of manual scavengers that belonged to Other Backward Classes and Dalit populations. Media regularly published articles and pictures of persons cleaning manholes and sewers without protective gear. On March 16, the Ministry of Social Justice and Empowerment stated that there were 12,737 manual scavengers in 13 states and union territories. NGOs maintained the actual numbers were higher.

HRW reported that children of manual scavengers faced discrimination, humiliation, and segregation at village schools. Their occupation often exposed manual scavengers to infections that affected their skin, eyes, respiratory, and gastrointestinal systems. Health practitioners suggested children exposed to such bacteria were often unable to maintain a healthy body weight and suffered from stunted growth.

The law prohibits the employment of scavengers or the construction of dry (nonflush) latrines, and penalties range from imprisonment for up to one year, a fine of 2,000 rupees ($32), or both.

Indigenous People

The constitution provides for the social, economic, and political rights of disadvantaged groups of indigenous persons. The law provides special status for indigenous individuals, but authorities often denied them their rights.

In most of the northeastern states, where indigenous groups constituted the majority of the states' populations, the law provides for tribal rights, although some local authorities disregarded these provisions. The law prohibits any nontribal person, including citizens from other states, from crossing a government-established inner boundary without a valid permit. No one may remove rubber, wax, ivory, or other forest products from protected areas without authorization. Tribal authorities must approve the sale of land to nontribal persons.

Country Reports on Human Rights Practices for 2017
United States Department of State • Bureau of Democracy, Human Rights and Labor

294 | Page

Acts of Violence, Discrimination, and Other Abuses Based on Sexual Orientation and Gender Identity

The law criminalizes homosexual sex. The country recognizes Hijras (male-to-female transgender persons) as a third gender, separate from men or women. Lesbian, gay, bisexual, transgender, and intersex (LGBTI) persons faced physical attacks, rape, and blackmail. Some police committed crimes against LGBTI persons and used the threat of arrest to coerce victims not to report the incidents. With the aid of NGOs, several states offered education and sensitivity training to police.

LGBTI groups reported they faced widespread societal discrimination and violence, particularly in rural areas. Activists reported that transgender persons, who were HIV positive, continued to face difficulty obtaining medical treatment.

In January 2015 a high court dismissed petitions challenging the 2013 Supreme Court judgment reinstating a colonial-era legal provision criminalizing homosexual sex. It has since agreed to review that ruling. Additionally, in an August ruling that the country's citizens have a constitutional right to privacy, the Supreme Court termed sexual orientation "an essential attribute of privacy."

In February the Ministry of Health and Family Welfare unveiled the *2017 Saathiya Education Plan*, resource material related to sex education, which recognized that persons can feel attraction for any individual of the same or opposite sex.

In April K. Prithika Yashini became India's first transgender individual to join a state police force in Dharmapuri, Tamil Nadu. She was initially denied police service employment until the Madras High Court intervened and ruled in her favor.

In May the Kerala government hired 21 transgender citizens in Kochi, but several weeks later many of the transgender workers quit their jobs, reportedly because of difficulty finding rental accommodation in Kochi due to their gender identities.

HIV and AIDS Social Stigma

The number of new HIV cases decreased by 57 percent over the past decade. The epidemic persisted among the most vulnerable populations: high-risk groups, which include female sex workers; men who have sex with men; transgender persons; and persons who inject drugs.

Country Reports on Human Rights Practices for 2017
United States Department of State • Bureau of Democracy, Human Rights and Labor

295 | P a g e

Additionally, antiretroviral drug stock outages in a few states led to treatment interruption. On April 11, the government passed the HIV and AIDS (Prevention and Control) Bill. The bill is designed to prevent discrimination in regards to health care, employment, education, housing, economic participation, or political representation.

The National AIDS Control Program prioritized HIV prevention, care, and treatment interventions for high-risk groups and rights of persons living with HIV. The National AIDS Control Organization worked actively with NGOs to train women's HIV/AIDS self-help groups.

Police engaged in programs to strengthen their role in protecting communities vulnerable to human rights violations and HIV.

Other Societal Violence or Discrimination

Societal violence based on religion and caste and by religiously associated groups continued to be a serious concern. Ministry of Home Affairs 2016-17 data showed 703 incidents of communal (religious) violence took place, which killed 86 persons and injured 2,321.

On July 26, the upper house of parliament issued a statement in response to hate crimes, expressing the need for the Union and the Ministry of Home Affairs to take proactive measures in order to create a heightened sense of security and inclusion for citizens from the northeastern region. In response to a recommendation of the Supreme Court, a committee was established to address such concerns.

The year saw an increase in cow vigilante attacks, typically associated with Hindu extremists. Since 2010 61 of the 63 reported attacks targeted Muslims, and 24 out of 28 of those killed in the attacks were Muslim. According to HRW cow vigilante violence has resulted in the death of at least 10 Muslims since 2015, including a 12-year-old boy. In several instances police filed charges against the assault victims under existing laws prohibiting cow slaughter. According to a report by IndiaSpend, an independent journalism outlet, mob lynchings of minorities took place in Jharkhand, Madhya Pradesh, Rajasthan, and Uttar Pradesh. In the first six months of the year, 20 cow-related vigilante attacks were reported, a more than 75-percent increase over 2016.

According to media reports, on June 22, 16-year-old Junaid Khan was stabbed to death on a train in Haryana by a mob who accused him and his three companions

Country Reports on Human Rights Practices for 2017
United States Department of State • Bureau of Democracy, Human Rights and Labor

296 | P a g e

of transporting beef. The Haryana police arrested six accused individuals in connection with the case. On July 9, Maharashtra police arrested Naresh Kumar, the prime suspect in the case, and as of August, four of the six accused had been granted bail.

On September 11, UN High Commissioner for Human Rights Zeid Ra'ad al-Hussein told the 36th opening session of the Human Rights Council he was dismayed by a broader rise of intolerance towards religious and other minorities in the country. He stated, "The current wave of violent, and often lethal, mob attacks against persons under the pretext of protecting the lives of cows is alarming."

Section 7. Worker Rights

a. Freedom of Association and the Right to Collective Bargaining

The law provides for the right to form and join unions and bargain collectively, although there is no legal obligation for employers to recognize a union or engage in collective bargaining. In the state of Sikkim, trade union registration was subject to prior permission from the state government. The law limits the organizing rights of federal and state government employees.

The law provides for the right to strike but places restrictions on this right for some workers. For instance, in export processing zones (EPZs), a 45-day notice is required because of the EPZs' designations as "public utilities." The law also allows the government to ban strikes in government-owned enterprises and requires arbitration in specified "essential industries." Definitions of essential industries vary from state to state. The law prohibits antiunion discrimination and retribution for involvement in legal strikes and provides for reinstatement of employees fired for union activity.

Enforcement of the law varied from state to state and from sector to sector. Enforcement was generally better in the larger, organized-sector industries. Authorities generally prosecuted and punished individuals responsible for intimidation or suppression of legitimate trade union activities in the industrial sector. Civil judicial procedures addressed abuses because the Trade Union Act does not specify penalties for such abuses. Specialized labor courts adjudicate labor disputes, but there were long delays and a backlog of unresolved cases.

Employers generally respected freedom of association and the right to organize and bargain collectively in the formal industrial sector but not in the large, informal

Country Reports on Human Rights Practices for 2017
United States Department of State • Bureau of Democracy, Human Rights and Labor

297 | P a g e

economy. Most union members worked in the formal sector, and trade unions represented a small number of agricultural and informal-sector workers. An estimated 80 percent of unionized workers affiliated with one of the five major trade union federations. Unions were independent of the government, but four of the five major federations were associated with major political parties. According to the Ministry of Labor and Employment, there were 163 strikes in 2015. State and local authorities occasionally used their power to declare strikes illegal and force adjudication. Membership-based organizations, such as the Self Employed Women's Association, successfully organized informal-sector workers and helped them to gain higher payment for their work or products.

On May 31, 425 workers of Aisin Automotive company in Rohtak, Haryana, were arrested while protesting the dismissal of coworkers who had sought to form a trade union. The arrested workers were charged with assault and obstructing the functioning of government officials and released on bail. Labor groups reported that some employers continued to refuse to recognize established unions and some, instead, established "workers' committees" and employer-controlled unions to prevent independent unions from organizing. EPZs often employed workers on temporary contracts. Additionally, employee-only restrictions on entry to the EPZs limited union organizers' access. On August 22, nearly one million employees of state owned banks went on strike to protest the federal government's plans to merge various banks.

b. Prohibition of Forced or Compulsory Labor

The law prohibits all forms of forced or compulsory labor, but this problem, including bonded child labor (see section 7.c.), remained widespread.

Estimates of the number of bonded laborers varied widely, although some NGOs placed the number in the tens of millions. Most bonded labor occurred in agriculture. Nonagricultural sectors with a high incidence of bonded labor were stone quarries, brick kilns, rice mills, construction, embroidery factories, and beedi (hand-rolled cigarettes) production.

Enforcement and compensation for victims is the responsibility of state and local governments and varied in effectiveness. The government generally did not effectively enforce laws related to bonded labor or labor trafficking laws, such as the Bonded Labor System (Abolition) Act. When inspectors referred violations for prosecution, court backlogs, inadequate prosecution, and a lack of prioritization sometimes resulted in acquittals. Prosecutions were rare.

Country Reports on Human Rights Practices for 2017
United States Department of State • Bureau of Democracy, Human Rights and Labor

The Ministry of Labor and Employment continued to work with the International Labor Organization to combat bonded labor, including the "convergence program" in the states of Andhra Pradesh and Odisha to target workers vulnerable to bonded labor.

The Ministry of Labor and Employment reported the federally funded, state-run Centrally Sponsored Scheme allowed the release of 2,607 bonded laborers during the period April 2016 through March. Some NGOs reported delays in obtaining release certificates for rescued bonded laborers that were required to certify employers held them in bondage and entitled them to compensation under the law. The distribution of rehabilitation funds was uneven across states. In May 2016 the government revised its bonded labor rehabilitation program and increased the compensation for victims from 20,000 rupees ($320) to 100,000 rupees ($1,600) for male victims, 200,000 rupees ($3,200) for women and child victims, and 300,000 rupees ($4,800) for sexually exploited women and child victims.

Bonded labor, particularly in brick kilns, continued to be a concern in several states. In March, Uttar Pradesh authorities, with assistance from an NGO, rescued 149 bonded laborers from two brick kilns in the state.

On March 10, a Karnataka district court sentenced a brick kiln owner who employed 12 workers as bonded laborers to 10 years in prison with hard labor. The court imposed a penalty of approximately 15,500 rupees ($250) for employing bonded labor in his premises. Authorities had charged the perpetrator under the Bonded Labor System (Abolition) Act along with Section 370 of the Indian Penal Code.

On July 24, nearly 88 bonded laborers, including 25 children and 29 women, were rescued from a brick kiln following a complaint received by the Delhi-based National Campaign Committee for Eradication of Bonded Labor.

SC and ST members lived and worked under traditional arrangements of servitude in many areas of the country. Although the central government had long abolished forced labor servitude, these social groups remained impoverished and vulnerable to forced exploitation, especially in Arunachal Pradesh.

Also see the Department of State's *Trafficking in Persons Report* at www.state.gov/j/tip/rls/tiprpt/.

c. Prohibition of Child Labor and Minimum Age for Employment

The government amended the Child Labor (Abolition) Act in August 2016 to ban employment of children below the age of 14. The amended law also prohibits the employment of children between the ages of 14 and 18 in hazardous work except in mines. Children are prohibited from using flammable substances, explosives, or other hazardous material, as defined by the law. In March the Ministry of Labor and Employment added 16 industries and 59 processes to the list of hazardous industries where employment of children below the age of 18 is prohibited and where children under 14 are prohibited from helping, including family enterprises. The law, however, permits employment of children in family-owned enterprises, involving nonhazardous activities, after school hours. Nevertheless, child labor remained widespread.

State governments enforced labor law and employed labor inspectors, while the Ministry of Labor and Employment provided oversight and coordination. Nevertheless, violations were common. The amended law establishes a penalty in the range of 20,000 rupees ($320) to 50,000 rupees ($800) per child employed in hazardous industries. Such fines were often insufficient to deter violations, and authorities sporadically enforced them. The fines are deposited in a welfare fund for formerly employed children.

The Ministry of Labor and Employment coordinated its efforts with states to raise awareness about child labor by funding various outreach events such as plays and community activities. On June 13, the government ratified two instrumental conventions of the International Labor Organization, Conventions 138 and 182, which set the minimum age for admission to employment and prohibit the worst forms of child labor, respectively.

According to news reports, the Rajasthan government's antihuman trafficking unit rescued more than 500 children from roadside eateries, grocery shops, and vehicle repair shops in Kota, Bundi, Baran, and Jhalawar Districts during a month-long campaign in May and June.

The majority of child labor occurred in agriculture and the informal economy, in particular in stone quarries, in the rolling of cigarettes, and in informal food service establishments. Commercial sexual exploitation of children occurred (see section 6, Children).

The V. V. Giri National Institute of Labor reported that the two cities with the highest numbers of cases in the country were Hyderabad with 67,366 child workers and Jalore with 50,440.

Forced child labor, including bonded labor, also remained a serious problem. Employers engaged children in forced or indentured labor as domestic servants and beggars, as well as in quarrying, brick kilns, rice mills, silk-thread production, and textile embroidery.

Also see the Department of Labor's *Findings on the Worst Forms of Child Labor* at www.dol.gov/ilab/reports/child-labor/findings/.

d. Discrimination with Respect to Employment and Occupation

The law and regulations prohibit discrimination with respect to employment and occupation, with respect to race, sex, gender, disability, language, sexual orientation, and/or gender identity, or social status. The law does not prohibit discrimination against individuals with HIV/AIDS or other communicable diseases, color, religion, political opinion, national origin, or citizenship. The government effectively enforced the law and regulations within the formal sector. The law and regulations, however, do not protect those working within the informal sector, who made up an estimated 90 percent of the workforce.

Discrimination occurred in the informal sector with respect to Dalits, indigenous persons, and persons with disabilities. Legal protections are the same for all, but gender discrimination with respect to wages was prevalent. Foreign migrant workers were largely undocumented and typically did not enjoy the legal protection available to workers who are nationals of the country.

e. Acceptable Conditions of Work

Federal law sets safety and health standards, but state government laws set minimum wages, hours of work, and additional state-specific safety and health standards. The daily minimum wage varied but was more than the official estimate of poverty level income. State governments set a separate minimum wage for agricultural workers.

Laws on wages, hours, and occupational health and safety do not apply to the large informal sector.

Country Reports on Human Rights Practices for 2017
United States Department of State • Bureau of Democracy, Human Rights and Labor

301 | P a g e

The law mandates a maximum eight-hour workday and 48-hour workweek, as well as safe working conditions, which include provisions for restrooms, cafeterias, medical facilities, and ventilation. The law mandates a minimum rest period of 30 minutes after every four hours of work and premium pay for overtime, but it does not mandate paid holidays. The law prohibits compulsory overtime, but it does not limit the amount of overtime a worker can work. Occupational safety and health standards set by the government were generally up to date and covered the main industries in the country.

State governments are responsible for enforcing minimum wages, hours of work, and safety and health standards. The number of inspectors generally was insufficient to enforce labor law. State governments often did not effectively enforce the minimum wage law for agricultural workers. Enforcement of safety and health standards was poor, especially in the informal sector but also in some formal sector industries. Penalties for violation of occupational safety and health standards range from a fine of 100,000 rupees ($1,600) to imprisonment for up to two years, but they were not sufficient to deter violations.

Violations of wage, overtime, and occupational safety and health standards were common in the informal sector (industries and/or establishments that do not fall under the purview of the Factories Act), which employed an estimated 90 percent of the workforce. Small, low-technology factories frequently exposed workers to hazardous working conditions. Undocumented foreign workers did not receive basic occupational health and safety protections. In many instances workers could not remove themselves from situations that endangered health or safety without jeopardizing their employment.

On March 15, two contracted sanitation workers of the Vijayawada Municipal Corporation in Andhra Pradesh died of suffocation inside an underground sewage line. Police registered a case of negligent death against their employer. According to an estimate by NGO Safai Karmachari Andolan, a longtime campaigner for eradication of manual scavenging, an estimated 1,500 individuals died cleaning septic tanks across the country between 2014 and 2016.

According to a 2016 Asian Human Rights Commission report, although the Supreme Court ordered enforcement of the law prohibiting employment as manual scavengers, calling for their rehabilitation, and banning manual cleaning of sewage lines, authorities rarely enforced the law. The commission quoted a Dalit rights activist who asserted that at least 700 deaths in manholes occurred every year.

ABOUT THE AUTHOR

Brian D. Lerner is an Immigration Lawyer and runs a National Immigration Law Firm for nearly 30 years. He is an attorney who is a certified specialist that might help in Immigration & Nationality Law as issued by the California State Bar, Board of Legal Specialization. Attorney Lerner is an expert in Immigration Law, Removal and Deportation, Citizenship, Waiver and Appeals.

He has been a licensed attorney since 1992 and started the Law Offices of Brian D. Lerner, APC. The immigration practice consists of Immigration and Nationality Law, and everything involved with and regarding immigration which includes citizenship, investment visas, family and employment visas, removal and deportation hearings, appeals, waivers, adjustment, consulate processing and all types of immigration and citizenship matters.

He has represented clients from all over the U.S. and in many countries around the world. One side of his practice is dedicated to keeping people in the U.S. and fighting for their immigration rights, while another side is to get people back who have been deported and removed from the U.S.

Also, there is the affirmative part of Immigration Law which Brian Lerner has helped numerous people come into the U.S. on business visas, investment visas, student visas, fiancée and marriage visas, religious visas and many more. Attorney Lerner has helped immigrants who are victims of crime and domestic violence or ones that are married to abusers.

In other words, Attorney Lerner has a firm that helps people all over the U.S. He has dedicated significant time to preparing numerous petitions and applications for you to get at a fraction of the price of hiring an attorney. He says it is the next best thing to a real attorney because they are real petitions prepared by an expert.

www.ingramcontent.com/pod-product-compliance
Lightning Source LLC
Chambersburg PA
CBHW060926210326
41597CB00042B/4514